THE LIBERAL TRADITION IN AMERICA

The great advantage of the Americans is, that they have arrived at a state of democracy without having to endure a democratic revolution; and that they are born equal, instead of becoming so.
                    —Alexis de Tocqueville, *Democracy in America*

The
Liberal Tradition
in America

AN INTERPRETATION OF AMERICAN POLITICAL
THOUGHT SINCE THE REVOLUTION

Louis Hartz

Harcourt, Brace & World, Inc.
New York

FOR STEVE

Preface

I first advanced the concept of a liberal society in a series
of articles on the American Revolution, the early Whigs,
and the Civil War which appeared in 1952 in the *American Political Science Review* and the *Western Political
Quarterly*. These articles are reprinted here, with the
permission of those journals, but a special word is necessary concerning one. The essay on the Revolution, which
is the first of two chapters on that subject, was written
before I had the argument of the book clearly in mind
and therefore tends to generalize also about problems
dealt with in other places. Since it is a unit in itself, I
have permitted it to stand essentially as it was written.

It is a pleasure to acknowledge here the debt I owe to
Samuel Beer, whose wide erudition and keenness of mind
have helped me over much difficult terrain, especially in
the European field. I have also gained much from numer-
ous discussions with Adam Ulam largely concerning Europe, and with Robert McCloskey, William Dowling, and
Rush Welter mainly in connection with the American materials. I am profoundly grateful, too, to Earl Latham,
whose personal interest and scholarly criticism have been
continuous, and to David Owen, who read certain chapters of the book in manuscript. A good deal of my work
was done in the course of a Faculty Research Fellowship
of the Social Science Research Council, sponsored by

Merle Fainsod, and all of it was argued out over a long period in my graduate seminar in American political thought. Finally I cannot fail to associate this book with Benjamin F. Wright, my Harvard tutor, now president of Smith College, who years ago communicated to me a lasting interest in the comprehensive interpretation of American history.

LOUIS HARTZ

Cambridge, Massachusetts
July, 1954

Contents

Part Three. The Emergence of Democracy

Part Four. The Feudal Dream of the South

CONTENTS

Part Five. The American World of Horatio Alger

Part Six. Depression and World Involvement

PART ONE

Feudalism and the American Experience

CHAPTER ONE

The Concept of a Liberal Society

---

1. *America and Europe*

The analysis which this book contains is based on what might be called the storybook truth about American history: that America was settled by men who fled from the feudal and clerical oppressions of the Old World. If there is anything in this view, as old as the national folklore itself, then the outstanding thing about the American community in Western history ought to be the non-existence of those oppressions, or since the reaction against them was in the broadest sense liberal, that the American community is a liberal community. We are confronted, as it were, with a kind of inverted Trotskyite law of combined development, America skipping the feudal stage of history as Russia presumably skipped the liberal stage. I know that I am using broad terms broadly here. "Feudalism" refers technically to the institutions of the medieval era, and it is well known that aspects of the decadent feudalism of the later period, such as primogeniture, entail, and quitrents, were present in America even in the eighteenth century.* "Liberalism" is an even

---

* There is no precise term for feudal institutions and feudal ideas as they persisted into the modern period amid the national states and economic movements which progressively undermined them. The phrases

3

vaguer term, clouded as it is by all sorts of modern social reform connotations, and even when one insists on using it in the classic Lockian sense, as I shall insist here, there are aspects of our original life in the Puritan colonies and the South which hardly fit its meaning. But these are the liabilities of any large generalization, danger points but not insuperable barriers. What in the end is more interesting is the curious failure of American historians, after repeating endlessly that America was grounded in escape from the European past, to interpret our history in the light of that fact. There are a number of reasons for this which we shall encounter before we are through, but one is obvious at the outset: the separation of the study of American from European history and politics. Any attempt to uncover the nature of an American society without feudalism can only be accomplished by studying it in conjunction with a European society where the feudal structure and the feudal ethos did in fact survive. This is not to deny our national uniqueness, one of the reasons curiously given for studying America alone, but actually to affirm it. How can we know the uniqueness of anything except by contrasting it with what is not unique? The rationale for a separate American study, once you begin to think about it, explodes the study itself.

In the end, however, it is not logic but experience, to use a Holmesian phrase, which exposes the traditional

"quasi-feudal" and "ancien régime" are nebulous enough. Some historians speak of "corporate society," but since a good deal more is involved than a congeries of associational units and since "corporate" is often used to describe current fascist states, the term has disadvantages. Under the circumstances it seems best to retain the simple word "feudal," realizing that its technical meaning is stretched when one applies it in the modern era.

approach. We could use our uniqueness as an excuse for evading its study so long as our world position did not really require us to know much about it. Now that a whole series of alien cultures have crashed in upon the American world, shattering the peaceful landscape of Bancroft and Beard, the old non sequitur simply will not do. When we need desperately to know the idiosyncrasies which interfere with our understanding of Europe, we can hardly break away from "European schemes" of analysis, as J. Franklin Jameson urged American historians to do in 1891 (not that they ever really used them in the first place) on the ground that we are idiosyncratic. But the issue is deeper than foreign policy, for the world involvement has also brought to the surface of American life great new domestic forces which must remain inexplicable without comparative study. It has redefined, as Communism shows, the issue of our internal freedom in terms of our external life. So in fact it is the entire crisis of our time which compels us to make that journey to Europe and back which ends in the discovery of the American liberal world.

2. "Natural Liberalism": The Frame of Mind

One of the central characteristics of a nonfeudal society is that it lacks a genuine revolutionary tradition, the tradition which in Europe has been linked with the Puritan and French revolutions: that it is "born equal," as Tocqueville said. And this being the case, it lacks also a tradition of reaction: lacking Robespierre it lacks Maistre, lacking Sydney it lacks Charles II. Its liberalism is what Santayana called, referring to American democracy, a "natural" phenomenon. But the matter is curiously broader than this, for a society which begins with Locke, and thus transforms him, stays with Locke, by virtue of an absolute and irrational attachment it develops for him, and becomes as indifferent to the challenge of socialism in the later era as it was unfamiliar with the heritage of feudalism in the earlier one. It has within it, as it were, a kind of self-completing mechanism, which insures the universality of the liberal idea. Here, we shall see, is one of the places where Marx went wrong in his historical analysis, attributing as he did the emergence of the socialist ideology to the objective movement of economic forces. Actually socialism is largely an ideological phenomenon, arising out of the principles of class and the revolutionary liberal revolt against them which the old European order inspired. It is not accidental that America which has uniquely lacked a feudal tradition has uniquely lacked also a socialist tradition. The hidden origin of socialist thought everywhere in the West is to be found in the feudal ethos. The *ancien régime* inspires Rousseau; both inspire Marx.

Which brings us to the substantive quality of the natural liberal mind. And this poses no easy problem. For when the words of Locke are used and a prior Filmer is absent, how are we to delineate the significance of the latter fact? In politics men who make speeches do not go out of their way to explain how differently they would speak if the enemies they had were larger in size or different in character. On the contrary whatever enemies they fight they paint in satanic terms, so that a problem sufficiently difficult to begin with in a liberal society becomes complicated further by the inevitable perspectives of political battle. Take the American Revolution. With

6

John Adams identifying the Stamp Act with the worst of the historic European oppressions, how can we distinguish the man from Lilburne or the philosophers of the French Enlightenment? And yet if we study the American liberal language in terms of intensity and emphasis, if we look for silent omissions as well as explicit inclusions, we begin to see a pattern emerging that smacks distinctively of the New World. It has a quiet, matter of fact quality, it does not understand the meaning of sovereign power, the bourgeois class passion is scarcely present, the sense of the past is altered, and there is about it all, as compared with the European pattern, a vast and almost charming innocence of mind. Twain's "Innocents Abroad" is a pretty relevant concept, for the psyche that springs from social war and social revolution is given to far suspicions and sidelong glances that the American liberal cannot easily understand. Possibly this is what people mean when they say that European thought is "deeper" than American, though anyone who tries to grapple with America in Western terms will wonder whether the term "depth" is the proper one to use. There can be an appalling complexity to innocence, especially if your point of departure is guilt.

Now if the *ancien régime* is not present to begin with, one thing follows automatically: it does not return in a blaze of glory. It does not flower in the nineteenth century in a Disraeli or a Ballanche, however different from each other these men may be. I do not mean to imply that no trace of the feudal urge, no shadow whatsoever of Sir Walter Scott, has been found on the hills and plains of the New World. One can get into a lot of useless argument if he affirms the liberalness of a liberal society in

7

absolute mathematical fashion. The top strata of the American community, from the time of Peggy Hutchinson to the time of Margaret Kennedy, have yearned for the aristocratic ethos. But instead of exemplifying the typical Western situation, these yearnings represent an inversion of it. America has presented the world with the peculiar phenomenon, not of a frustrated middle class, but of a "frustrated aristocracy"—of men, Aristotelian-like, trying to break out of the egalitarian confines of middle class life but suffering guilt and failure in the process. The South before the Civil War is the case par excellence of this, though New England of course exemplifies it also. Driven away from Jefferson by abolitionism, the Fitzhughs of the ante-bellum era actually dared to ape the doctrinal patterns of the Western reaction, of Disraeli and Bonald. But when Jefferson is traditional, European traditionalism is a curious thing indeed. The Southerners were thrown into fantastic contradictions by their iconoclastic conservatism, by what I have called the "Reactionary Enlightenment," and after the Civil War for good historical reasons they fell quickly into oblivion. The South, as John Crowe Ransom has said, has been the part of America closest to Old World Europe, but it has never really been Europe. It has been an alien child in a liberal family, tortured and confused, driven to a fantasy life which, instead of disproving the power of Locke in America, portrays more poignantly than anything else the tyranny he has had.

But is not the problem of Fitzhugh at once the problem of De Leon? Here we have one of the great and neglected relationships in American history: the common fecklessness of the Southern "feudalists" and the modern socialists. It is not accidental, but something rooted in the logic

8

of all of Western history, that they should fail alike to leave a dent in the American liberal intelligence. For if the concept of class was meaningless in its Disraelian form, and if American liberalism had never acquired it in its bourgeois form, why should it be any more meaningful in its Marxian form? This secret process of ideological transmission is not, however, the only thing involved. Socialism arises not only to fight capitalism but remnants of feudalism itself, so that the failure of the Southern Filmerians, in addition to setting the pattern for the failure of the later Marxists, robbed them in the process of a normal ground for growth. Could De Leon take over the liberal goal of extended suffrage as Lasalle did in Germany or the crusade against the House of Lords as the Labor Party did in England? Marx himself noted the absence of an American feudalism, but since he misinterpreted the complex origins of European socialism in the European *ancien régime,* he did not grasp the significance of it.

Surely, then, it is a remarkable force: this fixed, dogmatic liberalism of a liberal way of life. It is the secret root from which have sprung many of the most puzzling of American cultural phenomena. Take the unusual power of the Supreme Court and the cult of constitution worship on which it rests. Federal factors apart, judicial review as it has worked in America would be inconceivable without the national acceptance of the Lockian creed, ultimately enshrined in the Constitution, since the removal of high policy to the realm of adjudication implies a prior recognition of the principles to be legally interpreted. At the very moment that Senator Benton was hailing the rise of America's constitutional fetishism, in France Royer Collard and the Doctrinaires were desperately trying to build

9

precisely the same atmosphere around the Restoration Charter of 1814, but being a patchwork of Maistre and Rousseau, that constitutional document exploded in their faces in the July Revolution. *Inter arma leges silent.* If in England a marvelous organic cohesion has held together the feudal, liberal, and socialist ideas, it would still be unthinkable there that the largest issues of public policy should be put before nine Talmudic judges examining a single text. But this is merely another way of saying that law has flourished on the corpse of philosophy in America, for the settlement of the ultimate moral question is the end of speculation upon it. Pragmatism, interestingly enough America's great contribution to the philosophic tradition, does not alter this, since it feeds itself on the Lockian settlement. It is only when you take your ethics for granted that all problems emerge as problems of technique. Not that this is a bar in America to institutional innovations of highly non-Lockian kind. Indeed, as the New Deal shows, when you simply "solve problems" on the basis of a submerged and absolute liberal faith, you can depart from Locke with a kind of inventive freedom that European Liberal reformers and even European socialists, dominated by ideological systems, cannot duplicate. But the main point remains: if Fitzhugh and De Leon were crucified by the American general will, John Marshall and John Dewey flourished in consequence of their crucifixion. The moral unanimity of a liberal society reaches out in many directions.

At bottom it is riddled with paradox. Here is a Lockian doctrine which in the West as a whole is the symbol of rationalism, yet in America the devotion to it has been so irrational that it has not even been recognized for what it is: liberalism. There has never been a "liberal movement" or a real "liberal party" in America: we have only had the American Way of Life, a nationalist articulation of Locke which usually does not know that Locke himself is involved; and we did not even get that until after the Civil War when the Whigs of the nation, deserting the Hamiltonian tradition, saw the capital that could be made out of it. This is why even critics who have noticed America's moral unity have usually missed its substance. Ironically, "liberalism" is a stranger in the land of its greatest realization and fulfillment. But this is not all. Here is a doctrine which everywhere in the West has been a glorious symbol of individual liberty, yet in America its compulsive power has been so great that it has posed a threat to liberty itself. Actually Locke has a hidden conformitarian germ to begin with, since natural law tells equal people equal things, but when this germ is fed by the explosive power of modern nationalism, it mushrooms into something pretty remarkable. One can reasonably wonder about the liberty one finds in Burke.

I believe that this is the basic ethical problem of a liberal society: not the danger of the majority which has been its conscious fear, but the danger of unanimity, which has slumbered unconsciously behind it: the "tyranny of opinion" that Tocqueville saw unfolding as even the pathetic social distinctions of the Federalist era collapsed before his eyes. But in recent times this manifestation of irrational Lockianism, or of "Americanism," to use a favorite term of the American Legion, one of the best expounders of the national spirit that Whiggery discovered after the Civil War, has neither slumbered nor been unconscious. It has been very much awake in a red scare

11

hysteria which no other nation in the West has really been able to understand. And this suggests a very significant principle: that when a liberal community faces military and ideological pressure from without it transforms eccentricity into sin, and the irritating figure of the bourgeois gossip flowers into the frightening figure of an A. Mitchell Palmer or a Senator McCarthy. Do we not find here, hidden away at the base of the American mind, one of the reasons why its legalism has been so imperfect a barrier against the violent moods of its mass Lockianism? If the latter is nourished by the former, how can we expect it to be strong? We say of the Supreme Court that it is courageous when it challenges Jefferson, but since in a liberal society the individualism of Hamilton is also a secret part of the Jeffersonian psyche, we make too much of this. The real test of the Court is when it faces the excitement both of Jefferson and Hamilton, when the Talmudic text is itself at stake, when the general will on which it feeds rises to the surface in anger. And here, brave as the Court has been at moments, its record has been no more heroic than the logic of the situation would suggest.

The decisive domestic issue of our time may well lie in the counter resources a liberal society can muster against this deep and unwritten tyrannical compulsion it contains. They exist. Given the individualist nature of the Lockian doctrine, there is always a logical impulse within it to transcend the very conformitarian spirit it breeds in a Lockian society: witness the spirit of Holmes and Hand. Given the fact, which we shall study at length later, that "Americanism" oddly disadvantages the Progressive despite the fact that he shares it to the full, there is always a strategic impulse within him to transcend it: witness the spirit of Brandeis, Roosevelt, and Stevenson. In some sense the tragedy of these movements has lain in the imperfect knowledge they have had of the enemy they face, above all in their failure to see their own unwitting contribution to his strength. The record of Brandeis was good on civil liberties, but anyone who studies his Progressive thought will see that he was, for good or bad, on that score a vital part of the compulsive "Americanism" which bred the hysteria he fought. The Progressive tradition, if it is to transcend the national general will, has got to realize, as it has not yet done, how deeply its own Jacksonian heroes have been rooted in it.

But the most powerful force working to shatter the American absolutism is, paradoxically enough, the very international involvement which tensifies it. This involvement is complex in its implications. If in the context of the Russian Revolution it elicits a domestic redscare, in the context of diplomacy it elicits an impulse to impose Locke everywhere. The way in which "Americanism" brings McCarthy together with Wilson is of great significance and it is, needless to say, another one of Progressivism's neglected roots in the Rousseauan tide it often seeks to stem. Thus to say that world politics shatters "Americanism" at the moment it intensifies it is to say a lot: it is to say that the basic horizons of the nation both at home and abroad are drastically widened by it. But has this not been the obvious experience of the recent past? Along with the fetish that has been made of Locke at peace conferences and at Congressional investigations has not Locke suffered a relativistic beating at the same time? You can turn the issue of Wilsonianism upside

13

down: when has the nation appreciated more keenly the limits of its own cultural pattern as applied to the rest of the world? You can turn the issue of McCarthyism upside down: when has the meaning of civil liberties been more ardently understood than now? A dialectic process is at work, evil eliciting the challenge of a conscious good, so that in difficult moments progress is made. The outcome of the battle between intensified "Americanism" and new enlightenment is still an open question.

Historically the issue here is one for which we have little precedent. It raises the question of whether a nation can compensate for the uniformity of its domestic life by contact with alien cultures outside it. It asks whether American liberalism can acquire through external experience that sense of relativity, that spark of philosophy which European liberalism acquired through an internal experience of social diversity and social conflict. But if the final problem posed by the American liberal community is bizarre, this is merely a continuation of its historic record. That community has always been a place where the common issues of the West have taken strange and singular shape.

3. *The Dynamics of a Liberal Society*

So far I have spoken of natural liberalism as a psychological whole, embracing the nation and inspiring unanimous decisions. We must not assume, however, that this is to obscure or to minimize the nature of the internal conflicts which have characterized American political life. We can hardly choose between an event and its context, though in the study of history and politics there will always be some who will ask us to do so. What we learn from the concept of a liberal society, lacking feudalism and therefore socialism and governed by an irrational Lockianism, is that the domestic struggles of such a society have all been projected with the setting of Western liberal alignments. And here there begin to emerge, not a set of negative European correlations, but a set of very positive ones which have been almost completely neglected.

We can thus say of the right in America that it exemplifies the tradition of big propertied liberalism in Europe, a tradition familiar enough though, as I shall suggest in a moment, much still remains to be done in studying it along transnational lines. It is the tradition which embraces loosely the English Presbyterian and the English Whig, the French Girondin and the French Liberal: a tradition which hates the *ancien régime* up to a certain point, loves capitalism, and fears democracy. Occasionally, as a matter of fact, American Hamiltonianism has been called by the English term "Whiggery," though no effort has been made to pursue the comparative analysis which this label suggests.* Similarly the European "petit-bourgeois" tradition is the starting point for an understanding of the American left. Here, to be sure, there are critical problems of identification, since one of the main things America did was to expand and transform the European "petit-

---

* Because no term has been coined to describe as a whole the wealthier, conservative strand in the liberal movement I often use the term "Whig" for it in this study, which, of course, extends the technical meaning of the term very much. There is, however, a unity in social thought to this tradition which makes a common label necessary. Even in the case of the post-Civil War Republicans in the United States, where the materials seem uniquely American, it is possible to interpret them in terms of the general problem that the wealthier phase of the liberal movement faced in the West.

15

bourgeois" by absorbing both the peasantry and the proletariat into the structure of his personality. It is only the beginning of comparative analysis to link up American Progressivism with the tradition of the French Jacobins and to counterparts elsewhere in Europe. But even though agrarian and proletarian factors complicate this issue enormously, bringing us for all practical purposes out of the petit-bourgeois world of Europe, the basic correlation remains a sound one.

One of the reasons these European liberal correlations have gone neglected is quite obvious once you try to make them. America represents the liberal mechanism of Europe functioning without the European social antagonisms, but the truth is, it is only through these antagonisms that we recognize the mechanism. We know the European liberal, as it were, by the enemies he has made: take them away in American fashion and he does not seem like the same man at all. This is true even of the Whig who prior to 1840 poses the easiest problem in this respect. Remove Wellington from Macaulay, and you have in essence Alexander Hamilton, but the link between the latter two is not at first easy to see. After 1840, when the American Whig gives up his Hamiltonian elitism and discovers the Horatio Alger ethos of a liberal society, discovers "Americanism," the task of identification is even harder. For while it is true that the liberals of England and France ultimately accepted political democracy, Algerism and "Americanism" were social ideologies they could hardly exploit. So that the continuing problem of a missing Toryism, which is enough to separate the American Republicans from the reactionary liberals of Victorian England and the Neo-Girondins of the Third Republic, is complicated further by the unique ideological shape that the Whig tradition is destined to take in a liberal society.

The American democrat, that "petit-bourgeois" hybrid of the American world, raises even more intricate questions. To take away the Social Republic from the French Montagnards changes their appearance just about as much as taking away the feudal right from the English Whigs. But the American democrat, alas, deviated sharply from the Montagnards to begin with, since in addition to being "petit-bourgeois" in their sense he was a liberal peasant and a liberal proletarian as well: indeed the whole of the nation apart from the Whig, a condition hardly vouchsafed to the Montagnards. And yet even in the face of such tremendous variations, comparative analysis can continue. We have to tear the giant figure of Jackson apart, sorting out not only the "petit-bourgeois" element of the man but those rural and urban elements which the American liberal community has transformed. Ultimately, as with the Whigs, for all of the magical chemistry of American liberal society, we are dealing with social materials common to the Western world.

That society has been a triumph for the liberal idea, but we must not assume that this ideological victory was not helped forward by the magnificent material setting it found in the New World. The agrarian and proletarian strands of the American democratic personality, which in some sense typify the whole of American uniqueness, reveal a remarkable collusion between Locke and the New World. Had it been merely the liberal spirit alone which inspired the American farmer to become capitalistically oriented, to repudiate save for a few early remnants the village organization of Europe, to produce for a market

17

and even to enter capitalist occupations on the side such as logging and railroad building, then the difficulties he encountered would have been greater than they were. But where land was abundant and the voyage to the New World itself a claim to independence, the spirit which repudiated peasantry and tenantry flourished with remarkable ease. Similarly, had it merely been an aspect of irrational Lockianism which inspired the American worker to think in terms of the capitalist setup, the task would have been harder than it was.

But social fluidity was peculiarly fortified by the riches of a rich land, so that there was no small amount of meaning to Lincoln's claim in 1861 that the American laborer, instead of "being fixed to that condition for life," works for "a while," then "saves," then "hires another beginner" as he himself becomes an entrepreneur.[1] And even when factory industrialism gained sway after the Civil War, and the old artisan and cottage-and-mill mentality was definitely gone, it was still a Lockian idea fortified by material resources which inspired the triumph of the job mentality of Gompers rather than the class mentality of the European worker. The "petit-bourgeois" giant of America, though ultimately a triumph for the liberal idea, could hardly have chosen a better material setting in which to flourish.

But a liberal society does not merely produce old Whig and new democrat, does not merely cast a strange set of lights and shadows on them. More crucially it shapes the outcome of the struggle in which they engage. We cannot say this about the Civil War, which involved in

[1] The notes will be found on pages 313-20.

any case a different alignment, because socially the Civil War was unique to America and there is no comparative material on the basis of which to analyze it. It was not, as some have said, comparable to the French and Puritan revolutions, and if we list it as one of the triumphs of nineteenth-century nationalism, Lincoln becoming a counterpart of Cavour as in some sense he undoubtedly was, we remove the issue to a different plane of comparative analysis where results are equally meager. The liberal society analysis can interpret many of the forces and ideologies that went into the war, but it is asking too much of it to account strategically for its military outcome. The picture changes, however, when we come back to the historic Whig-democrat battle which is the characteristic upshot of a liberal society. There the analysis has a lot to say about strategy.

Firstly America, by making its "petit-bourgeois" hybrid the mass of the nation, makes him unconquerable, save in two instances: when he is disorganized, as prior to Jefferson and Jackson, or when he is enchanted with the dream of becoming a Whig himself, as prior to the crash of 1929. Which is merely another way of saying that the historic Whig technique of *divide et impera* which comes out perhaps most vividly at the time of the First Reform Act and the July Revolution—of playing the mass against the *ancien régime*, the *ancien régime* against the mass, and the mass against itself—cannot work in a society where the mass embraces everything but Whiggery. This is what the Hamiltonian Federalists, who actually tried to pursue this course in America, ultimately had to learn. And this is also why, when they learned it, even their existing resemblance to European Whiggery disappeared and they

19

became distinctively American operators. What they learned was the Alger mechanism of enchanting the American democrat and the "Americanistic" mechanism of terrifying him, which was the bounty they were destined to receive for the European strategies of which they were deprived. For the defeat of Hamilton, so long as the economy boomed, they were bound to get the victory of McKinley. One might call this the great law of Whig compensation inherent in American politics. The record of its functioning takes up a large part of American history.

So one cannot say of the liberal society analysis that by concentrating on national unities it rules out the meaning of domestic conflict. Actually it discovers that meaning, which is obscured by the very Progressive analysis that presumably concentrates on conflict. You do not get closer to the significance of an earthquake by ignoring the terrain on which it takes place. On the contrary, that is one of the best ways of making sure that you will miss its significance. The argument over whether we should "stress" solidarity or conflict in American politics misleads us by advancing a false set of alternatives.

4. *The Problem of a Single Factor*

It will be said that this is a "single factor" analysis of American history and politics, and probably the only way of meeting this charge is to admit it. Technically we are actually dealing with two factors: the absence of feudalism and the presence of the liberal idea. The escape from the old European order could be accompanied by other ideas, as for instance the Chartist concept which had some effect in the settlement of Australia.* But in terms of European history itself the abstraction of the feudal force implies the natural development of liberalism, so that for all practical purposes we are dealing with a single factor.

Now there is nothing wrong with this, provided we do not claim for our factor any more than it can actually account for on the basis of comparative analysis. It is reasonable to reject the essentially religious claims of ultimate causality that single factor theories such as those of Marx and Hobbes advance. There is no "secret" or "key" to the historical process, or if there is, we certainly cannot know it. But we must not, because of this, brand as fruitless any attempt to isolate a significant historical variable and to study it by consistently comparing cases. If we do, we shall have thrown out, along with the bath water of false monisms, the very baby of scientific analysis. Granted that a single factor cannot illuminate all situations, it can still illuminate many. And these, given what we want to know at any moment, may be very relevant indeed.

Viewed in these terms the feudal issue is one whose

* What is needed here is a comparative study of new societies which will put alongside the European institutions left behind the positive cultural concepts brought to the various frontier settings. There are an infinite variety of combinations possible, and an infinite variety of results. Veblen, in a sentence he never followed up, caught some of the significance of this problem when he said that "it was the fortune of the American people to have taken their point of departure from the European situation when the system of Natural Liberty was still 'obvious and simple,'" while other colonial enterprises "have had their institutional point of departure blurred with a scattering of the holdovers that were brought in again by the return wave of reaction in Europe, as well as by these later-come stirrings of radical discontent that have questioned the eternal fitness of the system of Natural Liberty itself." *What Veblen Taught,* ed. W. Mitchell (New York, 1947), pp. 368-69.

consideration in American history is long overdue. This is not only because of the chain of insights it yields, as long as the course of our national development itself, but also because without it other elements have been burdened with work which it alone can do. Consider that ancient question: the early triumph of American democracy. Turner's frontier, of course, has been advanced to explain this phenomenon but, discovering alas that frontiers are to be found in Canada where feudalism was originally imported and in Russia, historians have revolted against the Turner approach. Actually, as I have suggested on the basis of the comparative European data, the speedy victory of manhood suffrage in America was dictated by the inevitable frustration of elitist Whiggery in a liberal context. Which suggests that Turner was not wrong but, in a way he scarcely understood, half right, for how could American liberalism flourish as it did without a frontier terrain free of Old World feudal burdens?[2] By claiming its own, in other words, the liberal society concept puts the frontier in proper perspective, dissolving both the exaggerated enthusiasms and the exaggerated hostilities that it has engendered.

It does the same thing with other factors, as for example capitalist growth. Reacting against Turner (to continue with the democratic illustration) some recent historians have pointed to the growth of industrialism and an Eastern urban proletariat to explain the swift appearance of American manhood suffrage. Certainly there were pressures here. But if we do not find them in Canada and Russia prior to Jackson, we do in England and France, and on a larger scale, so that the theory advanced to supplant Turner fares no better than his own. Indeed if we check back to the comparative analysis yielded by the liberal society concept we see that it was the nonproletarian outlook of the early American working class, the fact that it did not frighten the mass of small property owners above it, as the Social Republic frightened the French Mountain in 1848, which saved the democratic forces of the nation from being split to the advantage of Whiggery, as they so often were in Europe. Or take the explanation from capitalist growth of the national Alger ideology after the Civil War. Capitalism was surely related to Alger, but if it produced him, why did it not do so in Germany where it was booming at the same time or in England where it boomed earlier? Actually the Alger spirit is the peculiar instinct of a Lockian world, and what capitalist growth did, once the Whigs began to articulate it, was to fortify their case. Puritanism, to shift to another well known factor, does not serve as a substitute for the liberal society concept in this case or indeed in others. If it is the titanic explanatory force that some critics found it to be, why did it not lead to an American history in England where it first appeared? The answer, of course, as Lord Morley once eloquently observed in connection with the failure of Cromwell, was that the ancient social order of England hemmed it in so that it could not permeate the national spirit as it did in the New World.

These sample instances illustrate the utility of the liberal society concept in relation to familiar problems. Though concerned with a "single factor," its effect is actually to balance distorted emphases that we have traditionally lived with in the study of American history and politics.

23

5. *Implications for Europe*

If Europe provides data for checking America, America provides data for checking Europe: we are dealing with a two-way proposition. So that the liberal society analysis, at the same moment it stresses the absence of the feudal factor in America, stresses its presence abroad. Modern European historians have never evolved an interpretation of their subject from precisely this point of view. To some extent, no doubt, this is because they have been no more transatlantic in their orientation than their American brethren. But there is also a superficial logical reason for this: if modern history begins with liberalism, why stress feudalism, which after all is "medieval history"? And yet, quite apart from the lessons of the American experience, is not the fallacy of this reasoning patent? Merely to state that the feudal structure was the target of modern forces is to affirm the fact, by any sophisticated logic, that it determined the shape these forces took. One hardly needs to read Mannheim to realize that the status quo determines the categories of revolution, or Hegel to realize that the thesis is not unrelated to the sort of antithesis that arises. If the feudal factor is the mother factor of modern life, how can its influence be anything less than permanent and inescapable?

Now I am not advocating here a "conservative interpretation" of European history, which will lay the ghost of the Whigs, making a hero out of Eldon and a villain out of Grey. As a purely normative matter I concede virtues in the European feudal ethos, some of which are tragically missing in America, but I am less enthusiastic about them than, say, Mr. Peter Viereck. What I have in mind is neutral to the question of the goodness or badness of the feudal factor, which is perhaps why none of its partisans have bothered to develop it. There are "analytic" historical interpretations of a movement which, if charged with enough secular religiosity, can blend norm and fact and insure the triumph of the movement itself. Condorcet's was one of these, and so was Marx's. But it would take a lot of Hegelian magic to produce out of any analysis of the medieval influence in modern history a retrogressive apocalypse which would insure the return of the medieval spirit itself. A study of this factor, though it would illumine modern history fundamentally, would scarcely serve a partisan reactionary purpose. Indeed it might be shocking to a good Bonaldian to discover how much of feudalism went into the shaping of the sinful movements of liberalism and proletarian socialism he is wont to fight against.

And yet whatever its strategic value may be for conservatism, the American experience suggests that a study of modern European history from the feudal angle might yield interesting results. One of these, curiously enough, is a point of departure, not merely for the comparative study of America and Europe, but for the comparative study of European nations themselves. With the crystallization of national states, the European nations have been studied almost as independently as America itself, the idea being apparently that since the "medieval unity" had broken down there was no use preserving it in historical study. The result is that many of the most primitive correlations among the European countries, in economics and politics, have not been made. But if the "medieval unity" is found actually to be a decisive factor in the epoch that followed it, the basis for these correlations automatically appears. Now this is not to suggest that national differences in Western Europe are not crucial. As in the case of America we must be careful to avoid useless debate over a situation and its context. To stress feudalism in Europe is no more to deny that wide variations take place within it than to stress liberalism in America is to deny that wide variations take place within that. One can still emphasize the differences between Burke and Haller, or Jaurès and Bernstein, just as one can still emphasize the differences between Bryan and William Howard Taft. Indeed, were it not for the fact that a uniform liberalism does not see itself at all, while a uniform feudalism sees itself considerably by virtue of the antagonisms it engenders, one might even argue for a certain similarity between America and Europe on this very score. Here Locke has been so basic that we have not recognized his significance, there Filmer. And the two issues dovetail: to discover the one yields the perspective for discovering the other.

Needless to say, I have not tried in this book to explore in special detail the European pattern. But as one tries to piece together the nature of American liberal society, one cannot help being astonished at the small degree to which the relevant European relationships have been organized for study. This is less true in the simple matter of social movements than in the case of their interplay with each other, and less true on the latter count in connection with the great revolutions than with the periods which followed them. We have had a number of studies of the "Enlightenment" and the "Reaction" and "Liberalism," though it is astonishing, when one tries to break the issue down into a matter like the comparison between French Radicalism and Engish Liberal Reform, how little work really is available. But when we come to comparative dynamic analyses such as the correlation between the First Reform Act and the July Revolution, we are in a poverty-stricken area indeed. It is interesting that such analyses should primarily have been focused on the Puritan, French, and even the Russian revolutions, the assumption being that because "great revolutions" took place in these instances there is a larger ground for comparative study. Actually these revolutionary situations vividly foreshadow the dynamic alignments of the relatively peaceful periods which follow them, and if it is reasonable to relate 1642 to 1789, it is just as reasonable to relate 1830 to 1832.

But what has been lacking has been the common point of departure, which the American liberal experience, by contrast, supplies at once. Indeed one is struck with another similarity between the problem of America and Western Europe in the realm of self-analysis. Historically European hegemony has provided much the same atmosphere for European analysis that American isolation has provided for American analysis: the common environment could be left inarticulate and internal contrasts stressed, as if reality itself were being studied. But when the big wide world rushes in on America and Europe, not to speak of their rushing in on each other, is not this happy arrogance fated by a similar logic to end in both cases?

6. *The Progressive Scholarship*

In American social studies we still live in the shadow of the Progressive era. Historians have openly assailed

Beard, challenging economic motivations here and there and often transforming "radicals" into "conservatives." But after all is said and done Beard somehow stays alive, and the reason for this is that, as in the case of Marx, you merely demonstrate your subservience to a thinker when you spend your time attempting to disprove him. The way to fully refute a man is to ignore him for the most part, and the only way you can do this is to substitute new fundamental categories for his own, so that you are simply pursuing a different path. Such categories represent the only hope for a genuine escape from the pervasive frustration that the persistence of the Progressive analysis of America has inspired.

It is not unreasonable to suspect that our own time will discover such categories and that they may well lie in the relation of America to other nations. Everyone knows the old saw about each age rewriting history from its own angle, and everyone agrees that the peculiar angle of our own age is the involvement of America with the world. What is really wrong with the Progressive analysis, insofar as the questions we want answered today are concerned, is not that it is Progressive but that it is American. And here there is an interesting paradox, for one of the advances that the Progressives thought they were making lay in the explosion of the old nationalist history, what John Spencer Bassett called the "patriotic" school of historians. No doubt they did corrode many of the premises of this school. But at the same time they carried on a profound nationalism of their own. Even the "objectivists" among American historical writers, who rejected theses of any kind, did the same thing, for they did not, as Jameson urged, look at American history "from the standpoint of the outsider." [3] Rankian fact-gathering is not the same as getting "outside" your subject. The truth is, the American historian at practically every stage has functioned quite inside the nation: he has tended to be an erudite reflection of the limited social perspectives of the average American himself.

Where then lay the nativism of Beard and J. Allen Smith? It is not simply in the fact that they did not attempt the European correlations. This hid something deeper: their theory was a projection of the Progressive social orientation, which was compact of America's irrational liberalism. The agitation of Brandeis and Wilson was the agitation of Western Liberal Reform altered by the fact that, fighting only Whiggery, rather than Toryism and socialism too, it was able no more than Whiggery to perceive the nature of its liberalism. It was as if Lloyd George were fighting only the reactionary members of the Liberal party who, in any case, had no Tory party to enter if they were dissatisfied with him. Hence, with the whole scheme of liberal unity blacked out, Whiggery became for the Progressives a frightful "conservatism," whereas it itself became "progressive" or "radical," a set of terms which meant nothing insofar as Western history of Western political alignments as a whole went. Armed with these intellectual tools, and as blind as the Progressives themselves to the natural liberalism of the nation, Beard and Smith went back to the origins of American history, splitting it up into two warring camps, discovering a "social revolution" in the eighteenth century, and in general making it impossible to understand the American liberal community. Their treatment of the Constitution may have lacked the piety of the "patriotic" historians, but it was as "American" as anything those historians developed. Indeed one might even argue that the others, by stressing a kind of happy national family, were a shade closer to the Lockian solidarity of the nation, which indeed was flourishing as never before in a commonly accepted "Americanism."

The Bentley group analysis, which was to have so great an influence on our political science, was a variation of the same process: the projection of irrational "Americanism" into the study of America. It was not, to be sure, a political weapon, as the Beardian analysis was, but its elevation of peculiar American phenomena into absolute categories of political analysis was of the same kind as we found there. A multiplicity of groups flourishes in a liberal society, habitually determining the outcome of policy, since class lines of the European type are not present. To interpret America in terms of the groups it peculiarly evolves is to miss the nature of the national liberal world as badly as to interpret it in terms of "conservative" and "radical." Had the disciples of Bentley tried to apply his analysis to the Dreyfus Affair as they did to the Smoot-Hawley Tariff, they would hardly have found the procedure so easy, although of course they could always call classes "groups" if they wanted to.*

Being reflections of America's irrational liberalism, these analyses cannot illuminate the questions of domestic freedom and international policy which that liberalism in our own time poses. One cannot help noticing the sudden efflorescence in the last few years of historical anthologies of the memoirs of foreign travelers who came to America

* For a wider discussion of the Progressive scholarship, see Chapter Nine.

—some of them excellent. A hunger has finally appeared for getting outside the national experience. But is it not a sad commentary on our historical writing that, when the nation wants really to see itself, about all that can be offered are the fleeting impressions of foreigners who may have stayed in Cincinnati for a day or two? Surely the American historian would not be satisfied with such impressions in regard to the fur trade; he would demand mountains of evidence. In this connection one cannot help noticing an interesting fact: no school of American historians has ever come out of the well known work of the greatest foreign critic America ever had—Tocqueville. We find in him a series of deep insights into the American liberal community. And yet while American students have lavished unlimited praise on Tocqueville, have indeed edited and re-edited him, they have deserted him when they have come to serious work, gladly substituting the Beardian notion of social conflict for his famous notion of equality. They have lived a happily divided life on this score. But given the nationalist forces which have shaped American studies, could anything different really be expected?

There were many comforts in the old Progressive history which the liberal society analysis can never claim. The Progressives, for one thing, always had an American hero available to match any American villain they found, a Jefferson for every Hamilton. Which meant that in their demonology the nation never really sinned: only its inferior self did, its particular will, to use the language of Rousseau. The analyst of American liberalism is not in so happy a spot, for concentrating on unities as well as conflict, he is likely to discover on occasion a national villain, such as the tyrannical force of Lockian sentiment, whose treatment requires a new experience for the whole country rather than the insurgence of a part of it. Actually there was amid all the smoke and flame of Progressive historical scholarship a continuous and almost complacent note of reassurance. A new Jefferson would arise as he had always arisen before. The "reactionaries" would be laid low again. Needless to say, when you are dealing with problems inspired by an unprecedented set of world forces, you cannot take this line. So that the liberal society analyst is destined in two ways to be a less pleasing scholar than the Progressive: he finds national weaknesses and he can offer no absolute assurance on the basis of the past that they will be remedied. He tends to criticize and then shrug his shoulders, which is no way to become popular, especially in an age like our own. But even if there were not an integrity to criticism which ought to be kept inviolate at any cost, this mood is not without constructive virtue. It reminds us of a significant fact: that instead of recapturing our past, we have got to transcend it. As for a child who is leaving adolescence, there is no going home again for America.

PART TWO

Revolution in a
New World

CHAPTER TWO

The Perspectives of 1776

1. *Hebraism: The Chosen People*

When Tocqueville wrote that the "great advantage" of the American lay in the fact that he did not have "to endure a democratic revolution," [1] he advanced what was surely one of his most fundamental insights into American life. However, while many of his observations have been remembered but not followed up, this one has scarcely even been remembered. Perhaps it is because, fearing revolution in the present, we like to think of it in the past, and we are reluctant to concede that its romance has been missing from our lives. Perhaps it is because the plain evidence of the American revolution of 1776, especially the evidence of its social impact that our newer historians have collected, has made the comment of Tocqueville seem thoroughly enigmatic. But in the last analysis, of course, the question of its validity is a question of perspective. Tocqueville was writing with the great revolutions of Europe in mind, and from that point of view the outstanding thing about the American effort of 1776 was bound to be, not the freedom to which it led, but the established feudal structure it did not have to destroy. He was writing too, as no French liberal of the nineteenth century could fail to write, with the shattered hopes of the Enlightenment in mind. The American revolution had been one of the greatest of them all, a precedent constantly appealed to in 1793. In the age of Tocqueville there was ground enough for reconsidering the American image that the Jacobins had cherished.

Even in the glorious days of the eighteenth century, when America suddenly became the revolutionary symbol of Western liberalism, it had not been easy to hide the free society with which it started. As a matter of fact, the liberals of Europe had themselves romanticized its social freedom, which put them in a rather odd position; for it Raynal was right in 1772, how could Condorcet be right in 1776? If America was from the beginning a kind of idyllic state of nature, how could it suddenly become a brilliant example of social emancipation? Two consolations were being extracted from a situation which could at best yield only one. But the mood of the Americans themselves, as they watched the excitement of Condorcet seize the Old World, is also very revealing. They did not respond in kind. They did not try to shatter the social structure of Europe in order to usher in a tenth and final epoch in the history of man. Delighted as they were with the support that they received, they remained, with the exception of a few men like Paine and Barlow, curiously untouched by the crusading intensity we find in the French and the Russians at a later time. Warren G. Harding, arguing against the League of Nations, was able to point back at them and say, "Mark you, they were not reforming the world." [2] * And James Fenimore Cooper, a

* For a fuller discussion of Harding and the whole era of the First World War on this count see p. 297.

keener mind than Harding, generalized their behavior into a comment about America that America is only now beginning to understand: "We are not a nation much addicted to the desire of proselytizing." [8]

There were, no doubt, several reasons for this. But clearly one of the most significant is the sense that the Americans had themselves of the liberal history out of which they came. In the midst of the Stamp Act struggle, young John Adams congratulated his colonial ancestors for turning their backs on Europe's class-ridden corporate society, for rejecting the "canon and feudal law." [4] The pervasiveness of Adams's sentiment in American thought has often been discussed, but what is easily overlooked is the subtle way in which it corroded the spirit of the world crusader. For this was a pride of inheritance, not a pride of achievement; and instead of being a message of hope for Europe, it came close to being a damning indictment of it. It saturated the American sense of mission, not with a Christian universalism, but with a curiously Hebraic kind of separatism. The two themes fought one another in the cosmopolitan mind of Jefferson, dividing him between a love of Europe and fear of its "contamination"; but in the case of men like Adams and Gouverneur Morris, the second theme easily triumphed over the first. By the time the crusty Adams had gotten through talking to politicians abroad, he had buried the Enlightenment concept of an oppressed humanity so completely beneath the national concept of a New World that he was ready to predict a great and ultimate struggle between America's youth and Europe's decadence. As for Morris, our official ambassador to France in 1789, he simply inverted the task of the Comintern agent. Instead of urging the French on to duplicate the American experience, he badgered them by pointing out that they could never succeed in doing so. "They want an American constitution" he wrote contemptuously, "without realizing they have no Americans to uphold it." [5]

Thus the fact that the Americans did not have to endure a "democratic revolution" deeply conditioned their outlook on people elsewhere who did; and by helping to thwart the crusading spirit in them, it gave to the wild enthusiasms of Europe an appearance not only of analytic error but of unrequited love. Symbols of a world revolution, the Americans were not in truth world revolutionaries. There is no use complaining about the confusions implicit in this position, as Woodrow Wilson used to complain when he said that we had "no business" permitting the French to get the wrong impression about the American revolution. On both sides the reactions that arose were well-nigh inevitable. But one cannot help wondering about something else: the satisfying use to which our folklore has been able to put the incongruity of America's revolutionary role. For if the "contamination" that Jefferson feared, and that found its classic expression in Washington's Farewell Address, has been a part of the American myth, so has the "round the world" significance of the shots that were fired at Concord. We have been able to dream of ourselves as emancipators of the world at the very moment that we have withdrawn from it. We have been able to see ourselves as saviors at the very moment that we have been isolationists. Here, surely, is one of the great American luxuries that the twentieth century has destroyed.

2. *Utopia, Power, and the Sense of Time*

When the Americans celebrated the uniqueness of their own society, they were on the track of a personal insight of the profoundest importance. For the nonfeudal world in which they lived shaped every aspect of their social thought: it gave them a frame of mind that cannot be found anywhere else in the eighteenth century, or in the wider history of modern revolutions.

One of the first things it did was to breed a set of revolutionary thinkers in America who were human beings like Otis and Adams rather than secular prophets like Robespierre and Lenin. Despite the European flavor of a Jefferson or a Franklin, the Americans refused to join in the great Enlightenment enterprise of shattering the Christian concept of sin, replacing it with an unlimited humanism, and then emerging with an earthly paradise as glittering as the heavenly one that had been destroyed. The fact that the Americans did not share the crusading spirit of the French and the Russians, as we have seen, is already some sort of confirmation of this, for that spirit was directly related to the "civil religion" of Europe and is quite unthinkable without it. Nor is it hard to see why the liberal good fortune of the Americans should have been at work in the position they held. Europe's brilliant dream of an impending millennium, like the mirage of a thirst-ridden man, was inspired in large part by the agonies it experienced. When men have already inherited the freest society in the world, and are grateful for it, their thinking is bound to be of a solider type. America has been a sober nation, but it has also been a comfortable one, and the two points are by no means unrelated.

39

Sam Adams, for example, rejects the hope of changing human nature: in a mood of Calvinist gloom, he traces the tyranny of England back to "passions of Men" that are fixed and timeless.[6] But surely it would be unreasonable to congratulate him for this approach without observing that he implicitly confines those passions to the political sphere—the sphere of parliaments, ministers, and stampmasters—and thus leaves a social side to man which can be invoked to hold him in check. The problem was a different one for Rousseau and Marx, who started from the view that the corruption of man was complete, as wide as the culture in which he lived, with the result that revolutions became meaningless unless they were based on the hope of changing him. Here, obviously, is a place where the conclusions of political thought breathe a different spirit from the assumptions on which they rest. Behind the shining optimism of Europe, there are a set of anguished grievances; behind the sad resignation of America, a set of implicit satisfactions.

One of these satisfactions, moreover, was crucially important in developing the sober temper of the American revolutionary outlook. It was the high degree of religious diversity that prevailed in colonial life. This meant that the revolution woud be led in part by fierce Dissenting ministers, and their leadership destroyed the chance for a conflict to arise between the worldly pessimism of Christianity and the worldly ambitions of revolutionary thought. In Europe, especially on the continent, where reactionary church establishments had made the Christian concept of sin and salvation into an explicit pillar of the status quo, liberals were forced to develop a political religion—as Rousseau saw—if only in answer to it. The Americans not only avoided this compulsion; they came close, indeed, to reversing it. Here, above all in New England, the clergy was so militant that it was Tories like Daniel Leonard who were reduced to blasting it as a dangerous "political engine," a situation whose irony John Adams caught when he reminded Leonard that "in all ages and countries" the church is "disposed enough" to be on the side of conservatism.[7] Thus the American liberals, instead of being forced to pull the Christian heaven down to earth, were glad to let it remain where it was. They did not need to make a religion out of the revolution because religion was already revolutionary.

Consider the case of Rev. William Gordon of Roxbury. In 1774, when all of Boston was seething with resentment over the Port Bill, Gordon opened one of his sermons by reminding his congregation that there were "more important purposes than the fate of kingdoms" or the "civil rights of human nature," to wit, the emancipation of men from the "slavery of sin and Satan" and their preparation "for an eternal blessedness." But the Sons of Liberty did not rise up against him; they accepted his remarks as perfectly reasonable. For instead of trying to drug Bostonians with a religious opiate, Gordon proceeded to urge them to prepare for open war, delivering a blast against the British that the Tories later described as a plea for "sedition, rebellion, carnage, and blood." [*] When Christianity

---

[*] J. Thornton (ed.), *The Pulpit of the American Revolution* (Boston, 1876), pp. 196-197. The point I am making here about America in contrast to Europe is much the same point that Halévy makes about England in contrast to the continent. We must not, of course, confuse French and English thought on this score. But the role of nonconformity in discouraging the rise of political religions was actually more marked in America than it was in England.

is so explosive, why should even the most ardent revolutionary complain if heaven is beyond his grasp?

Of course, the Gordons and the Mayhews of America were quite unaware that their work had this significance —the indirect significance of keeping political thought down to earth. If anything impressed them in their role as religious figures, it was undoubtedly the crusade they were carrying forward against the "popery" of the Anglican Tories—in other words what mattered to them was not that they were helping America to avoid the eighteenth century, but that they were helping it to duplicate the seventeenth. However, their achievement on the first count was actually far more important than their achievement on the second. The revolutionary attack on Anglicanism, with its bogey of a Bishop coming to America and its hysterical interpretation of the Quebec Act of 1774, was half trumped up and half obsolete; but the alliance of Christian pessimism with liberal thought had a deep and lasting meaning. Indeed, the very failure of the Americans to become seventeenth-century prophets like the English Presbyterians enhances this point considerably. For when we add to it the fact that they did not become latter-day prophets like the Jacobins and the Marxists, they emerge, if we wish to rank them with the great revolutionaries of modern history, as in a curious sense the most secular of them all.

Perhaps it was this secular quality that Joel Barlow was trying to describe when he declared, in a Fourth of July oration in Boston in 1778, that the "peculiar glory" of the American revolution lay in the fact that "sober reason and reflection have done the work of enthusiasm and performed the miracles of Gods." [8] In any case, there was something fateful about it. For if the messianic spirit does not arise in the course of a country's national revolution, when is it ever going to arise? The post-revolutionary age, as the experience of England, France, and even in some sense Russia shows, is usually spent trying to recuperate from its effects. The fact that the Americans remained politically sober in 1776 was, in other words, a fairly good sign that they were going to remain that way during the modern age which followed; and if we except the religiosity of the Civil War, that is exactly what happened. There have been dreamers enough in American history, a whole procession of "millennial Christians," as George Fitzhugh used to call them; but the central course of our political thought has betrayed an unconquerable pragmatism.

Sir William Ashley, discussing the origins of the "American spirit," once remarked that "as feudalism was not transplanted to the New World, there was no need for the strong arm of a central power to destroy it." * This is a simple statement but, like many of Ashley's simple statements, it contains a neglected truth. For Americans usually assume that their attack on political power in 1776 was determined entirely by the issues of the revolution, when as a matter of fact it was precisely because of the things they were not revolting against that they were able to carry it through. The action of England inspired the American colonists with a hatred of centralized authority; but had that action been a transplanted American feudalism, rich in the chaos of ages, then they would surely have had to dream of centralizing authority themselves.

They would, in other words, have shared the familiar

agony of European liberalism—hating power and loving it too. The liberals of Europe in the eighteenth century wanted, of course, to limit power; but confronted with the heritage of an ancient corporate society, they were forever devising sharp and sovereign instruments that might be used to put it down. Thus while the Americans were attacking Dr. Johnson's theory of sovereignty, one of the most popular liberal doctrines in Europe, cherished alike by Bentham and Voltaire, was the doctrine of the enlightened despot, a kind of political deism in which a single force would rationalize the social world. While the Americans were praising the "illustrious Montesquieu" for his idea of checks and balances, that worthy was under heavy attack in France itself because he compromised the unity of power on which so many liberals relied. Even the English Whigs, men who were by no means believers in monarchical absolutism, found it impossible to go along with their eager young friends across the Atlantic. When the Americans, closing their eyes to 1688, began to lay the ax to the concept of parliamentary sovereignty, most of the Whigs fled their company at once.

A philosopher, it is true, might look askance at the theory of power the Americans developed. It was not a model of lucid exposition. The trouble lay with their treatment of sovereignty. Instead of boldly rejecting the concept, as Franklin was once on the verge of doing when he said that it made him "quite sick," they accepted the concept and tried to qualify it out of existence. The result was a chaotic series of forays and retreats in which a sovereign Parliament was limited, first by the distinction between external and internal taxation, then by the distinction between revenue and regulation, and finally by the remarkable contention that colonial legislatures were as sovereign as Parliament was. But there is a limit to how much we can criticize the Americans for shifting their ground. They were obviously feeling their way; and they could hardly be expected to know at the time of the Stamp Act what their position would be at the time of the First Continental Congress. Moreover, if they clung to the concept of sovereignty, they battered it beyond belief, and no one would confuse their version of it with the one advanced by Turgot or even by Blackstone in Europe. The meekness of the American sovereign testifies to the beating he had received. Instead of putting up a fierce and embarrassing battle against the limits of natural law and the separation of powers, as he usually did in the theories of Europe, he accepted those limits with a vast docility.

If we look at what happened to America's famous idea of judicial control when the physiocrats advanced it in France, we will get an insight into this whole matter. Who studies now the theory of legal guardianship with which La Rivière tried to bind down his rational and absolute sovereign? Who indeed remembers it? American students of the judicial power rarely go to Cartesian France to discover a brother of James Otis—and the reason is evident enough. When the physiocrats appealed to the courts, they were caught at once in a vise of criticism: either they were attacked for reviving the feudal idea of the *parlements* or they were blasted as insincere because they had originally advanced a despot to deal with the feudal problem. They had to give the idea up.[10] But in America, where the social questions of France did not exist and the absolutism they engendered was quite unthinkable, the claim of Otis in the Writs of Assistance Case, that laws against reason and the Constitution were "void" and that the "Courts must pass them into disuse," met an entirely different fate.[11] It took root, was carried forward by a series of thinkers, and blossomed ultimately into one of the most remarkable institutions in modern politics.*

The question, again, was largely a question of the free society in which the Americans lived. Nor ought we to assume that its impact on their view of political power disappeared when war and domestic upheaval finally came. Of course, there was scattered talk of the need for a "dictator," as Jefferson angrily reported in 1782;[12] and until new assemblies appeared in most places, committees of public safety had authoritarian power. But none of this went deep enough to shape the philosophic mood of the nation. A hero is missing from the revolutionary literature of America. He is the legislator, the classical giant who almost invariably turns up at revolutionary moments to be given authority to lay the foundations of the free society. He is not missing because the Americans were unfamiliar with images of ancient history, or because they had not read the Harringtons or the Machiavellis and Rousseaus of the modern period. Harrington, as a matter of fact, was one of their favorite writers. The legislator is missing because, in truth, the Americans had no need for his services. Much as they liked Harrington's republicanism, they did not require a Cromwell, as Harring-

* If one is primarily concerned with judicial review one must relate this interpretation to the fact, stressed throughout this book, that the moral unanimity of a liberal society nourishes a legalistic frame of mind and an acquiescence in restraints on the part of the majority. See especially pp. 103-04. These points, of course, fit together. You could not have social agreement if you had an earlier society to destroy, and if you had such a society, you would need a sharpened view of sovereign power.

ton thought he did, to erect the foundations for it. Those foundations had already been laid by history.

The issue of history itself is deeply involved here. On this score, inevitably, the fact that the revolutionaries of 1776 had inherited the freest society in the world shaped their thinking in an intricate way. It gave them, in the first place, an appearance of outright conservatism. We know, of course, that most liberals of the eighteenth century, from Bentham to Quesnay, were bitter opponents of history, posing a sharp antithesis between nature and tradition. And it is an equally familiar fact that their adversaries, including Burke and Blackstone, sought to break down this antithesis by identifying natural law with the slow evolution of the past. The militant Americans, confronted with these two positions, actually took the second. Until Jefferson raised the banner of independence, and even in many cases after that time, they based their claims on a philosophic synthesis of Anglo-American legal history and the reason of natural law. Blackstone, the very Blackstone whom Bentham so bitterly attacked in the very year 1776, was a rock on which they relied.

The explanation is not hard to find. The past had been good to the Americans, and they knew it. Instead of inspiring them to the fury of Bentham and Voltaire, it often produced a mystical sense of Providential guidance akin to that of Maistre—as when Rev. Samuel West, surveying the growth of America's population, anticipated victory in the revolution because "we have been prospered in a most wonderful manner." [13] The troubles they had with England did not alter this outlook. Even these, as they pointed out again and again, were of recent origin, coming after more than a century of that "salutary neglect" which Burke defended so vigorously. And in a specific sense, of course, the record of English history in the seventeenth century and the record of colonial charters from the time of the Virginia settlement provided excellent ammunition for the battle they were waging in defense of colonial rights. A series of circumstances had conspired to saturate even the revolutionary position of the Americans with the quality of traditionalism—to give them, indeed, the appearance of outraged reactionaries. "This I call an innovation," thundered John Dickinson, in his attack on the Stamp Act, "a most dangerous innovation." [14]

Now here was a frame of mind that would surely have troubled many of the illuminated liberals in Europe, were it not for an ironic fact. America piled on top of this paradox another one of an opposite kind and thus, by misleading them twice as it were, gave them a deceptive sense of understanding.

Actually, the form of America's traditionalism was one thing, its content quite another. Colonial history had not been the slow and glacial record of development that Bonald and Maistre loved to talk about. On the contrary, since the first sailing of the *Mayflower*, it had been a story of new beginnings, daring enterprises, and explicitly stated principles—it breathed, in other words, the spirit of Bentham himself. The result was that the traditionalism of the Americans, like a pure freak of logic, often bore amazing marks of antihistorical rationalism. The clearest case of this undoubtedly is to be found in the revolutionary constitutions of 1776, which evoked, as Franklin reported, the "rapture" of European liberals everywhere. In America, of course, the concept of a written constitution, including many of the mechanical devices it embodied, was the end-product of a chain of historical experience that went back to the Mayflower Compact and the Plantation Covenants of the New England towns: it was the essence of political traditionalism.[15] But in Europe just the reverse was true. The concept was the darling of the rationalists—a symbol of the emancipated mind at work.

Thus Condorcet was untroubled. Instead of bemoaning the fact that the Americans were Blackstonian historicists, he proudly welcomed them into the fraternity of the illuminated. American constitutionalism, he said, "had not grown, but was planned"; it "took no force from the weight of centuries but was put together mechanically in a few years." When John Adams read this comment, he spouted two words on the margin of the page: "Fool! Fool!"[16] But surely the judgment was harsh. After all, when Burke clothes himself in the garments of Sieyès, who can blame the loyal rationalist who fraternally grasps his hand? The reactionaries of Europe, moreover, were often no keener in their judgment. They made the same mistake in reverse. Maistre gloomily predicted that the American Constitution would not last because it was created out of the whole cloth of reason.

But how then are we to describe these baffling Americans? Were they rationalists or were they traditionalists? The truth is, they were neither, which is perhaps another way of saying that they were both. For the war between Burke and Bentham on the score of tradition, which made a great deal of sense in a society where men had lived in the shadow of feudal institutions, made comparatively little sense in a society where for years they had been

49

creating new states, planning new settlements, and, as Jefferson said, literally building new lives. In such a society a strange dialectic was fated to appear, which would somehow unite the antagonistic components of the European mind; the past became a continuous future, and the God of the traditionalists sanctioned the very arrogance of the men who defied Him.

This shattering of the time categories of Europe, this Hegelian-like revolution in historic perspective, goes far to explain one of the enduring secrets of the American character: a capacity to combine rock-ribbed traditionalism with high inventiveness, ancestor worship with ardent optimism. Most critics have seized upon one or the other of these aspects of the American mind, finding it impossible to conceive how both can go together. That is why the insight of Gunnar Myrdal is a very distinguished one when he writes: "America is . . . conservative. . . . But the principles conserved are liberal and some, indeed, are radical." [17] Radicalism and conservatism have been twisted entirely out of shape by the liberal flow of American history.

3. *The Mentality of a Victorious Middle Class*

What I have been doing here is fairly evident: I have been interpreting the social thought of the American revolution in terms of the social goals *it did not need to achieve*. Given the usual approach, this may seem like a perverse inversion of the reasonable course of things; but in a world where the "canon and feudal law" are missing, how else are we to understand the philosophy of a liberal revolution? The remarkable thing about the "spirit of 1776," as we have seen, is not that it sought emancipation but that it sought it in a sober temper; not that it opposed power but that it opposed it ruthlessly and continuously; not that it looked forward to the future but that it worshiped the past as well. Even these perspectives, however, are only part of the story, misleading in themselves. The "free air" of American life, as John Jay once happily put it, penetrated to deeper levels of the American mind, twisting it in strange ways, producing a set of results fundamental to everything else in American thought. The clue to these results lies in the following fact: the Americans, though models to all the world of the middle class way of life, lacked the passionate middle class consciousness which saturated the liberal thought of Europe.

There was nothing mysterious about this lack. It takes the contemptuous challenge of an aristocratic feudalism to elicit such a consciousness; and when Richard Price glorified the Americans because they were men of the "middle state," men who managed to escape being "savage" without becoming "refined," [18] he explained implicitly why they themselves would never have it. Franklin, of course, was a great American bourgeois thinker; but it is a commonplace that he had a wider vogue on this score in Paris and London than he did in Philadelphia; and indeed there is some question as to whether the Europeans did not worship him more because he seemed to exemplify Poor Richard than because he had created the philosophy by which Poor Richard lived. The Americans, a kind of national embodiment of the concept of the bourgeoisie, have, as Mr. Brinkmann points out,[19] rarely used that concept in their social thought, and this is an entirely natural state of affairs. Frustration produces the social passion, ease does not. A triumphant middle class, unassailed by the agonies that Beaumarchais described, can take itself for granted. This point, curiously enough, is practically never discussed, though the failure of the American working class to become class conscious has been a theme of endless interest. And yet the relationship between the two suggests itself at once. Marx himself used to say that the bourgeoisie was the great teacher of the proletariat.

There can, it is true, be quite an argument over whether the challenge of an American aristocracy did not in fact exist in the eighteenth century. One can point to the great estates of New York where the Patroons lived in something resembling feudal splendor. One can point to the society of the South where life was extraordinarily stratified, with slaves at the bottom and a set of genteel planters at the top. One can even point to the glittering social groups that gathered about the royal governors in the North. But after all of this has been said, the American "aristocracy" could not, as Tocqueville pointed out, inspire either the "love" or the "hatred" that surrounded the ancient titled aristocracies of Europe.[20] Indeed, in America it was actually the "aristocrats" who were frustrated, not the members of the middle class, for they were forced almost everywhere, even in George Washington's Virginia, to rely for survival upon shrewd activity in the capitalist race. This compulsion produced a psychic split that has always tormented the American "aristocracy"; and even when wealth was taken for granted there was still, especially in the North, the withering impact of a colonial "character" that Sombart himself once described as classically bourgeois.[21] In Massachusetts, Governor Hutchinson used to lament that a "gentleman" did not meet even with "common civility" from his inferiors.[22] Of course, the radicals of America blasted their betters as "aristocrats," but that this was actually a subtle compliment is betrayed in the quality of the blast itself. Who could confuse the anger of Daniel Shays with the bitterness of Francis Place even in the England of the nineteenth century?

Thus it happened that fundamental aspects of Europe's bourgeois code of political thought met an ironic fate in the most bourgeois country in the world. They were not so much rejected as they were ignored, treated indifferently, because the need for their passionate affirmation did not exist. Physiocratic economics is an important case in point. Where economic parasites are few, why should men embark on a passionate search for the productive laborer? Where guild restrictions are comparatively slight and continental tariffs unknown, why should they embrace the ruthless atomism of Turgot? America's attack on the English Acts of Trade was couched in terms of Locke, not in terms of Quesnay; and though Franklin and Jefferson were much taken by the "modern economics," they did not, here as in certain other places, voice the dominant preoccupation of American thought. It had often been said, of course, that the Americans were passionately laissez faire in their thinking, but this is to confuse either bourgeois ease with bourgeois frustration or a hatred of absolute power with the very economic atomism which, in physiocratic terms, was allied to it. Turgot himself saw that the Americans did not long to smash a feudal world into economic atoms any more than they longed for a unified sovereign to accomplish this feat. A lover of the Americans who, like most European liberals, could not quite imagine life outside the *ancien régime,* he complained bitterly on both counts. His complaint on the count of sovereignty is legendary, but his complaint on the count of laissez faire has, alas, been entirely forgotten. This is because John Adams replied to the one in his *Defence of the Constitutions* but did not mention the other. And yet it appears in the same place, in Turgot's famous letter to Richard Price: *"On suppose partout le droit de regler le commerce . . . tant on est loin d'avoir senti que la loi de la liberté de tout commerce est un corollaire du droit de propriété."* [23]

The lament of Turgot reveals that America's indifference to the bourgeois fixations of Europe had in itself a positive meaning: the failure to develop a physiocratic conscience led to a quiet and pragmatic outlook on the question of business controls. This is the outlook that characterizes a whole mass of early economic legislation that American historians are now beginning to unearth in what should have been, reputedly, the most "laissez faire" country in the world.[24] But it is in connection with materialism and idealism, utilitarianism and natural law, that the inverted position of the Americans comes out most clearly. There was no Bentham, no Helvetius, among the superlatively middle-class American thinkers. On the contrary, they stuck with Puritan passion to the dogma of natural law, as if an outright hedonism were far too crass for consideration. In a purely political sense this may be interesting, because the Americans, at least during the Stamp Act phase of their struggle, were fighting that corrupt system of parliamentary representation which in England Benthamism later rose to assail. But it is in terms of the wider significance of utility as an attack on feudal norms, as an effort to make of "business a noble life," as Crane Brinton has put it,[25] that America's indifference to it takes on its deepest meaning. Benjamin Franklins in fact, the Americans did not have to become Jeremy Benthams in theory. Unchallenged men of business, they did not have to equate morality with it. And this has been a lasting paradox in the history of American thought. The American tradition of natural law still flourishes after a century and a half of the most reckless material exploitation that the modern world has seen. A persistent idealism of mind, reflected in Emerson's remark that utilitarianism is a "stinking philosophy," has been one of the luxuries of a middle class that has never been forced to become class conscious.

But this is not all. If the position of the colonial Americans saved them from many of the class obsessions of Europe, it did something else as well: it inspired them with a peculiar sense of community that Europe had never known. For centuries Europe had lived by the spirit of solidarity that Aquinas, Bossuet, and Burke romanticized: an organic sense of structured differences, an essentially Platonic experience. Amid the "free air" of American life, something new appeared: men began to be held together, not by the knowledge that they were different parts of a corporate whole, but by the knowledge that they were similar participants in a uniform way of life—by that "pleasing uniformity of decent competence" which Crèvecoeur loved so much.[26] The Americans themselves were not unaware of this. When Peter Thacher proudly announced that "simplicity of manners" was the mark of the revolutionary colonists,[27] what was he saying if not that the norms of a single class in Europe were enough to sustain virtually a whole society in America? Richard Hildreth, writing after the leveling impact of the Jacksonian revolution had made this point far more obvious, put his finger directly on it. He denounced feudal Europe, where "half a dozen different codes of morals," often in flagrant contradiction with one another, flourished "in the same community," and celebrated the fact that America was producing "one code, moral standard, by which the actions of all are to be judged. . . ." [28] Hildreth knew that America was a marvelous mixture of many peoples and many religions, but he also knew that it was characterized by something more marvelous even than that: the power of the liberal norm to penetrate them all.

Now a sense of community based on a sense of uniformity is a deceptive thing. It looks individualistic, and in part it actually is. It cannot tolerate internal relationships of disparity, and hence can easily inspire the kind of advice that Professor Nettels once imagined a colonial farmer giving his son: "Remember that you are as good as any man—and also that you are no better." [29] But in another sense it is profoundly anti-individualistic, because the common standard is its very essence, and deviations from that standard inspire it with an irrational fright. The man who is as good as his neighbors is in a tough spot when he confronts all of his neighbors combined. Thus William Graham Sumner looked at the other side of Professor Nettels's colonial coin and did not like what he saw: "public opinion" was an "impervious mistress. . . . Mrs. Grundy held powerful sway and Gossip was her prime minister." [30]

Here we have the "tyranny of the majority" that Tocqueville later described in American life; here too we have the deeper paradox out of which it was destined to appear. Freedom in the fullest sense implies both variety and equality; but history, for reasons of its own, chose to separate these two principles, leaving the one with the old society of Burke and giving the other to the new society of Paine. America, as a kind of natural fulfillment of Paine, has been saddled throughout its history with the defect which this fulfillment involves, so that a country like England, in the very midst of its ramshackle class-ridden atmosphere, seems to contain an indefinable germ of liberty, a respect for the privacies of life, that America cannot duplicate. At the bottom of the American experience of freedom, not in antagonism to it but as a constituent element of it, there has always lain the inarticulate premise of conformity, which critics from the time of Cooper to the time of Lewis have sensed and furiously attacked. "Even what is best in America is compulsory," Santayana once wrote, "the idealism, the zeal, the beautiful happy unison of its great moments." [31] Thus while millions of Europeans have fled to America to discover the freedom of Paine, there have been a few Americans, only a few of course, who have fled to Europe to discover the freedom of Burke. The ironic flaw in American liberalism lies in the fact that we have never had a real conservative tradition.

One thing, we might suppose, would shatter the unprecedented sense of uniform values by which the colonial American was beginning to live: the revolution itself. But remarkably enough, even the revolution did not produce this result; John Adams did not confront Filmer as Locke did, or Maistre, as the followers of Rousseau did. He confronted the Englishmen of the eighteenth century;

and most of these men, insofar as the imperial struggle went, themselves accepted the Lockian assumptions that Adams advanced. Nor did the American Tories, with the fantastic exception of Boucher, who stuck to his thesis that Filmer was still "unrefuted," confront him with a vision of life completely different from his own. Samuel Seabury and Joseph Galloway accepted the Lockian principles, even sympathized with the American case, insisting only that peaceful means be used to advance it. Among their opponents, indeed, there were few who would fundamentally deny the "self-evident" truths the Americans advanced in 1776. The liberals of Europe always had a problem on their hands, which they usually neglected, to be sure, of explaining how principles could be "self-evident" when there were obviously so many people who did not believe them. Circumstance nearly solved this problem for the Americans, giving them, as it were, a national exemption from Hume's attack on natural law—which may be one of the reasons they almost always ignored it. When one's ultimate values are accepted wherever one turns, the absolute language of self-evidence comes easily enough.

This then is the mood of America's absolutism: the sober faith that its norms are self-evident. It is one of the most powerful absolutisms in the world, more powerful even than the messianic spirit of the continental liberals which, as we saw, the Americans were able to reject. That spirit arose out of contact with an opposing way of life, and its very intensity betrayed an inescapable element of doubt. But the American absolutism, flowing from an honest experience with universality, lacked even the passion that doubt might give. It was so sure of itself that it hardly needed to become articulate, so secure that it could actually support a pragmatism which seemed on the surface to belie it. American pragmatism has always been deceptive because, glacierlike, it has rested on miles of submerged conviction, and the conformitarian ethos which that conviction generates has always been infuriating because it has refused to pay its critics the compliment of an argument. Here is where the joy of a Dewey meets the anguish of a Fenimore Cooper; for if the American deals with concrete cases because he never doubts his general principles, this is also the reason he is able to dismiss his critics with a fine and crushing ease. But this does not mean that America's general will always lives an easy life. It has its own violent moments—rare, to be sure, but violent enough. These are the familiar American moments of national fright and national hysteria when it suddenly rises to the surface with a vengeance, when civil liberties begin to collapse, and when Cooper is actually in danger of going to jail as a result of the Rousseauan tide. Anyone who watches it then can hardly fail to have a healthy respect for the dynamite which normally lies concealed beneath the free and easy atmosphere of the American liberal community.

When we study national variations in political theory, we are led to semantic considerations of a delicate kind, and it is to these, finally, that we must turn if we wish to get at the basic assumption of American thought. We have to consider the peculiar meaning that American life gave to the words of Locke.

There are two sides to the Lockian argument: a defense of the state that is implicit, and a limitation of the state that is explicit. The first is to be found in Locke's basic social norm, the concept of free individuals in a state of nature. This idea untangled men from the myriad associations of class, church, guild, and place, in terms of which feudal society defined their lives; and by doing so, it automatically gave to the state a much higher rank in relation to them than ever before. The state became the only association that might legitimately coerce them at all. That is why the liberals of France in the eighteenth century were able to substitute the concept of absolutism for Locke's conclusions of limited government and to believe that they were still his disciples in the deepest sense. When Locke came to America, however, a change appeared. Because the basic feudal oppressions of Europe had not taken root, the fundamental social norm of Locke ceased in large part to look like a norm and began, of all things, to look like a sober description of fact. The effect was significant enough. When the Americans moved from that concept to the contractual idea of organizing the state, they were not conscious of having already done anything to fortify the state, but were conscious only that they were about to limit it. One side of Locke became virtually the whole of him. Turgot ceased to be a modification of Locke and became, as he was for John Adams, the destruction of his very essence.

It was a remarkable thing—this inversion of perspectives that made the social norms of Europe the factual premises of America. History was on a lark, out to tease men, not by shattering their dreams, but by fulfilling them with a sort of satiric accuracy. In America one not only found a society sufficiently fluid to give a touch of meaning to the individualist norms of Locke, but one also found letter-perfect replicas of the very images he used. There was a frontier that was a veritable state of nature. There were agreements, such as the Mayflower Compact, that were veritable social contracts. There were new communities springing up *in vacuis locis,* clear evidence that men were using their Lockian right of emigration, which Jefferson soberly appealed to as "universal" in his defense of colonial land claims in 1774. A purist could argue, of course, that even these phenomena were not enough to make a reality out of the presocial men that liberalism dreamed of in theory. But surely they came as close to doing so as anything history has ever seen. Locke and Rousseau themselves could not help lapsing into the empirical mood when they looked across the Atlantic. "Thus, in the beginning," Locke once wrote, "all the world was America. . . ." [32]

In such a setting, how could the tremendous, revolutionary social impact that liberalism had in Europe be preserved? The impact was not, of course, missing entirely; for the attack on the vestiges of corporate society in America that began in 1776, the disestablishment of the Anglican church, the abolition of quitrents and primogeniture, the breaking up of the Tory estates, tinged American liberalism with its own peculiar fire. Nor must we therefore assume that the Americans had wider political objectives than the Europeans, since even their new governmental forms were, as Becker once said, little more than the "colonial institutions with the Parliament and king left out." [33] But after these cautions have been taken, the central point is clear. In America the first half of Locke's argument was bound to become less a call to arms than a set of preliminary remarks essential to establishing a final conclusion: that the power of the state must be limited. Observe how it is treated by the Americans in their great debate with England, even by original thinkers like Otis and Wilson. They do not lavish upon it the fascinated inquiry that we find in Rousseau or Priestley. They advance it mechanically, hurry through it, anxious to get on to what is really bothering them: the limits of the British Parliament, the power of taxation. In Europe the idea of social liberty is loaded with dynamite; but in America it becomes, to a remarkable degree, the working base from which argument begins.

Here, then, is the master assumption of American political thought, the assumption from which all of the American attitudes discussed in this essay flow: the reality of atomistic social freedom. It is instinctive to the American mind, as in a sense the concept of the polis was instinctive to Platonic Athens or the concept of the church to the mind of the middle ages. Catastrophes have not been able to destroy it, proletariats have refused to give it up, and even our Progressive tradition, in its agonized clinging to a Jeffersonian world, has helped to keep it alive. There has been only one major group of American thinkers who have dared to challenge it frontally: the Fitzhughs and Holmeses of the pre-Civil War South who, identifying slavery with feudalism, tried to follow the path of the European reaction and of Comte. But American life rode roughshod over them—for the "prejudice" of Burke in America was liberal and the positive reality of Locke in America transformed them into the very metaphysicians they assailed. They were soon forgotten, massive victims of the absolute temper of the American mind, shoved off the scene by Horatio Alger, who gave to the

Lockian premise a brilliance that lasted until the crash of 1929. And even the crash did not really shatter it.

It might be appropriate to summarize with a single word, or even with a single sentence, the political outlook that this premise has produced. But where is the word and where is the sentence one might use? American political thought, as we have seen, is a veritable maze of polar contradictions, winding in and out of each other hopelessly: pragmatism and absolutism, historicism and rationalism, optimism and pessimism, materialism and idealism, individualism and conformism. But, after all, the human mind works by polar contradictions; and when we have evolved an interpretation of it which leads cleanly in a single direction, we may be sure that we have missed a lot. The task of the cultural analyst is not to discover simplicity, or even to discover unity, for simplicity and unity do not exist, but to drive a wedge of rationality through the pathetic indecisions of social thought. In the American case that wedge is not hard to find. It is not hidden in an obscure place. We find it in what the West as a whole has always recognized to be the distinctive element in American civilization: its social freedom, its social equality. And yet it is true, for all of our Jeffersonian nationalism, that the interpretation of American political thought has not been built around this idea. On the contrary, instead of interpreting the American revolution in terms of American freedom, we have interpreted it in terms of American oppression, and instead of studying the nineteenth century in terms of American equality, we have studied it in terms of a series of cosmic Beardian and Parringtonian struggles against class exploitation. We have missed what the rest of the world has seen and what we ourselves have seen whenever we have contrasted the New World with the Old. But this is a large issue which brings us not only to the Progressive historians but to the peculiar subjectivism of the American mind that they reflect, and it is beyond the scope of our discussion now.

4. *The Flight from the European Struggle*

The liberals of Europe in 1776 were obviously worshiping a very peculiar hero. If the average American had been suddenly thrust in their midst, he would have been embarrassed by the millennial enthusiasms that many of them had, would have found their talk of classes vastly overdone, and would have reacted to the Enlightenment synthesis of absolutism and liberty as if it were little short of dishonest doubletalk. Bred in a freer world, he had a different set of perspectives, was animated by a different set of passions, and looked forward to different goals. He was, as Crèvecoeur put it, a "new man" in Western politics.

But, someone may ask, where did the liberal heritage of the Americans come from in the first place? Didn't they have to create it? And if they did, were they not at one time or another in much the same position as the Europeans?

These questions drive us back to the ultimate nature of the American experience, and, so doing, confront us with a queer twist in the problem of revolution. No one can deny that conscious purpose went into the making of the colonial world, and that the men of the seventeenth century who fled to America from Europe were keenly aware of the oppressions of European life. But they were revolutionaries with a difference, and the fact of their fleeing is no minor fact: for it is one thing to stay at home and

64

fight the "canon and feudal law," and it is another to leave it far behind.* It is one thing to try to establish liberalism in the Old World, and it is another to establish it in the New. Revolution, to borrow the words of T. S. Eliot, means to murder and create, but the American experience has been projected strangely in the realm of creation alone. The destruction of forests and Indian tribes—heroic, bloody, legendary as it was—cannot be compared with the destruction of a social order to which one belongs oneself. The first experience is wholly external and, being external, can actually be completed; the second experience is an inner struggle as well as an outer struggle, like the slaying of a Freudian father, and goes on in a sense forever.† Moreover, even the matter of creation is not in the American case a simple one. The New World, as Lord Baltimore's ill-fated experiment with feudalism in the seventeenth century illustrates, did not merely offer

---

* In a real sense physical flight is the American substitute for the European experience of social revolution. And this, of course, has persisted throughout our national history, although nothing in the subsequent pattern of flight, the "safety-valve" notwithstanding, has approximated in significance the original escape from Europe. It is interesting how romance has been thrown alike around the European liberals who stayed home to fight and the American liberals who fled their battle. There are two types of excitement here, that of changing familiar things and that of leaving them, which both involve a trip into the unknown. But though one may find a common element of adventure in flight and revolution, it is a profound mistake to confuse the perspectives they engender. They are miles apart—figuratively as well as literally.

† Note the words of Goethe:

> Amerika, du hast es besser
> Als unser Kontinent, das Alte
> Hast keine verfallene Schloesser
> Und keine Basalte.
> Dich stoert nicht im Innern
> Zu lebendiger Zeit
> Unnuetzes Erinnern
> Und vergeblicher Streit.

the Americans a virgin ground for the building of a liberal system: it conspired itself to help that system along. The abundance of land in America, as well as the need for a lure to settlers, entered it so completely at every point, that Sumner was actually ready to say, "We have not made America, America has made us." [34]

It is this business of destruction and creation which goes to the heart of the problem. For the point of departure of great revolutionary thought everywhere else in the world has been the effort to build a new society on the ruins of an old one, and this is an experience America has never had. We are reminded again of Tocqueville's statement: the Americans are "born equal."

That statement, especially in light of the strange relationship which the revolutionary Americans had with their admirers abroad, raises an obvious question. Can a people that is born equal ever understand peoples elsewhere that have become so? Can it ever lead them? Or to turn the issue around, can peoples struggling for a goal understand those who have inherited it? This is not a problem of antitheses such, for example, as we find in Locke and Filmer. It is a problem of different perspectives on the same ideal. But we must not for that reason assume that it is any less difficult of solution; it may in the end be more difficult since antitheses define each other and hence can understand each other, but different perspectives on a single value may, ironically enough, lack this common ground of definition. Condorcet might make sense out of Burke's traditionalism, for it was the reverse of his own activism, but what could he say about Otis, who combined both concepts in a synthesis that neither had seen? America's experience of being born equal has put it in a strange relationship to the rest of the world.

CHAPTER THREE

America's "Social Revolution"

1. The Pattern of Internal Conflict

,The old days are gone when it used to be the fashion to refer to the American Revolution as a distinctively "political revolution." New historians have uncovered beneath our struggle for national independence a whole series of domestic conflicts, so that now one hears it said again and again, often with a peculiar passion, as if America too long has been denied its rightful heritage of violence, that America, too, had a "social revolution." Whatever these terms may mean, one thing is clear: if we identify the social upheavals of 1776 in America with those of the great European revolutions, we shall never be able to understand them. It is the fact that feudal relics such as primogeniture abolished by the American revolutionaries were indeed relics—which explains the nature of their abolition. And this fact ramifies outward into every other phase of the revolutionary experience. It is reflected in the remarkable achievements of the American radical liberal, the American Jacobin and the American Independent, as it were, since it meant that he did not need to knuckle under to the conservative liberals for long in a battle against the *ancien régime*. It is reflected in the

67

bourgeois ethos even of the outermost limit of American radicalism, since it meant that Daniel Shays lacked the ideological resources to generate anything like the socialist visions of Winstanley or Babeuf. Above all it is reflected in the Whig-Girondin nature of the American "reaction," since it meant that there was no significant *ancien régime* at the beginning to come marching back at the end. A great anticlimax awaits us, to be sure, when we come to Federalist social thought itself. There we find a Hobbesian picture of social conflict which literally turns upside down the revolutionary process of which the Federalists are a part. But this, too, in its own way, is a datum of the American world.

The "social revolution" theory buys its glamour at an especially high price in connection with the American attack on the British monarchy, Tory estates, quitrents, primogeniture and entail, and the Anglican church in the South. Straining to identify this movement with the antifeudal movements of Europe—"as in France," to use Beard's phrase when he describes "newly rich merchants," swarming over the estates of the Jessups and the Morrises [1]—it makes the remarkable success of the movement practically unintelligible. Where else has monarchy ever been destroyed with the quick dispatch and the few regrets that we find here? Where else has a landed and ecclesiastical "aristocracy" been destroyed in the same way? Even the famous Virginia "aristocrats" of 1785, who were not like most of the Tories driven from the country forever, went under with scarcely a blow, evoking, as Jefferson himself reported, more "pity than anger" from the people of the state.[2] The French aristocracy had an inner

68

weakness, perhaps even an obscure hunger for its own destruction, but it did not behave like this. Furthermore the fact that these were "pale replicas" of the old European order, as Becker has put it, rather than the real thing, explains more than the speed of their demolition. It explains the frame of mind that accompanied that demolition, which was not the European passion toned down but something entirely different. For while a frontal attack against feudalism involves a rejection of the past, a mopping up campaign against feudal relics in a liberal society involves the fulfillment of it. While the one creates deep social scars, the other leads to a comfortable sense of fuller social integration. The "social revolution" theory, in other words, cannot by qualification be whittled into an effective analytic tool.

"As in France" unfortunately is not a slogan often applied to the internal struggles of the American revolution where European correlations have usually gone abegging. But the Girondin-Jacobin, Presbyterian-Independent splits within the European liberal ranks are indeed analogous to the "conservative-radical" split in America, and their nature confirms the falseness of the feudal parallels. Were not the Jacobins and the Independents originally wedded to the European moderates by the initial struggles against the *ancien régime?* Did they even discover their democratic dreams until those battles were fought? And what blocked the fulfillment of those dreams if not the leap from the old European order which they required? It is a commonplace of American liberal history that the victory of the American radicals was swift, that it was the culmination of tensions familiar throughout the colonial past, and that even the "reaction" left many of its institutions standing. Nor is the socialist strand in the European revolutions, which fed in ideology on feudal and liberal sources, without significance. Dangerous as it is to overstress the significance of the Diggers and Babeuvisme, it is surely a mark of the American world that it could only produce Daniel Shays, an extension himself of populist liberalism.

The Whig-Girondin nature of the American "reaction" completes the cycle. We do not need to interpret it in terms of Washington's self-abnegation with respect to monarchy and dictatorship or in terms of a lucky Providence which saved America from aristocracy. Madison explained the first issue when he said that the country would not stand for autocratic rule and John Dickinson explained the second when he said that you could not manufacture an aristocracy overnight. A liberal society could only produce, anomalous as the language seems, a liberal reaction. Of course the Hobbesian cosmos of Federalist political thought, though it reflects Federalist liberalism, shows little understanding of these processes. It is filled with "levellers" even worse than Babeuf, just as the anti-Federalist world is filled with "aristocrats" even worse than the Guises. But Federalist political thought, ironically called "realism" by the Progressives, does not alter American reality, which in the end supports the Federal Constitution and shatters the Federalist party. Federalist thought is relevant to the achievements and failures of Federalism, but it does not explain them, any more indeed than it explains the whole of America's strange "social revolution."

2. *Feudal Relics, Democratic Liberalism, and the Problem of Daniel Shays*

Mr. Geoffrey Gorer, the English anthropologist who described George III as a father figure for the Americans, has been criticized for using Freudian language, but the truth is, he used it in the wrong way. For of all the kings unseated by great modern revolutions, George III was probably the only one without real Oedipal significance, as is shown by the fact that when the revolution was over and the nation presumably saturated with guilt, opinion was "decidedly adverse," as Elbridge Gerry put it, to any monarchical restoration.[3] Actually of course there was practically no guilt with respect to any of the feudal relics eliminated by America's evolving liberal society during the revolution, due to the fact that the fundamental liberal decisions had been made long before they were overthrown. A nation that had a great social revolution and was untroubled by it would baffle the social Freudian, but a nation "born equal" does not, save of course for the fact that it poses the unusual problem of a fatherless tribe. It is only because history had already accomplished the ending of the old European order in America that its "social revolution," instead of tearing the soul of the nation apart, integrated it further.

This experience produces a particular kind of polemic: the smashing blow rather than the subtle argument, the technique of the mopping up campaign rather than the full blown battle. Take for example Jefferson's famous attack on primogeniture in the Virginia Assembly in 1785 on the ground that first-born sons worked no more and ate no more than their brothers did. This is supposed to have shattered Edmund Pendleton, that hard-bitten leader of the tidewater "aristocracy," but why? Given the feudal and familial premises of primogeniture, Jefferson's argument is absurd, and in other societies at other times (in Britain, indeed, rather late) it would have elicited considerable laughter. The answer lies in the fact that in Virginia, even in Virginia, the premises of Benjamin Franklin had already superseded those of Bishop Laud, so that the European laughter was replaced by an American explosion. Jefferson's attack on the Virginia Church Establishment is a case of the same thing. He said nothing new. What he did was to achieve a kind of sledge-hammer effect, by piling up against the principle of religious intolerance, one after another, the familiar ideas of natural right, individual conscience, and equitable taxation. He had won his argument, or at least a large part of it, long before he began to speak.

Here, too, I think, we uncover the secret of Paine. The amazing success he had with his attack on monarchy in 1776 seems mysterious only because we overlook the fact that colonial history had long been preparing the nation for it. Of course on the surface the Americans behaved like the best of monarchical peoples, blaming their troubles on ministers and refusing to blame their king until the very end. Even when royal troops were quartered in the colonies, Sam Adams stressed America's unflinching loyalty to the British crown. And yet is it not clear, for all this, and for all the distance of the British monarchy from American life, which surely helped to undermine it, that the bourgeois spirit of the nation had for years been piling up a silent hostility to the rationale on which it rested? What Paine did was to make this hostility explicit—the most powerful technique any propagandist can use. He discussed the "business of a king" as a Connecticut farmer might discuss the business of a grocer, he sized up the civil list as a Boston merchant might size up the salary of a clerk.[4] It was another case of Jefferson and primogeniture: a liberal argument meaningless in a feudal setting became crashingly "self-evident" in a liberal one.

Paine, because he contributed both to the peculiar turmoils of America and Europe, is a good man to think about in this connection. A common sense philosopher, he had come to the most common sense country in the world, but this did not lead to personal fulfillment: he was less happy than Jefferson. For the irony of common sense in Europe was that being frustrated it ceased to be commonsensical, and Paine found himself curiously out of tune with the political temper of his American paradise. America could use a European bourgeois match to explode its latent antimonarchical dynamite, but the rest of Paine's rationalism, his faith in unified legislatures and the like, found a cool reception here, save for a fiery moment in Pennsylvania. If his successes were traceable to the inverted Freudianism of the American revolutionary experience, so were his failures. Actually when this "citizen of the world" plunged himself into the French Revolution, for all of the troubles he had in the course of it, he returned to the instinctive experience of his life: liberal Europe's rejection of the past, not liberal America's fulfillment of it.

With an *ancien régime* as pathetic as this, little wonder that the American radical liberal got out from under the moderate liberals so quickly and so successfully. Not the fighting of the foreign armies of George III, not the fighting of the Tories could force the American radical into a united front with the Whig-Girondin force in the revolution for the length of time that the Levellers or the Jacobins were forced into it by the initial battles against the old European order. With less to accomplish at the extreme right, and with plenty of experience from the colonial past, the backcountry farmers and the city artisans took things into their own hands with remarkable speed. And they left a mark that did not suddenly fade, as did the dreams of the Levellers and the Jacobins, but endured from that time onward in the institutional development of American politics.

We see in the very nature of the social forces which went into the personality of the American radical the nonfeudal world from which he derived his strength. This "petit-bourgeois" was centrally a man of the land, a small capitalist in the American backwoods, breathing the Jacobin spirit of the "shop" as it were, in a novel agrarian setting. Nothing in the French peasantry, and certainly in the English tenant, could compare with the way the American farmer absorbed the land into small-scale capitalism. In many ways this was the most distinctive mark of the American situation. The artisan, too, in the East, showed a liberal, nonproletarian orientation pregnant with significance for the New World. Here, incipiently, is the American democrat whose power was to be writ large over subsequent chapters of the national history.

Here too are the beginnings of his tension, the price he pays for American advantages. In some sense he is even more fearful than the revolutionary peasant or "petit-bourgeois" of France. For already living in the world's closest approximation to a Lockian state of nature, economically he fears loss almost more than he cherishes gain. It is not a glorious dream, but a "conviction of great uneasiness" that the stalwarts of Shays Rebellion complain of when they gather at Hatfield, Massachusetts, during the stormy days of 1785.[5] If they do not have the feudal lord to hate, they have the money-lender to fear. Bentham once said that it is more painful to be deprived of what you have than it is pleasurable to get what you do not have, and when one considers the emotion that went into the radical drive for antiforeclosure legislation, stay laws, and currency inflation, one is tempted to agree with him. Of course, the American radical also wanted more than he had, but this produced not a larger outburst but more acquiescence, since then he identified himself with his only American enemy: the richer liberal. When good times come and the democratic capitalist appetite is whetted, a tempest like the one that Shays represents dies down quickly. You can trace within the revolutionary age itself, culminating in the prosperity of the constitutional "reaction," that manic depressive mentality reflecting the business cycle, which has always characterized the American democratic movement.

Politically there are also tensions, such as the persistent one between extended mass rule and an individualism enshrined in all bills of rights, but here the outstanding mark of the American world will always be the high degree of permanence in the radical achievement. In almost every case, even in the hotbed of revolutionary radicalism, Pennsylvania, the main lines of the constitutionalism they created survived the impact of the American "reaction." The Pennsylvania Convention of 1790 abolished the unicameral legislature and plural executive of the revolutionary days, but it did not touch the essential principle of democracy. In Georgia, the most radical state of the South, the situation was much the same. Contrast these victories with the fate of the glorious republic Lilburne dreamed of or the virtuous republic Robespierre tried to introduce, and the result is remarkable. Morley in his discussion of Cromwell hit the point when he said that in America the democratic idea "was checked by no encounter with an old social state too deeply laid to be speedily modified." [6] The Europeans were trying to implement a law of combined development all of their own, a leap from feudalism all the way to a democratic republic, which is why they were passing explosions on the historical scene. The Americans, having already profited from a law of combined development which eliminated feudalism, were moving only one step leftward, so that it is hardly surprising that they left a more lasting residue behind them. But is not this the reason for the swift destruction of Old World relics and the quick emancipation of the radicals in the first place? We are merely restating here the general principle of America's "social revolution."

We restate it again when we explain why Daniel Shays, frightening as he was to Governor Bowdoin and the Continental Congress, could not become anything like Babeuf or even Winstanley. It is misleading to concentrate here exclusively on the fact that the insurgent American farmers owned property and hence were not likely to dream of Babeuf's "community of wealth." Actually, as M. Mathiez has shown, most of the Babeuvistes were members of the bourgeoisie itself, though the miseries of the Parisian mob were involved in their plea. Behind the issue of proletarian economics lies the larger distinction between the American and the French revolutions: Babeuf was heir to a social experience that Daniel Shays, even in his most turbulent moments, never dreamed of.

Quite apart from the fact of feudal and liberal content, the simple fact of social upheaval is relevant here. "It is scarcely six years that you have begun to breathe, in the expectation of independence, happiness, equality!" runs the famous Manifesto of Equals to the French people in 1795. "The French Revolution is but the precursor of another, and a greater and more solemn revolution, which will be the last!" [7] Obviously Sylvain Maréchal, the author of this Babeuviste document, wanted to complete a social transformation already begun, and while there is no need to twist a religious collectivist dreamer like Winstanley into the French pattern, one can agree with Mr. Petegorsky that the Diggers cherished the same notion. In America, where no such transformation had ever been begun, how could the idea of completing it arise? Of course, the Shays forces pointed to the events of 1776 and after, and their own contributions to them, but these could not teach the European lessons of class upheaval.

Perform an experiment: put the patterns of French and American liberal thought alongside each other and relate them to the socialist idea. Is it not clear that Babeuf got the whole apparatus of socialist thought from liberalism itself revolting against the *ancien régime?* Did he have to go farther than the French Enlightenment to discover his notions of class oppression, concentrated power, millennial secular salvation? It was only a brief step ideologically, if historically rather fateful, to substitute the Pence for

77

the Tiers Etat. Indeed Maréchal cited Condorcet at the very head of the Manifesto of Equals. But if this is true, is it not equally plain that Shays had no such incipient socialist inspiration on which to draw? Where was he to find it—in the psychological pessimism of Adams, the power hatred of Otis, the bourgeois self-satisfaction of Franklin? The great differences which as we have seen separate American from European liberalism killed the socialist dream here at its very bourgeois roots. Indeed what American liberalism offers Shays is a fixed acceptance of Locke deeply antagonistic to anything like the vision of Babeuf and Maréchal. Even had he had some inner yearning in the socialist direction, Shays could not have found the materials to satisfy it.

There is a kind of Biblical irony here. European liberalism, because it was cursed with feudalism, was forced to create the mentality of socialism, and thus was twice cursed. American liberalism, freed of the one was freed of the other, and hence was twice blessed. But as the nineteenth century evolved, as we shall see, the problem of socialism in America and Europe took on a much greater complexity than this.* It is enough to note now that when the Massachusetts radicals frightened the nation they did so in the mood of unhappy kindred spirits, not in the mood of wholesale antagonists. They were inside, rather than outside, the liberal process of American politics.

3. *The Phantom World of the Federalists*

Nothing is better designed to confuse this process, as it embraces Paine and Sam Adams and Shays alike, than

* See pp. 244-53.

the social thought of the constitutional era in which Federalist cries "leveller" and anti-Federalist cries "aristocrat." Nor is the situation helped any by the Federalist denunciation of the French Revolution which superficially seems to link the Whiggery of America with the European reaction and hence indeed with "aristocracy." Some of this, to be sure, is very understandable. As we shall see more clearly later,* the Whig-Girondin temperament seeks to retain some of the old aristocratic order at the very moment it assails it, and while this is meaningful in Europe, in America it is misleading. When the American radicals see Dickinson longing after aristocracy, how are they to know, since there are no aristocrats present, that Dickinson instead of being an aristocrat himself is merely a frustrated liberal who wants to lean on a bit of aristocracy? And yet the ideological confusion of the constitutional era, with its Hobbesian image of man in a land of high cultural solidarity, cannot mislead the student of comparative history for very long.

First of all, in spite of all the excitement of the Federalists over the French Revolution, in spite of all their blasting of the Jacobin clubs and their turmoil over Citizen Genet, they are obviously not in a class with Bonald, Haller, or even Burke. Burke assailed the revolutionary "shopkeepers" of Paris and the continental reactionaries, defined the commercial way of life as a satanic plot against God. Is this the mood of Alexander Hamilton? Of the Hartford Convention? Two things have led to confusion here. One is the fact that the American constitutionalists have a pessimistic view of human nature,

* See Chapter Three.

which Bonald and Maistre also shared, but this is to over-look the fact that all pessimistic views of human nature are not alike. There is a feudal bleakness about man which sees him fit only for external domination, and there is a liberal bleakness about man which sees him working autonomously on the basis of his own self-interest; Maistre believed in the one, Adams believed in the other. The difference between the two boils down to a question of historic development and human rationality, nor ought it to be obscured by the fact that Adams assails the French rationalists for ignoring the lesson of pragmatic evolution. American historicism was charged with the creativeness of the American political past, and Adams was a great believer in the "political science" Burke hated and the man-made constitutionalism Maistre denounced. Indeed 1787 inspired the revolutionaries of France almost as much as 1776 and M. Aulard writes as if there is little difference between the two. Everything goes to show that the difference between Federalism and the European reaction is the difference between liberal Whiggery and the European *ancien régime*.

And yet, of course, rationalist as Federalist Hobbesian-ism was, it premised a type of conflict fully as keen as if the Federalists had indeed been European reactionaries and their opponents European "levellers." Now I do not mean here to underestimate the statemanship the Founding Fathers showed on many specific issues. The frame of mind that went into the Connecticut Compromise apportioning representation among the states, or into the Virginia Plan for a national government which in principle was ultimately accepted, deserves at least most of the praise that Acton and Gladstone gave it. At the same time their deeper philosophy of human nature cannot be called "realistic" unless we define realism by how far away a man gets from the communal optimism of Fourier, which is hardly reasonable, since community is just as real a conflict and Hobbes in his own way just as utopian as the early French socialists. One thing can be said for Hobbes, however, as against Hamilton. Hobbes identified the spirit of the English Civil Wars with the whole of human personality, while Hamilton had to conjure up a set of Civil Wars in order to make the same mistake.

There will always be a dualism here. For the very Americans who tear the community apart when they think about politics at home are forever putting it back together again when they think about politics abroad. We have already seen that one of the earliest sources of American nationalism was a sense of equality that came from knowing that the social conflicts of Europe were not established here. Franklin, who in 1787 saw Americans struggling with each other because of "the love of power" had only a few years before, when he was in Ireland and Scotland, spoken lyrically of the "happiness of New England, where every man is a freeholder. . . ." [8] The same thing can be said about John Adams, Gouverneur Morris, and many others. Historians have praised the Americans for both of these perspectives, but surely there is something wrong with one of them. If the Americans are "realistic" when they celebrate their solidarity in London or Paris, can they also be "realistic" when they forget it in Philadelphia?

What happens, of course, when the Americans come home is that they lose their comparative perspectives and plunge themselves into the shadow world of their own social conflict. This about-face in social thought is accompanied as well, however, by a revolution in philosophic outlook. When the Americans are in feudal Europe, or think of feudal Europe, one might say, despite their difference from Maistre, that their mood is the relativistic mood he described so well when he said that he had seen Frenchmen, Italians, Russians, but never "man." When they come back to America they become universalist children of the Enlightenment once again, and instead of thinking about Americans and Europeans, they think of "man." Man is the hero, or perhaps one ought to say the villain, of American thought in the Constitutional era. True, national relativism is never alone an adequate basis for social thought, and when John Adams says that "Human nature is as incapable now of going through revolutions with temper and sobriety, with patience and prudence, or without fury and madness, as it was among the Greeks so long ago," [9] he is not to be assailed simply because he is searching for constants in human nature. That is valid enough. He is open to sharp criticism, however, when he omits to consider the various milieus in which those constants function. America's "social revolution," as it happens, was carried through with very little Grecian fury and madness.

Greece raises the question of the erudition of the Founding Fathers, which has been praised almost as much as their "realism." Historical knowledge of this sort could be the basis for a relative understanding of American life, a kind of substitute for the contrasting environments that foreign travel offered, but it was rarely used in this way. On the contrary it was subordinated to the Hobbesian universalism of Constitutional thought, and instead of inspiring the Americans to learn how much they differed from the Greeks and the modern Europeans, it inspired them to put themselves in a category with both. Madison loved to talk of "experience," but he was essentially aprioristic. "Experience" for Madison seems to be exhausted by the human propensity to fight, and whether he is discussing the patrician-plebeian struggles of "Ancient Greece," the "feudal licentiousness of the middle ages," or indeed the "existing condition of the American savages," [10] he is always discussing "man": the same man of course who farms in Vermont or runs a printing shop in Philadelphia.

A small bombshell was thrown into the musty atmosphere of this erudition by Virginia's Charles Pinckney. A young man at the time, and possibly without the learning of his elder colleagues, he rose in the Constitutional Convention and asked: "Can the military habits and manners of Sparta be resembled to our habits and manners? Are the distinctions of patrician and plebeian known among us? Can the Helvetic or Belgic confederacies, or can the unwieldy, unmeaning body called the Germanic Empire, can they be said to possess either the same or a situation like ours?" Needless to say, these were relevant words, and Pinckney understood their larger meaning, for he said: "We have considered ourselves as the inhabitants of an old instead of a new country." [11]

Pinckney was the relativist side of the American psyche suddenly exploding through the crust of its abstract universalism. He was Franklin in Scotland suddenly confronting Franklin in Philadelphia. He was John Adams amid the feudalism of Europe suddenly confronting John Adams amid the "levellers" of Massachusetts. And the consequence of his approach was practically predetermined.

By fastening on the "equality" and "mediocrity of station" that the Americans emphasized abroad, he dissolved the Hobbesian image they had created at home. The American who emerged from the "one great and equal body of citizens" that Pinckney proceeded to talk about was the radical reverse of the American who emerged from the learned analyses of his colleagues. True, Pinckney's American was divided into the professional, commercial, and landed classes, but he was not a man who lusted through life for power and domination. His outstanding characteristic was a talent for mutual dependence in dealing with his countrymen.[12]

There is no need to make a great fuss over Pinckney's analysis here, especially since he himself did not stick to it consistently throughout the Convention debates, but it is worth observing that in certain respects, inchoate as it is, it surpasses the famous and much wider analysis that Madison makes in Federalist No. X. Madison discusses almost every kind of social alignment from the religious to the charismatic, but he is still speaking in abstract and universal terms: his concept of "faction" is as absolute as his concept of "man." Granted that the "sources of faction" are various, how much turmoil will they create at any given historic point? Madison does not help us much to answer this question when he says that property is the "most common and durable source" of conflict, since not only does he lump all economic conflicts in the same category, but he obviously believes that at any moment noneconomic issues can be of overwhelming importance. When he comes to the crucial question of specific societies at specific times, he simply says that the amount of conflict will depend on the "different circumstances of civil society." But that is a statement of the problem, not a solution of it.[13] What Pinckney was doing, at any rate, was investigating these "different circumstances" in the American case. And in the process he discovered the actual ethos that lay behind the world of America's "social revolution."

Insofar as the Constitution went, the Federalists should have been thankful that they were wrong. The fact that the document of 1787 is the oldest written constitution in existence, save that of Massachusetts, is pointed out no less frequently than the fact that the men who made it were "realists" in dealing with the stark facts of social conflict. But why has it survived so long? Why did it not go the way, for example, of the Restoration Charter in France? Has this not been precisely because fundamental value struggles have not been characteristic of the United States? Surely the Constitution did not fare very well in the only time any such struggles did appear in the United States, the time of the slavery controversy in the middle of the nineteenth century. Civil war broke out. Indeed one is bound to ask an even more telling question. Would the American Constitution have been able to survive in any nation save one characterized by so much of the "mutual dependence" that Pinckney found here? For the solution the constitutionalists offered to the frightful conflicts they imagined was a complicated scheme of checks and balances which it is reasonable to argue only a highly united nation could make work at all. Delay and deliberate confusion in government became intolerable in communities where men have decisive social programs that they want to execute. Thus a hidden and happy accident has lain at the bottom of the American constitutional experience.

The Founding Fathers devised a scheme to deal with conflict that could only survive in a land of solidarity. The truth is, their conclusions were "right" only because their premises were wrong.

Things did not work out so well however for the Federalist political party formed after 1787. For the very solidarity which supported the Constitution meant Whig elitism would be isolated as the democratic tide of the nation asserted itself once more. The mechanism of 1776 did not end in 1787; it merely went underground, as the victories of Jefferson and Jackson were to show. In this sense the mistaken views of American life that the Whigs cherished cost them heavily, for as they finally discovered when Harrison and Carnegie appeared on the scene, America had much that it could offer them if only they dared to understand it. But these are later chapters of American history. Here we have only to note that the Federalist philosophy of the late eighteenth century is no guide to the reality of the era: to the shattering of America's feudal relics, the triumph of the radicals, the absence of the socialist dream, or to the nature of Federalist "reaction" itself. The American liberal world pursues its own objective course behind the ideological smoke and flame that Federalism generates.

PART THREE

The Emergence of Democracy

CHAPTER FOUR

The Whig Dilemma

1. *Jacksonian Democracy, the July Revolution, and the First Reform Act*

In a society evolving along the American pattern of the Jeffersonian and Jacksonian eras, where the aristocracies, peasantries, and proletariats of Europe are missing, where virtually everyone, including the nascent industrial worker, has the mentality of an independent entrepreneur, two national impulses are bound to make themselves felt: the impulse toward democracy and the impulse toward capitalism. The mass of the people, in other words, are bound to be capitalistic, and capitalism, with its spirit disseminated widely, is bound to be democratic. This is one of the basic insights Tocqueville had about the actual behavior of the American people. The irony of early American history, however, is that these impulses, instead of supplementing each other, seemed to fight a tremendous political battle. The capitalist Whiggery of Hamilton was frightened of democracy, and the democratic tradition of Jackson, which was therefore able to destroy it, formulated a philosophy which seemed to deny its faith in capitalism. The result was a massive confusion in political thought, comparable to the one that we find in the constitutional era, and a set of victories and defeats which the Americans who experienced them scarcely understood. One is reminded of two boxers, swinging wildly, knocking each other down with accidental punches.

Looked at from one point of view, it is strange that Federalism and Neo-Federalism should have been shattered so badly in the liberal setting of American politics. For in the old society of Europe, where these movements were surrounded by a whole series of aristocratic and proletarian enemies, they were reaping their greatest triumphs at precisely the moment they were defeated here. The blood relationship between the Federalist-Whig tradition in America and the tradition of upper middle class liberalism in Europe, the tradition of the English Whigs and the French Liberals, has been as badly neglected in this case as in others. Parrington referred to it of course when he said that the Hamiltonian movement exemplified "English Whiggery." Henry Adams, in a characteristic flash of insight, once spoke of the "instinctive cousinship" that bound the Boston of the "upper class bourgeoisie" to the "London of Robert Peel, Macaulay, and John Stuart Mill" and to the "Paris of Louis Philippe, Guizot, and de Tocqueville." [1] But that is about as far as comparative analysis has gotten, even though the Federalists and the Whigs of America, in their love of capitalism and their fear of democracy, duplicate at virtually every point the European pattern of bourgeois thought.

And yet it is not, as I have said, this connection that in itself is really interesting. What is interesting is the fact that the Americans, unassailed by the manifold enemies their brethren have to face abroad, are defeated while their brethren are victorious. The eighteen thirties, which witness the Reform Act in England and the July Revolution in France, witness also the Jacksonian revolution in America. Just as the cry of "enrichissez-vous" goes up in Paris and London, the grim cry of "monopoly" goes up in the Boston that Adams compared them with. Just as Macaulay and Guizot are proclaiming that the day of universal suffrage will never come, Chancellor Kent and John Quincy Adams are bemoaning the disaster it has already brought. It would be hard to find a more vivid contrast than this, and what is curious is that Parrington and Adams, both imaginative minds, should have seen the basis for the contrast but should not have followed through to the contrast itself.

When we do, the peculiar mechanism of American politics begins to become apparent. We see that the American liberal community, if it did not confront its upper middle class with a set of European aristocracies, peasantries, and proletariats, was bound to confront it with something else which in certain ways was worse: a democratic movement of the lower middle class that it could not possibly master. The word "petit-bourgeois" comes to mind as always in this connection, but now we see more vividly even than in the eighteenth century why it cannot effectively be used. Jackson was not another edition of Flocon, Jefferson another version of Ledru-Rollin. In the very process of expanding the European category of the "petit-bourgeois" America shattered it, creating a movement so lusty and so powerful that it is more than a bit misleading to identify it with the continental shopkeepers on whom Marx and Engels poured their fine contempt in 1848. Of course small urban traders were enlisted in the American democratic movement, but they did not become its leaders. Two other groups, in Europe outside the "petit-bourgeois," clearly overshadowed them: the peasant who had been transformed into a capitalist farmer, and the laborer who had been transformed into an incipient entrepreneur. The result was a great new democratic hybrid unknown in any other land, America's unique contribution to the political culture of the West.

What America was doing here, one might say, was packing all of the traditional enemies of capitalist Whiggery into a single personality. From the angle of Whiggery nothing could have been worse. For the secret of its success in Europe, to put the matter a bit more bluntly than is justifiable, especially in the English case, lay in the fact that it could play its enemies off against one another. That was how it established a claim to national leadership. When the English Whigs and the French Liberals fought the aristocratic order of Europe, they became liberal heroes, rallying behind them the workers and small property owners both of England and France. When, on the other hand, they insisted on excluding their supporters from the suffrage—the workers from the Reform Act and both the workers and the petit-bourgeois from the July Charter—they became conservative heroes, rallying behind them the "existing institutions," as Brougham put it, that they had before assailed. If on the continent the petit-bourgeois sought an independent destiny, there was always the image of a hungry proletariat that might be used to frighten it, as the career of the French Mountain so pathetically reveals in 1848. Thus out of the very diversity of its opponents European Whiggery forged a foothold on which to rest, and out of their diversity, too, it managed to give its political thought a series of glorious overtones. Macaulay when he faced the Duke of Wellington developed a high liberal optimism. Guizot when he faced Ledru-Rollin developed a rich empirical traditionalism. Granted that these were rather contradictory types of glory, and in the French case were pursued with a shocking allegiance to class interest, they nevertheless provided the basis for some sort of genuine political thought.

Now what America did when it created the American democrat is fairly obvious. It removed the European foothold and, doing so, removed all chance for philosophic glory. Here there are no aristocracies to fight, and the Federalists and the Whigs are denied the chance of dominating the people in a campaign against them. Here there are no aristocracies to ally with, and they cannot use their help to exclude the people from political power. Here there are no genuine proletarian outbursts to meet, and they cannot frighten people into fleeing from them. They are isolated, put at the mercy of a strange new democratic giant they cannot possibly control. Their political thought loses entirely its "liberal" aspect, and its conservative denunciation of the people not only becomes suicidal, since it is precisely the people who are sure to shatter them, but loses most of its connection to reality. It is bad enough for Hamilton and Noah Webster to be denied the chance of developing Macaulay's liberalism, and thus to appear forever as conservatives only, but to be put in the position where their longing for a House of Lords, instead of being traditionalistic, is actually revolutionary, since none has ever existed, and where their denunciation of the "mob" is peculiarly absurd since the "mob" is as liberal as they are, is a horrible additional species of punishment. This knocks out all the props from under them, conservative as well as liberal.

And yet American Whiggery, had it not been strategically paralyzed over most of its early history, had it not had an impulse to duplicate European patterns which Henry Adams correctly described when he called it "instinctive," could have avoided all of this. It could have transformed the very liability of the American liberal community into a tremendous asset. For if the American democrat was unconquerable, he was so only because he shared the liberal norm. And this meant two things: one, that he was not a real social threat to Whiggery; and two, that Whiggery had much to offer him in the way of feeding his capitalist impulse. Thus what Whiggery should have done, instead of opposing the American democrat, was to ally itself with him: to give up the idea of exploiting many enemies, as in Europe, and try to exploit the presence of many friends. It should have made a big issue out of the unity of American life, the fact that all Americans were bitten with the capitalist ethos which it was trying to foster. It should, in other words, have developed some sort of theory of democratic capitalism which fit the Tocquevillian facts of American life.

But this, as we know, is precisely what Whiggery failed to do until it saw the light in 1840, and indeed, in any large sense, until the post-Civil War days of Horatio Alger and Andrew Carnegie. Over most of its early history it pursued a thoroughly European policy, and instead of emphasizing what it had in common with the American democrat, it emphasized precisely what it did not have in common with him. Instead of wooing this giant, it chose, quite without any weapons, to fight him. This would be a high species of political heroism, were it not associated with such massive empirical blindness. One can admire a man who will not truckle to the mob, even though the mob is sure to beat him, provided there is actually a mob in the first place. But in America there was no mob: the American democrat was as liberal as the Whigs who denounced him. Consequently the suicidal grandeur of Fisher Ames is tinged with a type of stupidity which makes admiration difficult. At best one can find in the Whigs a kind of quixotic pathos. One can treat them as Europeans living in an alien world, unwilling and unable to understand it. They have great liberal energies but America has no use for them. They pursue the usual conservative strategies but are baffled and dumfounded at every turn. It is the sort of pathos one might expect to find in Macaulay had he suddenly been shipped to America—except for the fact, alas, that Macaulay saw more about America from London than Fisher Ames saw about it from Boston.

This analysis gives us, it seems to me, a clue to the solution of an ancient problem: the speedy triumph of democracy in America. Our efforts to explain the rise of American democracy have foundered largely on the fact that they have been unable to withstand any comparative test. Turner's frontier theory breaks down because frontiers are to be found in other lands. An emphasis on urban industrialism, which some of our newer historians are supplanting it with, breaks down even more, since industrialism was farther advanced in England and possibly even in France than it was in the United States in the eighteen twenties. But if we assert that the quick emergence of democracy was inherent in the American liberal commu-

95

nity, we advance a proposition that comparative analysis cannot destroy. Indeed the inflexible European behavior of American Whiggery gives this proposition the kind of support that one might almost expect to get from a laboratory experiment. Had the Whigs adapted themselves at once to the unique reality of America, had they donned something like the garb of Carnegie in the age of Fisher Ames, they would have confused the issue considerably. We would have had to work entirely with assumptions that could not be empirically verified. As it is, however, since Fisher Ames tried his best to operate like Guizot, we can clearly say that in a liberal society the only type of antagonism to democracy that can appear is the antagonism of the upper middle class and that in such a society the upper middle class is robbed of the capacity to implement it. In other words, if we could imagine England or France in the eighteen thirties with their feudalisms gone and their masses unified around the liberal norm, we could expect to find, on the basis of their own history, the same sort of pattern that appeared in America. We could expect to find all of the familiar techniques of Whiggery exploding in its face, a huge new democrat emerging, and the early triumph of manhood suffrage.

2. *The Atrophy of Whig Progressivism*

Given its early strategy, then, there were three parts to the problem American Whiggery faced: the absence of an aristocracy to fight, the absence of an aristocracy to ally with, and the absence of a mob to denounce.

The first of these was in a sense the most crushing, and if we are to interpret the Whigs in terms of their pathos, here surely is a place where we can give them our deepest sympathy. Of course, looked at from one point of view, it is no minor blessing to have your Wellingtons and Polignacs removed for you in advance. On the rare occasions the American Whigs thought of the battles they had avoided, they breathed a sigh of relief. Rufus Choate, that arch apostle, with Story, of Massachusetts Whiggery, compared America with Europe and was delighted to discover that here there was no need to "reform" society "fundamentally." [2] But this was an ironic joy, as is often the case in politics, because enemies can of course perform a positive as well as a negative function. Had the need for fundamental reform actually existed, Choate would have been more than a mere "conservative," spinning negative theories of dubious validity. He would have been a crusading "liberal," developing something like Bentham's utilitarianism or, at the very least, something like the eclectic liberalism of the French Doctrinaires. He would not have gone down in history, since history has been written from the progressive point of view, as a villain merely, but as a hero as well.

This atrophy of Whiggery's liberal talent, this failure of Whiggery to develop the positive side of its personality, is an odd philosophic tragedy. Potentialities are everywhere, but instead of being developed, they are turned back upon themselves. Fisher Ames has a concept of "public liberty," but rather than carrying it forward, he proceeds to limit its application. Daniel Webster hails the revolutions of Europe, but after having done so, he laments the extension of suffrage in Massachusetts. The better half of Whiggery simply cannot flower, and one is reminded again and again of what Brougham might have looked like had his career been exhausted by the fear of

annual parliaments. American Whiggery, lacking a prov-
ing ground for its liberal energies, loses the hope and the
optimism that we find in the Whiggery of Europe. A life
of too much ease makes it negative, querulous, and bitter.

The way this shattered its claim to political leadership
becomes apparent when we consider the outlook of two
men like Francis Place and William Leggett. In England,
Place had little affection for a wealthy middle class that
was ready to exclude the people from power, but he was
at any rate watching it fight a tremendous battle against
the grip of Tory landlords, which made him feel that it
was at least on the right track, taking a step in his own
direction. But in America what has Leggett got to watch?
It is all right for Kent to tell him, as Macaulay told the
people of England, that "property and intelligence" ought
to govern the state, but what are property and intelligence doing in America to justify that honor here? It
makes no difference, alas, that under the right conditions
they might be doing everything they did abroad, that
Kent might actually be a legal reformer, and that Daniel
Webster might be delivering reformist speeches European
schoolboys would now be learning by heart. Leggett is
not concerned with that and, the truth is, neither is Kent.
In America the issue is America, not Europe. And here
Whiggery looks very much as if it is making the biggest
mistake in politics: claiming a privilege without perform-
ing a service.

As men, certainly, the big capitalists of America were
no worse than the big capitalists of England or the continent. Indeed they may well have been better: the proletarian miseries Engels found in Manchester he could not
have found in Lowell and the control of the state by

finance that Marx found in Paris he could not have found in Washington. But for all that, the inability of the Americans to match the claims of the Europeans dogged them to the end. In Europe during the thirties there was a kind of Aristotelian revival in social thought and theorists like James Mill and Royer-Collard glorified the wealthy middle class as the *juste-milieu* in politics, uncorrupted by the decadence of the aristocracy and unmoved by the turbulence of the mob. But in America the wealthy middle class is cruelly denied this chance of glorifying itself, because here, unfortunately, it is not in the middle but on top. A theory of the "middling class" such as Jonathan Wainwright developed, hurts it rather than helps it. Indeed in the liberal atmosphere of America it is itself the group that is blasted as an "aristocracy," and its dilemma is doubly and triply painful because it cannot even reply to the attack with the time-honored defense of a genuine aristocracy. A genuine aristocracy can claim at least the virtues of a public spirited paternalism, but how can a wealthy middle class ever hide the acquisitive code by which it lives? Thus what happens is this: America roasts its propertied liberals in a pair of completely incongruous fires. At one and the same time they are parasitic "aristocrats" and exploitative "capitalists."

This strange symbolic punishment, which can be documented in any work of Taylor or Leggett, was reflected also on the economic plane. Technically the American Whigs should have produced a Ricardo or a Say just as they should have produced a Macaulay or a Guizot. But because they did not confront the economic heritage of feudalism any more than they confronted its political heritage, they produced neither. True, this was not a story of energies that were totally lost: if they had a large measure of economic freedom, they still needed, because of America's underdeveloped economy, state economic aid, and so they exchanged the cry of "laissez faire" for the cry of tariffs and the "American system." In the process, however, the "aristocrat"-cum-"capitalist" torture was intensified a notch. They became at once the Corn Law "monopolists" of America, and symbols that looked very much like those they would have hurled at Europe's *ancien régime* were hurled at them by the American democrat. Here, indeed, is the source of our modern confusion of Jeffersonian theory with European theories of laissez faire—our inability to distinguish between a middle class attack on the established interests of corporate society and a democratic attack on the promotional aims of the middle class itself which are not even established. But words that look the same can be very misleading indeed. Even John Bright, the blood brother of the American Whigs, could not help confusing them with his aristocratic enemies. "The speeches of Henry Clay and Daniel Webster," Bright bitterly remarked in 1844, "might have done credit to the Dukes of Buckingham and Richmond themselves." [3]

Things have come to a pretty pass when Manchester can denounce Lowell as the seat of the English gentry. But in economics as in politics this was the price the Federalists and the Whigs paid for having their liberal victories handed to them on a silver platter, for having their Wellingtons and their Polignacs disappear into the thin historical air. Lacking the feudal enemies that might have made a nation follow them, they looked like the very villains they would have fought. It was an ironic situation, but one of the most ironic things about it is that it has dogged them all the way into our contemporary historical literature where at the hands of Beard and his disciples they receive much the same incongruous abuse they received at the hands of Taylor and Leggett. They are blasted as "reactionaries" when they are no more reactionary than the founders of European liberalism, they are denounced in the same breath as "aristocrats" and "capitalists" when in fact they are only capitalists, and in general they live the lives they led a hundred years ago. Our progressive historians, one is tempted to say, have not produced a study of American political thought: they have produced a replica of it.

But I am not trying, at this late hour, to rehabilitate the Federalists and the Whigs. They deserve all of the criticism they have received, but not for the reason they have received it. Their crime was not villainy but stupidity, and perhaps in politics a man ought to know that if he is guilty of the second, he is going to be charged with the first. What is remarkable is how long the American Whigs managed to endure the strange abuse of a liberal community without waking up to the logic behind it. Here they were in a setting where the democracy was closer to them than anywhere else in the West, and yet instead of embracing it, they feared it and they fought it as their comrades did in Europe, even though none of the European weapons were at hand. The lament of the Adamses, that they were born into the wrong sort of world, is not quite correct. They were born into the right sort of world and they were overwhelmed, not because they could not defeat their enemies but because they were too unenlightened to recognize their friends.

3. *The Search for an Aristocratic Anchor*

When we turn to the second part of the problem of American Whiggery, the absence of an aristocracy to ally with, we find a story no less subtle but one in which the gloom is occasionally broken by a ray of good fortune. The story begins, to be sure, on an even gloomier note than the other. The fact that Wellington is not available for a battle, whenever it occurs to the Whigs, is actually, as I have said, a source of conscious joy. But the fact that he is not available for an alliance, because it is directly related to the negative side of Whiggery which in America absorbed almost the whole of it, is a source of the keenest pain. It is a fact not easily forgotten. When John Dickinson, discussing aristocratic institutions in the Federal Convention, cried, "Can these be created by a breath or a stroke of the pen?" [4] he voiced a lament that echoed all the way down to the Jacksonian era. As late as 1837 Noah Webster, though dutifully rejecting "distinct orders or ranks of men," reopened the question of how the masses could ever be controlled without them.[5] Macaulay once said that the American political system was "all sail and no anchor," and it was precisely this which bothered his American brethren. They longed for an anchor, something that might hold in check the frightful proletarian rampages on which the American democrat was sure to embark.

Here, however, a strange thing happened, which rescued them a bit from their frustration. Their fear of the American democrat coincided with the American democrat's fear of himself, for he, no more than they, understood the liberal world that brought him to power, and hence could not see any better than they could that in such a world the majority would not want to annihilate the individualist way of life. And so the American democrat, in one of the strangest examples of political confusion and political collapse in the American record, permitted the Whigs to throw a set of chains around him. He would, of course, never accept the House of Lords that Hamilton and Dickinson wanted. But when they shifted their search for an anchor from aristocracy to the law, his resistance diminished considerably. That shift, as Hamilton maneuvered it, was little short of a strategic masterpiece. Denied the rock of aristocracy, confronted with a constitution that was a constantly moving set of wheels and mechanisms, he seized upon the one thing in this situation that did not move at all: the Constitution itself. Nor was this a purely metaphysical enterprise, a conceptual substitute for royalty such as Paine had once envisaged. Hamilton erected on the fixity of the fundamental law the judicial review of a set of life term judges who were very human indeed and who came as close to being a House of Lords as a purely liberal society could produce. Tocqueville, when he arrived in America, was able to call the "bench and the bar" the "American aristocracy."

Brilliant, amazing as all this was, we must not assume that it was a complete solution to Whiggery's problem. Hamilton was gloomy to the very end. And the American democrat, like any giant who has accepted a set of chains as a result of his own confusion, was restive under their restraint, striking out now and again in a way designed to terrify the smaller men around him. The Whigs, of course, lectured him passionately on how dangerous he was to everyone including himself. Story insisted that only the power of the fundamental law could serve in America as a substitute for Europe's "ecclesiastical and civil establishments, venerable from their antiquity." [6] Choate, doing his best to expend upon the law the mystic traditionalism those "establishments" got in Europe, said that it embodied the "national history" and the "national mind." [7] But the American democrat, though confused, was never thoroughly convinced. In the time of his Jacksonian anger he simplified common and statute law, he substituted Taney for Marshall, and if neither of these actions really went very far, they were enough to remind the Whigs that here, as elsewhere, their lot in America was a hard one. "I am the last of the old race of judges," Story bitterly lamented when he returned to Massachusetts from the Court. [8]

There was a hidden irony in Hamilton's disappointment at not having a real House of Lords to combine with. For the aristocrats of Europe soon showed that, even after being tamed by Whiggery, they could challenge it. They could join with the people themselves, forging a combination of extremes, and this is the source of that Tory humanitarianism, that "feudal socialism," as Marx and Engels called it, which arose in Europe in the nineteenth century. It would have been poetic justice if Hamilton, after bemoaning the absence of a solid aristocracy of the British type, had had to have a session with Lord Shaftesbury concerning the women and the children he wished to employ in American factories. His "judicial aristocracy," weak as it was, endangered always by the rising ire of the American democrat, would never at any rate provide him with a session like that. The worst thing that could happen in the case of judges was that they might collapse. They would not take the offensive, and in the name of an ancient society of status, demand the control of industrialism.

Thus another minor boon for the Whigs in the midst of their American misery: they did not have to confront either a Shaftesbury or a Berryer. We can hardly begrudge it to them. Orestes Brownson, a man who clearly caught their "middle class" character, on occasion seemed to do so. A "Duke of Wellington," he insisted, "is much more likely to vindicate the rights of labor than an Abbot Lawrence." [9] And in the American progressive tradition as a whole Brownson's lament has occasionally been echoed: we have missed the conservative humanitarianism of Europe, the sense of social responsibility it embodies. No one can deny, of course, that we have missed it, just as we have missed other things, the love of variety for example, which the tradition of Disraeli has given to the life of Europe. The closest in social theory that we have come to reproducing Disraeli are the Southern "feudalists" who read him with a passion before the Civil War, and surely they were very far from meeting the standard of Tory humanitarianism.* New England, with its Calvinist idea of stewardship, has never quite met that standard either. The Calvinist idea attaches social responsibility to the very exploitative wealth-getting that the Tory principle denounces.

But in the last analysis, what else do we have a right to expect? If liberal America is going to shatter its Whigs by removing the aristocrat and expanding the democrat, can we also ask that it shatter them again by restoring

* See p. 145 ff.

the aristocrat? A nation cannot have everything. A Wellington would have made a crusading "liberal" out of Abbot Lawrence and would probably have chained Brownson to his chariot as Cobbett was chained to the chariot of the English Whigs. In general Brownson was lucky that in America the rights of the people had to be vindicated by the people themselves—lucky, that is, until Whiggery, waking up to what it had in common with the "mob," discovering the facts of America's liberal life, began to defend the people itself. This changed the strategic picture entirely. But a lot of water went under the bridge, and the shade of Fisher Ames died a hundred deaths, before Brownson was struck the blow of 1840.

4. *The Attack on Popular Government*

The final dilemma of the Federalists and the Whigs, the fact that the people they denounced as lusting for Caesarism and the destruction of property were liberals like themselves, confronts us with a less intricate problem than the others. This was not a case of blows raining down from unknown sources, as with the absence of an aristocracy to fight, or of subtle adaptations to frustration, as with the absence of an aristocracy to ally with. It was a plain case of unjustly insulting a democracy that could not be controlled, and it reveals American Whiggery at its suicidal worst.

The truth is, the arguments of Whiggery against manhood suffrage were not even valid in Europe. The horror of Macaulay and Guizot at the thought of the universal vote overlooked the attachment of the European peasantry to the institution of property and exaggerated the hunger of the European proletariat. A shrewd conservative like

Bismarck saw this, and so did Berryer in France. What America did, when in the person of the American democrat it absorbed both of these groups into the liberal category, was to make the errors of Europe obvious. Indeed some of the European Whigs, unable to perceive these errors at home, actually perceived them here. Thomas Attwood, leader of the Birmingham Political Union in 1831, pointed out that America had "at least nine men interested in property to one man interested in labor alone," which was "exactly the reverse" of the situation in England,[10] and Macaulay agreed that this condition actually justified the adoption of universal suffrage.* But their American brethren, orthodox to the end, behaving "instinctively," advanced the European arguments nevertheless. Chancellor Kent, after concluding the familiar Platonic analysis of popular tyrannies and attacks on property in the New York Convention of 1821, asked: "And dare we flatter ourselves that we are a peculiar people . . . ?"[11] It did not occur to him that the answer might be yes.

Since it was such a patent distortion of the truth that even Macaulay and Attwood could see it, the argument of the Federalists and the Whigs was hardly designed to elicit a docile reaction from the American democrat. Of course the American democrat did not ordinarily defend himself by pleading that he was just as liberal as his opponents. He assailed them as "aristocrats" and defined himself as a downtrodden "laborer," thus shattering the Whigs with their own cosmology and in the end, alas, confusing himself almost as much as they were confused. But

* Macaulay's prediction as to the ultimate fate of American democracy was, of course, a gloomy one.

on occasion the plea of a common liberalism was stung out of him nevertheless. The American people, Leggett bitterly remarked, "are just as well acquainted with the rights of person and property and have as just a regard for them as the most illustrious lordling of the scrip nobility." In Virginia, John R. Cooke, replying to the charge that unpropertied men were potential "levellers," put his finger on a basic mechanism of American life: men who did not own property dreamed of doing so and hence it could never be to their "interest" to destroy it. And New York's General Root, infuriated by Chancellor Kent, declared: "We are all of the same estate—all commoners. . . ." [12]

All of the same estate: here in five words the basic fact that ruined Whiggery in America. But that Whiggery should have beaten those words out of the American democrat, if only for an angry and enlightened second, shows how blind it was. For if they were the key to Whiggery's collapse in European terms, they were the only key to its survival in American terms: unable to control the American democrat by leading him in a liberal movement and blasting him in a conservative movement, it could only control him by uniting with him in a capitalist movement. Instead of making him say, "we are all of the same estate," it should of course have said so itself—loudly and passionately and publicly.

The mind of Hamilton, for all of the ingenuity it displayed in the judicial realm, was unable to go as far as this. Defending manufactures he said that anything which enhances the "total mass of industry and opulence" in a country "is ultimately beneficial to every part of it." But not only did he stick to his unreal conception of the

American mob in politics, he extended it to economics as well. A national bank was good because it would "unite the interests and credit of rich individuals with those of the state." Manufactures were good because among other things they provided employment for the women and children of the poor. The idea of a national capitalist partnership in democratic terms was outside the path of his vision. His "nationalism," like Marshall's in McCulloch v. Maryland, was legal rather than social, defending a federal government but not embracing in any Rousseauan sense—as, ironically enough, Jefferson's "anti-nationalism" did—the American popular community.* Indeed so far did he go in ignoring the liberal capitalist impulse in the nation at large that Democratic politicians were able to steal many of his policies in the process of assailing them as "monopoly." The acceptance of much of Whiggery by the Jeffersonians is a familiar fact. In the states particularly they chartered corporations and constructed internal improvements with the happiest abandon.[12]

Thus so long as the Hamiltonian view prevailed the suicidal trend in American Whiggery was bound to persist. The fact that Americans were "all of the same estate," instead of being the key to glorious success, remained the key to bitter failure. The Whigs were "aristocrats" as well

---

* It is worth noticing that this legal aspect of Whig nationalism persisted into the sectional argument before the Civil War where a social or romantic theory would have been useful indeed in dealing with the Southern case—itself partially romantic. Webster, debating with Hayne, was an extension of Marshall. See p. 164. Of course the Whigs, once they discovered Horatio Alger, got hold of a really vibrant nationalism, the American Way of Life, but for the most part (although it is interesting that Webster himself helped to originate it) this came after the classic sectional battle in the context of which one ordinarily conceives their nationalist contribution to lie.

as "capitalists," they longed for stabilities they could not find, they aroused the very people who destroyed them. They were Europeans pursuing a strategy that even in Europe would soon become ineffective.

But whatever might be said about philosophers like Fisher Ames and Chancellor Kent, there is a limit to how many times politicians like Weed and Webster are willing to commit political suicide. As the Harrison campaign approached, these men, not out of any particular social insight but out of the sheer agony of defeat, discovered the facts of American life. Giving up the false aristocratic frustrations of the past, and giving up as well its false proletarian fears, they embraced America's liberal unity with a vengeance, and developed a philosophy of democratic capitalism. Willy-nilly, the difference between America and Europe swam into the ken of their vision, and Daniel Webster, pounding away at what he had in common with everyone else, insisted that the "visible and broad distinction" between the masses and the classes of the "old countries of Europe" was not to be found in the United States. Calvin Colton, also pointing to Europe, said that "every American laborer can stand up proudly, and say, I AM THE AMERICAN CAPITALIST. . . ." [14] Whiggery had finally hit on the secret of turning its greatest liability into its greatest advantage.

5. *The Idea of Democratic Capitalism*

If what I have said here is correct, the Whig Counter-reformation, as Arthur Schlesinger has aptly called it, has been rather badly misinterpreted. It has been denounced as insincere, and in the case of men like Colton and even Daniel Webster that may well have been true. But it has also been denounced as "unrealistic," as advancing a milk-and-water theory which obscured the facts and which was a sorry contrast to the grim Harringtonian theory of class conflict that Kent and Noah Webster stuck to. This would seem to be invalid. For while there can be no doubt that Edward Everett and Daniel Webster had overplayed the bond that existed between rich and poor in 1840, Kent and Webster had underplayed it even more. The whole trouble with the old Federalist theory of the "mob" was that in America it was thoroughly unrealistic, and if it was documented with many learned European sources, this merely suggests that it was more "realistic" in Europe than it was in America. Indeed what accounts for the nationalist slogan of "Americanism" so easily associated with the new Whig theory, and ultimately so effective a weapon in its armory, if not the fact that the Whigs had uncovered something basic in the temper of the national life? Our progressive historians will not give the Whigs a chance. They glory in the suicide the Whigs commit because they cannot understand America, but once they begin to understand it, the progressives denounce them for becoming unwise.

We think of the Whigs in the age of Harrison as stealing the egalitarian thunder of the Democrats, but actually they did more than that. They transformed it. For if they gave up Hamilton's hatred of the people, they retained his grandiose capitalist dream, and this they combined with the Jeffersonian concept of equal opportunity. The result was to electrify the democratic individual with a passion for great achievement and to produce a personality type that was neither Hamiltonian nor Jeffersonian but a strange mixture of them both: the hero of Horatio

Alger. Edward Everett emphasized that "in this country" the "wheel of fortune is in constant revolution, and the poor, in one generation, furnish the rich of the next." [15] A new social outlook took shape, dynamic, restless, competitive, and because it united the two great traditions of the American liberal community, its impact ultimately became enormous. The American democrat was unprepared to meet it, and one of the reasons why, ironically enough, was that he himself had ignored the fact that Americans were "all of the same estate." Exploiting an unreal demonology of "aristocrats" and "capitalists," he had missed the aristocratic and capitalistic impulses that burned in his own breast, and so without quite knowing why he found himself, as in 1840, harnessed to the chariot of a reformed Whiggery. The "judicial aristocracy" strategy was worked on him again, this time exploiting not a false fear but a genuine lust. To change our metaphor a bit, we might say that the tables of the American liberal community were turned upon the American democrat, and instead of capitalizing on Whiggery's blindness to America, Whiggery capitalized on his. This was the law of Whig compensation inherent in American life.

All of this, of course, reached its climax after the Civil War, when American capitalism surged forward rapidly, when no political movement, however perceptive, could withstand the appeal of the prizes it offered—when Carnegie and Harding took the place of Everett and Clay. But it is not without its relevance to our analysis here. It shows that a paradox apparently implicit in it did not in fact materialize: that the world's most capitalistic community should shatter the philosophy of capitalism. And for what a sentimental point is worth, it suggests that the

American Whigs were to be amply repaid for the humil-
iation they endured while their brethren were triumphant
abroad. In the late nineteenth and the twentieth centuries the situation would be reversed, and Chancellor Kent
would be watching the agonies of Guizot. While a new
movement, the movement of socialism, would be engulf-
ing the Whiggery of Europe, the age of Louis Philippe
would come with a vengeance to America—and it would
come precisely because the American Whigs had no aristocracy to fight, no aristocracy to ally with, and above all
no "mob" to denounce.

CHAPTER FIVE

The American Democrat: Hercules and Hamlet

1. Social Cross-Breeding and the Democratic Psyche

The clue to the American democrat lies in his hybrid character, and the clue to his hybrid character lies in the American liberal world. As we have seen, the Federalists and the Whigs are not a peculiar creation of American life. They are a familiar Western type, Whigs of the wealthy middle class, and what is remarkable about them is the fate that they experience: defeat in the age of Louis Philippe, success in the age of the Paris Commune. But the American democrat is the man who imposes this strange life on American Whiggery, and by doing so he displays in his own personality all of the nonliberal European elements that the American world has liberalized and inspirited with the ethos of Sydney and Locke. He is a liberal of the small propertied type, vastly expanded in size and character by a set of incongruous strains: the peasant who has become a capitalist farmer; the proletarian who has become an incipient entrepreneur; and in the time of Jefferson, even the Southern "aristocrat" who emerges to lead them both. It is not hard to see why the term "petit-bourgeois" loses its meaning in the case of a giant as rich, as complicated, and as various as this. When the European shopkeeper has absorbed practically the whole of a nation, what is to be gained by calling him a shopkeeper? Tocqueville, a man who came from the classic home of Europe's petit-bourgeois, from the Paris of Balzac and Marx, said that "what astonishes me in the United States is not so much the marvelous grandeur of some undertakings as the innumerable multitude of small ones."[1]

The truth is, there is not a term in the Western political dictionary that can be used to describe the American democrat, and he is therefore, for one thing, immune to all types of political insult. If the Marxist calls him a "humble and crouchingly submissive" small urban trader, he can point out at once that he is a man of the land, the factory, and the forge, a man who has all the proletarian virtues that Marx was forever contrasting with the pettiness of the petit-bourgeois. If the Marxist calls him a peasant, an agent of "barbarism within civilization," * he can reply, with Tocqueville, that he is an aggressive entrepreneur, buying "on speculation," combining "some trade with agriculture," making "agriculture itself a trade," indeed the leader of American progressivism.[2] Nor do bourgeois epithets bother him any more than socialist ones. If in the time of Jefferson you call him a landed aristocrat, he can reply that he is a radical democrat. If in the time of Jackson you call him a dangerous

---

* The Marxian terms here are taken from F. Engels, *Germany: Revolution and Counter-Revolution* (New York, 1933), pp. 13, 104; K. Marx, *The Class Struggles in France* (New York, 1936), p. 71.

proletarian, he can point to an undeviating attachment to liberalism and property rights.

There is, in other words, always something in the American democrat which redeems him from something else, so that the man who tries to attack him, or indeed even the man who tries to defend him, is confounded at every turn. At bottom, to lapse into Marxian language again, he has the "mesquin" outlook of a Flocon or a Ledru-Rollin, a certain smallness of entrepreneurial preoccupation which has never been glamorous in Western thought. But overlaid on this story there are two heroic dramas, the covered wagon drama of the American frontier and the strike-ridden drama of a rising labor movement, so that when we come to men like Jackson and Leggett we are never quite sure whether we are dealing with a petty hope or a glorious dream. But it is this very ethos of the small and independent liberal, this very shadow of the European "petit-bourgeois," which saves the American land and American labor from the charge of reaction and revolution. Whatever might be said about Jackson, he is not a Benjamin Disraeli; and whatever might be said about Leggett, he is something short of a Friedrich Lasalle. The American democrat, by compounding in his own small propertied liberal personality the ancient feudalism and the incipient socialism of Europe, is a man who may satisfy no one but he is also a man whom no one can thoroughly hate.

Here, of course, we have the reason the American democrat was able to demolish Whiggery during the time, prior to its conversion to the log-cabin faith, when it was pursuing the more genteel European strategies of Fisher Ames and J. Q. Adams. Swallowing up all of the social

116

forces that in Europe Whiggery would have played off against each other in order to keep him down, above all the feudal aristocracy and the unpropertied proletariat, he took the props from under Whiggery and left it helpless in a liberal world. Thus another clue to his personality suggests itself at once. Had he suddenly gone to Western Europe, instead of finding the many "instinctive cousins" that as Henry Adams noticed the American Whigs had there, he would not have found a man he could have called his brother. Imagine Daniel Webster and Andrew Jackson both in the England of the eighteen thirties or forties. It is not hard to conceive of Webster flourishing almost as much as Macaulay flourished, leading the masses against the aristocracy and joining with the aristocracy against the masses. But what would have happened to Jackson? Where would he have stood? Would he have stood with Disraeli and the land, or with Cobbett and the workers, or with the petty enterprisers who scarcely had an independent leadership? The fact is, he would not have known where to stand. He would have wandered homelessly over the face of Europe, a lost giant from another world, finding parts of his personality in various places but the whole of it nowhere. Victorious in the liberal society of America, he would have been, precisely for that reason, a massive misfit in the old society of Europe.

But the American democrat, for all of his giant size and his complex virtue, was a strangely pathetic figure even at home. First of all, there was a certain inherent logic to the Western European social divisions. It was not easy all at once to be a landed "aristocrat," a farmer, a laborer. Psychic tensions appeared. Moreover, even if the American democrat was thus placed in a position where he could isolate an elitist Whiggery, the premium this placed on wild claims of social war was bound further to confuse his social thought. When you do not know precisely who you are yourself, the invitation to call your enemies the worst of names has a curious effect all around. But finally, and above all, the historic petit-bourgeois dilemmas of the Western world remained: individualist fear despite a faith in the majority, capitalist hunger despite talk of "monopoly." These drives, as we know, ultimately enchained the American democrat to the very Whigs he was able to shatter in 1800 and 1828. They were painful enough impulses for the Flocons of Europe, but when they appeared in the breast of a New World democrat with a love of hyperbole, they became the clue to endless bewilderment and self-betrayal. They completed a pattern of theoretical confusion which will require from us the steadiest analytic hand to unravel.

Thus it happened that the American democratic giant bought his strength at the price of weakness, his power to defeat Whiggery at the price of losing to it in the end. Here was America's law of Whig compensation mirrored in reverse. And here, too, is why even the most romantic progressive historians have always missed fire somehow when they have come to the American democrat. The man is too thoroughly torn by inner doubt, too constantly in danger of selling out to his opponents, for a warrior legend ever successfully to be built around him. In itself I do not particularly care about the latter fact. Warrior giants, if they are legendary, are also frightening, and it is probably a virtue of the American democrat that he is not a frightening man. But as a symptom of American

118

liberalism, the failure of the progressive romanticists is signicant. It reminds us that when the New World began to cross the strands of the Old what emerged was not quite a Hercules but a Hercules with the brain of a Hamlet.

2. *"Aristocrat," Farmer, "Laborer"*

As the American democrat struggled to reconcile the conglomerate elements of Western society out of which he was built, he produced a scheme of social thought that reminds one of a house of mirrors: the more rooms you enter the more bewildered you get. Consider, first of all, the way in which he absorbed the land and the factory into the ethos of democratic liberalism. Americans take this so completely for granted, especially the liberal agrarianism of Jefferson, that it rarely occurs to them how remarkable it actually is. The role of the land in the politics of modern Europe still needs much historical study, but one thing would seem to be fairly clear. When it was not without a philosophy, as was true in the case of the peasantry and the tenantry, save for sporadic anarchist dreams like those of Proudhon or frustrated yeomen dreams like those of Cobbett, its spokesmen were usually conservative thinkers: men like Disraeli and Bonald. Liberalism was associated with the towns. The Jeffersonian theory, making land the indispensable base of liberal democracy, is quite an American matter, which shows us, as Whitney Griswold has pointed out,[3] how plastic the agrarian virtues of Aristotle are. Jefferson and Disraeli are agreed on many points. They agree that there is a peculiar goodness in the cultivation of the land, that industrial cities are dangerous things. But observe the way

119

they differ: Disraeli sees the land as fostering an ancient feudal order and the towns as fostering democracy, while Jefferson sees the land as fostering democracy and the towns a quasi-feudal kind of social dependence. The only irony that is needed to round this situation out is that capitalist Whiggery is blasted either way: Bright is assailed from the right, Daniel Webster from the left.

But this is not the main point. The main point is that the democratic-liberal transformation of the land in America was not quite complete, for the great early Southern agrarians were large plantation magnates who cherished, as much as America permitted it, the aristocratic ethos. This is not true in the case of Jefferson, whose faith in "small landholders" as the "most precious part of the state" cannot be seriously questioned. John Taylor, however, is a case of another kind. It is not hard to see that he is a radical democrat only because he cannot be an authentic aristocrat: because the land in America is predominantly in the hands of small entrepreneurs and if he wishes to defeat the Hamiltonian program he must join with a democracy that shares his debtor complex. He himself admitted as much as this when he said that a "multitude of proprietors" had made the American land "irretrievably republican," so that an "aristocracy cannot exist," which meant that a gentleman had "no alternative" but to move to the political left.[4] Here was a strange frustration: living on the radical edge of the Enlightenment only because you could not live on the conservative edge of the Reaction, supporting the independent farmer only because the "good discipline" of the English estate was impossible in a liberal world. What it meant, of course, was that the Mr. Hyde of an Edmund Burke was always struggling to explode beneath the Dr. Jekyll of a Thomas Paine. And eventually the explosion did in fact occur. When the tenants began to revolt in the Hudson Valley, James Fenimore Cooper, an "aristocrat," moved from blasting Whiggery's stake-in-society argument to supporting the good Burkian notion that the "column of society must have its capital as well as its base." [5] In the South, where slavery made the liberalism of the "aristocrats" doubly dubious, the explosion was tremendous. When abolitionism got under way, John Taylor, transforming himself into George Fitzhugh, did his best to dream the dream of Scott and the European reaction.

Even if these strange tensions within the agrarian part of his personality had never been resolved, however, the American democrat would have had to face the problem of uniting to it the urban part of his personality. This was no minor task in the realm of psychic integration. Had it been concerned alone with absorbing petty urban traders, the classic Western base of his political personality, the task might not have been so hard. But important as these became in the Jacksonian era when American business grew increasingly democratic, they were by no means of crucial importance. The crucial group that had to be dealt with was the growing group of urban laborers: the very "mobs of great cities," in other words, that Jefferson no less than Disraeli feared with an ardent fear. If half of the American democrat believed that the "workshops" of Europe ought to "remain in Europe," how was the other half, grounded in those workshops, ever to get along with it?

This is a well-known problem. We know that Jefferson was ultimately forced to change his mind about the urban worker. We know that in the Jacksonian era men like Ellery Sedgwick tried hard to dispel the old Jeffersonian bias, emphasizing the new opportunities that towns opened, their social contribution. But what seems to me the important thing is something else: the nature of the error Jefferson made. For what Jefferson was doing when he assailed the industrial worker was overlooking the magical alchemy of American life which was responsible for the very small liberal farmers that he loved. That alchemy, in addition to transforming passive peasants into dynamic liberal farmers, was going to transform bitter proletarians into incipient entrepreneurs. Jefferson emphasized the concrete fact of the ownership of property, which to be sure was not a characteristic of the industrial worker. But this was a kind of Marxian mistake, emphasizing economics at the price of thought, for the French peasant also owned property and he was far from being the enlightened liberal yeoman that Jefferson relied so heavily upon. The fact is, the liberalism of the American farmer was largely a psychological matter, a product of the spirit of Locke implanted in a new and nonfeudal world; and this spirit, freed as it was of the concept of class and the tyranny of ancient tradition, could infect the factory as well as it infected the land. There is no need in either case to underrate the importance of America's vast resources which produced, as Selig Perlman has put it, a "premise of abundance" hostile to the concept of class. But the ideological factor, the factor that Turner missed, is a matter of profound importance, and when Jefferson failed to understand it in the case of the urban worker he showed as well that he did not understand it in the case of the country farmer.

Jefferson's fear, in other words, was actually less real than the frustration of John Taylor. The American liberal world had a certain amount of pain to inflict on an "aristocratic" agrarianism as it confronted "small proprietors" but it had no pain to inflict on a democratic-liberal agrarianism as it confronted an urban working class. We need not now go over the familiar story, the lament of every Marxist, of how the early American labor movement stuck to the concepts of property and individualism. Stephen Skidmore, thrown out of the New York workingmen's party because of his radical educational schemes, wanted to guarantee inalienable the right of acquiring wealth. Orestes Brownson, certainly not the most moderate labor philosopher, dreamed of each worker being "an independent labourer on his own capital—on his own farm or in his own shop." [6] Indeed the irony of Jefferson's fear of an urban "mob" is that he himself became its philosophic idol when it began to develop, and not merely in a general egalitarian sense: in the sense also of his theory of agrarian independence. The labor literature would not give up the old idea of yeoman free-holding, and when as with Lucius Byllesby it was recognized to be impossible in the East, it was rediscovered with George Henry Evans in the new lands of the West. Jefferson had reason enough before he died to modify his fear of the American working class.

But even though he modified it he never really undid all of the damage it inflicted on the growing personality of the American democrat. During the Jacksonian era, while labor writers were clinging to Jefferson's small propertied individualism, Whigs were actually citing Jefferson in their campaign against working-class suffrage. In other words, if the "aristocrat" could flee from the democrat, the agrarian democrat could stick a dagger into the urban democrat, and the centrifugal forces in American democracy could move in several directions at once.

We have, however, to relate this complexity of soul to the symbolism produced by the battle against Whiggery. Under almost any circumstances, given a strategic situation in which power was stacked on the side of the American democrat so long as Whiggery maintained an elitist policy which isolated it from the American liberal world, the American democrat was bound to assist in that isolation. In other words, he was bound to dramatize the differences between Whiggery and himself as starkly and as vividly as possible and thus to obscure what he had in common with it: what any liberal of small property has in common with any liberal of large property, what the European shopkeeper has in common with the European industrialist. But being, precisely because of this strategic situation, a huge and various giant, an agrarian and a worker as well as a shopkeeper, the opportunities for confusing the American alignment were radically enhanced. I do not mean by this merely the opportunity he had, since no titled aristocracy existed, of blasting the Whigs as "aristocrats," a familiar polemical technique of the age, which is more than a bit incongruous when his own early leadership itself consists of frustrated Southern "aristocrats." When Taylor calls Hamilton an "aristocrat," it takes a moment or two to figure out what is going on. What I centrally have in mind is the way the American democrat dramatized himself as against both the "aristo-crat" and "capitalist" labels that he applied to American Whiggery.

In the first place, being an agrarian, he proceeded at once to describe the battle between himself and the Whigs as a battle between "agrarians" and "capitalists." This an-tithesis, which we find as polemic in the work of Jeffer-son and Taylor and as sober historical writing in the work of Beard and Parrington, was excellently designed to draw a red herring across the track of the American demo-crat's own liberal capitalist character. In a battle between "agrarians" and "capitalists," if a man is an "agrarian," how can he be a "capitalist?" Here is a devilish confusion indeed. It is true, of course, that capitalism as a system of economy and as a way of life produced an urban in-dustrialism, but the notion that "agrarianism" is a reason-able antithesis to it cannot be defended. English capital-ism first appeared on the land, and the originators of modern capitalist economics, the physiocrats, were middle class members of the French bureaucracy who invaded the feudal setup and tried to imitate the English. Taylor, up to a point, was one of their disciples. A feudal ethos and a feudal tradition did, indeed, persist on the English land, producing Disraeli's conservatism, but it is the ethos and the tradition, not the land, which was antithetical to cap-italism. And these, as we have seen, were exactly the things that were missing in America. That was why a Disraeli was a world apart from a Jefferson: the one had the feudal spirit, the other had the spirit of the small liberal entrepreneur.

One of the great ironies of America's class struggle be-tween the "agrarian" and the "capitalist" is that with John

Taylor it achieved the dignity of a historical philosophy. Taylor's historical theory is a kind of Marxism ending in a smashing anticlimax. The Roman masses overthrow the ancient aristocracy, the capitalists overthrow the feudal aristocracy, and capitalists are overthrown not by a propertyless proletariat but by a set of capitalist farmers. Of course Taylor is careful not to rank the American farmers with the capitalist men of "commerce," for this would expose the fact that the battle between him and Hamilton could be subsumed under one side of the battle between Locke and Filmer that preceded it: it would expose a sudden unity at precisely the time of apocalyptic conflict. But is it not obvious on the face of it that Taylor shared the property-owning, entrepreneurial ethos of Locke just as much as Hamilton did? Why else did he, and above all Jefferson, cherish the farmer and fear the "mob"? It was because the "mob," not as Marx but as everyone saw, was the true potential enemy of the capitalist.

But the American democrat did not belabor Whiggery merely by calling himself an "agrarian." He also called himself a "laborer." One might suppose that this was the result of the working-class component of his hybrid character, and hence would come into conflict with the theory of struggle produced on the rural side. The class struggle between "agrarian" and "capitalist," given the Jeffersonian fear of towns, ought not to be a convenient bedfellow for the class struggle between "laborer" and "capitalist." Actually, however, it was at this point that some accommodation between the two sides of the American democratic personality was theoretically made. For Taylor, in addition to defining himself as "agrarian," defined himself as a "laborer"—"my fellow laborers," as he put it—and thus shifted attention to a general struggle between men who produced and the "capitalists" who exploited men who produced.[7] During the Jacksonian era this became a rock of the urban labor literature. George Bancroft, after asserting that "farmers are the true material for a republic," lauded also the laboring "manufacturer." He contrasted them both with the "man who does but exchange."[8]

But the point made before has to be made again: did not the American farmer "exchange," the farmer that impressed Tocqueville so keenly with his speculative and entrepreneurial ambitions? And did not the American worker dream of doing so? Surely the latter instance is one of the greatest instances of confusion. The Marxist who is disappointed because of the "petit-bourgeois" nature of the early American labor movement is often comforted because he finds in its literature astonishing "anticipations of Marx," phrases of flashing insight into the nature of class struggle. At the very moment that the American worker betrays in a hundred ways his solidarity with the Whigs on the liberal individualist principle, and hence his solidarity with the Jeffersonian agrarians who feared him as much as the Whigs did, he speaks of class war. Seth Luther, a Boston labor leader influenced by his participation in Dorr's Rebellion, even went so far as to "anticipate" the concept that no class peacefully gives up power: "In all cases," he wrote, "the people have been compelled to take by force that which has been withheld from them by force."[9]

What all of this adds up to is fairly clear. The American liberal world practically led the small propertied liberal of America to a career of philosophic confusion. By making him, first of all, a huge and hybrid figure, he was never quite sure whether he was an "aristocrat," a farmer, or an urban worker, or whether in any of these roles he liked himself in the others. Then, by putting him as a result of this process into a strategic situation where Whiggery was his only opponent and the way to defeat it was to isolate it from him, it urged him to forget the liberal capitalism he shared with it and to concentrate on the new-found agrarianism and proletarianism of his social personality. The categories of farmer versus capitalist (aristocrat) and laborer versus capitalist (aristocrat) thus automatically appeared. And, of course, since the Whigs themselves, until around 1840, deliberately isolated themselves from the American democrat, fearing him, denouncing him, even persisting in the dream of an aristocratic alliance against him, the symbolism that he advanced served as a natural counterpart to the one that they advanced. William Leggett's attack upon the "capitalist" beautifully balanced Fisher Ames's attack upon the "mob." The liberalism of American life, by erecting a set of hidden traps and false façades, confounded not one group but all groups who lived within it. But insofar as the American democrat is concerned, this process reached its climax when, grappling with the issues raised by his own individualist fear and capitalist lust, he fell abjectly, confusedly, into the hands of the Whigs.

3. *Individualist Fear: The Problem of the Majority*

Being a liberal community, America, not unnaturally, has had as its central problem in political thought the classic liberal problem of majority rule and minority rights. What the issue of Enlightenment rationalism and feudal traditionalism has been for Europe the issue of majority rule has been for America, which shows us in a sense the relationship of American to European thought, for the reconciliation of majority rule and minority rights is an inner phase of the Enlightenment scheme. It is a problem which appears within the philosophy of Locke once his major premises have been granted. But though this has been the classic problem of American thought, it has rarely occurred to American thinkers that precisely for that reason there has been a classic solution to it: namely that when a nation is united on the liberal way of life the majority will have no interest in destroying it for the minority. Santayana, exploring America's "unison," caught at once the crucial fact that minorities on any issue could easily tolerate the outcome "either way." [10] But the American perspective has not been Santayana's, and so the very liberalism that restrains the majority has given rise to a vast neurotic fear of what the majority might do. What must be accounted one of the tamest, mildest, and most unimaginative majorities in modern political history has been bound down by a set of restrictions that betray fanatical terror. The American majority has been an amiable shepherd dog kept forever on a lion's leash.

But this has been a voluntary servitude and we must not assume, as our Progressive historians often imply, that it has been forced upon the American democrat by the subtle machinations of American Whiggery. Those machinations have taken place, but save for the cooperation of the American democrat himself, there is no reason why they should have been any more successful than the effort to limit suffrage through property qualifications. We are often told a story of the conquest of the American democrat by dark "capitalist" forces, which omits to explain how a man as powerful as he could be conquered against his will. In the last analysis it is Jefferson, not Hamilton, who is responsible for the harness in which Jefferson has been placed, and this is due to the fact that, missing the nature of American liberalism, he has shared to the full America's neurotic terror of the majority. In the case of Jefferson specifically, it is true, one has to qualify this remark. Amid his battle against "capitalists," "aristocrats," and the urban proletariat, he often had remarkable flashes of insight into the nature of the American community. When in his First Inaugural he said, "We are all Democrats, we are all Republicans," he got hold of something that was usually vouchsafed to him only in his days of foreign travel, and when in his correspondence with John Adams toward the end of his life he tried to explain to the latter that "here everyone owns property" or has a "sufficient interest in it" to guarantee its protection, he made explicit the nature of the mildness of the American liberal majority.[11] But on the whole this is not the theme of Jefferson. His theme is one of conflict. And so, when he insists that the "rights of the minority" are sacred, he leaves up in the air the problem of how the majority will be kept from constantly destroying them. This is the prelude to only one thing: binding the majority down by institutional restraints.

The American democrat, in other words, caught up in reverse in the class war subjectivism of Whiggery, has no way of finally answering the argument of Chancellor Kent. To be sure, he can give every answer but the final answer. He can hammer away at the inconsistency of accepting the liberal notion of equality and then excluding the masses from political power, the moral contradiction that everywhere in the West indicted the integrity of the Whigs. But once he has emancipated the majority morally, the empirical terror of Chancellor Kent, like a demon of the mind that will not die, confounds him at every turn. What if the majority does behave like a "mob"? In the midst of a war between "agrarians" and "capitalists" and "aristocrats," can the individual ever be really safe? The answer of course is that no such war is going on, that the Americans, as General Root said in New York, were "all of the same estate." But the remark of Root, like the reply of Jefferson to Adams, was something stung out of the American democrat in an off-guard moment of objectivity, and it contradicted the very polemical process by which he isolated the Whigs and destroyed them. Could William Leggett, who defended the majority against the oppression of "lordlings," seriously defend it also because it had comparatively little against its oppressors? Here was an ironic trap from which there was no escape: the successful political heroics of the American democrat moved in one direction, the solution of the majority problem moved in the other.

It is illuminating, and pathetic as well, to observe in several specific cases the agony with which the American democrat struggled with an issue that the blinders on his eyes prevented him from understanding. John Taylor tried to reason his fears away by saying that "a minority may live upon the labours of a majority" but that "a majority cannot subsist upon those of a minority." This argument, which drew no distinction between the French majority of 1789 and the American majority of 1800, was hardly satisfactory. A majority may not be able to live off the labors of a minority, but it can surely profit from them.

The fear of Hamilton was not to be exorcised by pointing out that some work would have to be done by the mob in any case. Taylor was on far solider ground when he simply dismissed with contempt those who "suffer imagination to conjure up a tumultuous populace, discharging its fury upon life, liberty, and property." [12] But this, alas, was the beginning of an analysis that someone else would have to end. Why would the American populace fail to be "tumultuous"? Clearly, because it had much in common with the man its opponents claimed it would destroy. Taylor was the last person who could possibly emphasize a point like this. In his theory the "aristocracy of the third age" was purely parasitic, and nothing less than its total annihilation was called for.

George Camp and Richard Hildreth skirted even closer to the real issue without touching it. Camp said that the majority was "an extremely fluctuating body," controlled in one moment by the threat of a new majority in another, and Hildreth said that it was limited by the realization that an oppressive act, operating "on the sympathies of the community," would deprive it of its power.[13] These were partial insights. Fluctuating majorities are indeed a protection for the minority, but what makes them fluctuate? It is a community where deep social conflicts do not freeze them into a permanent position. Kent's mythical mob was just such a frozen majority, and in the South the fear of Calhoun was that the North was becoming one too. The Civil War, the only instance in American history when Camp's analysis broke down, showed in part that Calhoun was right. Hildreth's point about "sympathy," was of much the same type. Sympathy does not operate in all cases; it operates, as Hildreth's own Benthamite analysis should have shown him, only when groups have enough in common to identify with each other. Both Camp and Hildreth, to develop their arguments to their logical conclusion, would have had to challenge fundamentally the whole social war trend of American thought.

And so it happened that the American democrat was barred by his own philosophy from discovering America's peculiar solution to the problem of majority rule. In 1837, at the flood tide of Jacksonian democracy, the *Democratic Review* painfully confessed that the majority concept "has ever been the point of the democratic cause most open to assault, and most difficult to defend." The characteristic anguish, evasions, bold fronts, and sudden collapses that we find in American democratic thought on this issue are nowhere better illustrated than in the editorial which contained this lament. Heroically announcing, "We are opposed to all restraints on the free exertion of the popular will," it then proceeded to say "except those which have for their sole object the prevention of precipitate legislation." And then, when elucidating these, it confessed that the "division of power" had to be ranked among them.[14] The institution of judicial review, Hamilton's American "aristocracy," it conveniently left unmentioned. We do not have to go very far to discover the psychic turmoil that lay behind this omission. On this issue the American democrat was always taking one step forward and two steps backward. Jefferson blasted judicial review as "the despotism of an oligarchy." Taylor's attack was even more vehement, and so was Van Buren's, but in the end the work of Marshall flourished and the symbolism of Court and Constitution became a national fetish.

There was one compensating factor, however, inherent

in this situation. If the American democrat threw himself, out of excessive terror, into the harness of Whiggery, the fact that the terror was excessive meant that the harness would not be unbearable. If he did not need the restraints that Hamilton devised for a "mob," the fact that he was not a "mob" meant that he could endure those restraints far more easily than any "mob" could. If Taney's Supreme Court had been able to settle the Civil War in the Dred Scott case, one might justify the restraints on the American majority in terms of the frightful premise which produced them. But it could not. The normal American majority has been able to endure these restraints precisely because its social ambitions have been mild. A false American fear, in other words, has produced a fantastic American system of checks, and the falsity of the fear, the liberal unity of the nation, has permitted those checks to survive. The European wonders at two things in America: our elaborate majoritarian controls, and our marvelous moral agreement. Who can ponder these two things for a moment without detecting the neurotic obsession and the objective reality which binds thems both together?

4. *Capitalist Lust: Conscience and Appetite*

In the last analysis there was probably nothing which could have prevented the American democrat from delivering himself up to Whiggery on the count of capitalist ambition. But it is still a fact that the philosophy of social war that he worked out in demolishing Fisher Ames confounded again and again the process by which he did so. Hidden hunger led to betrayals that were even more inglorious than those induced by hidden fear. There was, of course, the deepest connection between these two passions: the dream of new and greater wealth doubled the desire to protect wealth in general, so that the acceptance of the Hamiltonian restraints was based, half-consciously, on a judgment of the future. Fear was a part of lust, and lust a part of fear: the passion of the American democrat was an integrated force. Where trouble appeared was when it came into conflict with his polemical super-ego of "capitalists" and "aristocrats."

In the realm of economic policy, as if social thought were not already confused enough, another factor entered to confuse further. This was the program of state promotionalism that Whiggery in America was forced to advance. Now this program, as I have already said, was largely traceable to the underdeveloped nature of the American economy, and had the American Whigs been in England they not only would not have had to advance large parts of it, but fighting the vestiges of a corporate society, they would have become champions of laissez faire. The corporate charter with limited liability, one of the greatest bones of contention in America, was in England actually the objective of the "smaller capitalists" whom John Stuart Mill defended, men who wanted to compete with larger entrepreneurs—the English counterparts of the American democrat if England can be said to have any. But despite this, the American democrat seized upon the promotional principle as the historic clue to the rise of the "capitalist." The result was that a theory of class war which in the first instance was overdrawn became further confounded by a theory of class causality which cannot be defended. To John Taylor's philosophy of capitalist farmers overthrowing "capitalists" must be

135

added the additional idea that the "capitalists" arise out of the political action of legislatures.

This notion, which Jefferson also had and which even Beard concedes "reverses the facts," [15] easily arose in America for another reason as well. Starting with a comparatively free society, America had traditionally focused its fears upon the state, and so when the large capitalist began to emerge the instinctive American compulsion was to blame the state for him. The "reversal of the facts" that we find in American democratic thought was an extension of that preoccupation with the political conclusions of Locke which even in the eighteenth century the empirical nature of his social premises had made possible. Europe, on the other hand, starting with feudalism, could not miss the primacy of the social question. There the coercions of corporate society antedated the modern state, the state had been an instrument in their destruction, and the capitalist indeed had helped to destroy them. It is not accidental that the "capitalist" is for Taylor a pure villain while for Marx he is a hero and a villain at the same time. Nor is it accidental that the theorists in America who denounced most forcefully the Jeffersonian tendency to "reverse the facts" were the society-conscious followers of Fourier, men like Godwin and Brisbane, whose perspectives had been shaped in the atmosphere of Europe. The taken-for-granted social freedom of America had blinded it to the fact that society, just as much as politics, might be a source of evil.

Few things could be worse for the intellectual integrity of the American democrat than the identification of the "capitalist" and the "aristocrat" with the public action of legislatures. For when he himself began to adopt large

parts of the Whig program, he was put in the position
of grinding out the very demons who oppressed him. This
is the awful irony that cuts through the career of the
American democrat from the time of Jefferson onward—
from the time Jefferson said that "what is practicable must
often govern what is pure theory." It was worse than the
silent acceptance of judicial review after denouncing it.
There the American democrat merely submitted to an instrument of the "aristocrats," but here he actually created
the "aristocrats" themselves. He could, to be sure, advance
certain arguments in his behalf. He could say that his
own charters and internal improvements served both the
"high and the low," as Jackson once put it, and hence
were an "unqualified blessing." He could fight for free
incorporation, although this did not meet the argument
Taylor advanced when, assailing the purchase of bank
stock, he said that "every man may enlist in an army,
yet an army may enslave a nation." But whatever his
theoretical logic might be, the gap between theory and
practice was striking. A Pennsylvania Whig sardonically
asked of the Democrats in 1837: "Can it be possible that
a party which believes banks to be monopolies can go
on so rapidly creating them?" And a writer in the *Democratic Review,* in a moment of high humor, distinguished
between "a Democrat by trade" and "a Democrat in principle." "Heaven forfend," he added, "that any son of mine
should be a Democrat in principle—being a good Democrat by trade, he got a snug slice of the public de-
posites." [16]

The clash between capitalist hunger and anticapitalist
principle reached its climax, of course, on the banking
question. Charles A. Dana, a disciple of the easy credit

schemes of Proudhon, lamented that American democracy waged a "relentless war" on the banks of "discount and circulation" which the petit-bourgeois democracy of France realized to be in its own interest.[17] But the war was more relentless in theory than in practice. Mr. Bray Hammond has told the story brilliantly. The hard-money dreams of Taylor and Jackson were shattered by rising entrepreneurs, Western farmers, and private bankers who favored the assault on Biddle not in order to limit credit but rather to expand it at the hands of local banks. This type of pressure had been exerted even against the First Bank of the United States under Jefferson. By the time of Jackson, America's "acquisitive democracy"—its "millions of go-getting Americans," as Hammond puts it—overwhelmed the concept of credit control. The speculative boom of the thirties is an excellent commentary on the get-rich-quick compulsion of the American democrat. A writer of the time, describing that boom, said: "A young man who went to any of our large cities penniless was considered a blockhead if he did not report himself worth one or two hundred thousand dollars in a few years." [18] This is the sort of spirit that it is hard to reconcile with an attack on "capitalists."

Eighteen forty, as well as the age of Whig supremacy after the Civil War which it foreshadowed, was in this sense not a break with the past but a continuation of it. The open enchantment of the American democrat with Whiggery when he followed Harrison was a logical extension of his secret enchantment with it when he demolished John Quincy Adams. And this is precisely what Orestes Brownson saw. As he watched the log-cabin enthusiasms of 1840, he was struck with a flash of historic insight. All along, it had been the people, the "proletary," who had been responsible for his miseries. It had been they who had created "the immense system of corporations," they who had sustained the "ruinous system of paper money," they who had contracted abroad some "two hundred millions of dollars" of public works and corporation debts. And indeed if one went back as far as Jefferson, "will anyone tell us" wherein his policy "differed essentially from that of Mr. Adams"? Brownson had discovered at last the nature of the American liberal world. But being a classic intellectual, he did not blame his theory: he blamed the world. And so we find him fleeing from the principle of democracy, embracing Catholicism and conservatism, insisting in 1853 that the "distinction of classes" was "permanent and indestructible" and that the slavery of the South was a positive good.[19] One is reminded of the flight to conservatism on the part of intellectuals after the French Revolution in Europe. But there was this difference, inherent of course in the nature of things: in Europe the flight was due to an excess of radicalism; in liberal America Brownson's flight was due to the fact that there had not been enough. The disenchantment of the American intellectual has always been of an oddly inverted kind: ironically it has been hailed as proof that he is "European."

5. *The Problem of Unanimity*

We come back to our central point: the weakness of the American democrat was a part of his strength, his defeat a part of his victory. America isolated Whiggery by making the entire nation as liberal as it was, and this was also the reason that the entire nation, in the end, fell for its liberal fears and its capitalist dreams. An instinct of friendship, as it were, was planted beneath the heroic surface of America's political conflict, so that the contenders in it, just as they were about to deliver their most smashing blows, fell into each other's arms. American politics was a romance in which the quarrel preceded the kiss.

The strange thing about this story, however, will always be the intricate mechanism of philosophic confusion by which it unfolded. Starting with the moment the Federalists are robbed of their liberal personality, deprived of the House of Lords they look for, and sent assailing a set of "levellers" that do not exist, and then moving through the time of the emergence of the American democrat, with his inner "aristocratic"-democratic, rural-urban tensions, and his philosophy of assailing "capitalists" and "aristocrats," and coming finally to the age of Whiggery's democratization and the collapse of the American democrat, the record of American political thought is a veritable jig-saw puzzle of theoretical confusion. But throughout it all the liberal temper of American theory is vividly apparent. Locke dominates American political thought, as no thinker anywhere dominates the political thought of a nation. He is a massive national cliché. And as always in American history, when the Americans glance for a moment abroad, and see lands where this is not so, they are seized by a new objectivity. At the height of the Jacksonian "revolution," comparing America with Europe, James Fenimore Cooper said: "Every other enlightened nation of the earth is at this moment divided between great opposing principles; whereas here, if we except the trifling collisions of pecuniary interests, everybody is of the same mind except as to the ordinary immaterial question of a choice between men." [20]

Here, I think, we find the clue to Croly's judgment on the political thought of the Middle Period: that it was sterile. Some of the very writers who produced it conceded as much. Brownson said that "no work on politics of the slightest scientific value" had yet been written by an American and that "all questions relating to the origin and ground of the State" were sneered at by men in politics. We cannot explain this fact, as George Camp tried to explain it at the time and as many have tried to explain it since, by saying that the Americans "had the forest to subdue, a new continent to occupy," [21] and hence were too busy with material things to be political philosophers. The frontier, taken alone, no more explains the sterility of our political thought than it explains the speed of our democratic success. England during this same period unloosed immense material energies, pushing through an industrial revolution which reshaped the face of the nation, and yet largely because of that revolution it produced its Benthams, its Mills, and its Carlyles. When a nation has cause for political philosophy, nothing can stop it from producing it, and the clue to its absence in America lies in the absence of a cause. The absence of "opposing principles," the fact that beneath its political heroics the nation was of the "same mind" on the liberal formula, settled in advance the philosophic question.

But this in itself involves a problem: not the problem of the majority, which the Americans agonized themselves over so much, but the problem of virtual unanimity which, as Santayana saw, proved that their agony was excessive. It is interesting how this problem silently began to unfold beneath the heroic clashes of American Whiggery and American democracy. The collapse and transformation of the Whigs had this effect: it destroyed the only philosophy in America which, with the exception of the philosophy that the South produced in defense of slavery, enshrined the principle of diversity implicit in the principle of hierarchy. If Burke was not to be found in America, Adams at least was. And if the latter cherished delusions on the right and delusions on the left, they contained at any rate some hint of a dream of social diversity. The log-cabin passions of Harrison made Whiggery more realistic, but they swept even this dream away, so that the common American ethic, the "opinion" that frightened Tocqueville, became the conscious symbol by which the nation lived. Once the Southern philosophic challenge was liquidated, the "Americanism" that lay behind the shadow world of the Middle Period would come into its own amid the applause alike of Carnegie and Brandeis.

PART FOUR

The Feudal Dream
of the South

CHAPTER SIX

The Reactionary Enlightenment

1. Conservatism in a Liberal Society

"We begin a great conservative reaction," Virginia's George Fitzhugh proclaimed in 1863 on the eve of the battle of Gettysburg. "We attempt to roll back the Reformation in its political phases." The first American revolution, Fitzhugh argued, had been a mere "reform." But the "revolution of 1861," which raised the banner of Tories everywhere and resurrected even the dream of Filmer,* was a social upheaval that would ultimately shake the world.[1]

Here, surely, was a strange note to be coming out of America in the midst of its liberal tradition. What had happened? Had America suddenly produced, out of nowhere, a movement of reactionary feudalism? Was it beginning to experience, seventy-five years late and in an inverted way, a French Revolution that it had managed to escape before? Was its social thought, nourished for years in the easy atmosphere of liberal agreement, suddenly beginning to explode with all of the old historic tensions of Europe? If these things were true, the dis-

---

* Fitzhugh's acceptance of Filmer was qualified, but he did accept the notion of divinely appointed governors, which he held was the "doctrine of the South, and conservatives the world over." *Southern Literary Messenger*, Vol. 37 (1863), p. 720.

tinctive meaning of American history would have been canceled out at a single stroke. Tocqueville's statement that the Americans had been "born equal" would have become a fond illusion, the silent unity of Hamilton and Jefferson would have led nowhere, and the "promise of American life," to borrow the words that Croly used in another connection, would have become one of the falsest promises of modern times. By 1863, when Fitzhugh raised the Tory standard in the South, the battle over the "political phases" of the Reformation had ended even in Europe. The Holy Alliance had been dead for a generation.

Certainly we cannot deny that the American Southerners, when they began to break with their Jeffersonian past around 1830, duplicated in every essential aspect the argument of Europe's feudal reaction. We do not find here the mere parroting of a few of Burke's phrases. We find a most fantastic array of theoretical schemes, some of them to be sure as Aristotelian as they are Burkian, some of them passionately Hebraic in their emphasis on the Bible, but all of them dominated in the end by the basic concepts of the Western reaction. There are a group of ardent traditionalists who cherish the "conservative principle": the novelist N. Beverly Tucker, Governor Hammond of South Carolina, Albert Bledsoe. There are a group of "feudal socialists" * who lash out at Northern capitalism in the spirit of Disraeli and Carlyle: Fitzhugh, Chancellor Harper, George Sawyer, Edmund Ruffin.[2] There are even a group of "sociologists" determined after the fashion of Bonald and Comte to turn the law of nature upside down

---

* The "conservative principle" phrase is Fitzhugh's, and the "feudal socialism" label is the one applied by Marx to the Young England movement that heavily influenced Southern thought before the Civil War.

and prove that Locke is "metaphysical": Fitzhugh again, Professor George Frederick Holmes of the University of Virginia, and that Mississippi prodigy who published his system at the age of twenty-five, Henry Hughes. Nor is Holmes the only academic figure in the reactionary renaissance. College professors rush to the Tory standard from all sides, Dew of William and Mary giving it a Hegelian touch, Smith of Randolph-Macon showering it with an indiscriminate idealism, J. B. De Bow of Louisiana buttressing it with a solid array of statistics. We have here, indeed, one of the great and creative episodes in the history of American thought.

And yet it would be a mistake, even on the basis of this lush evidence, to jump to conclusions about the collapse of the American liberal tradition. When we penetrate beneath the feudal and reactionary surface of Southern thought, we do not find feudalism: we find slavery. The distinction is not unimportant. For it leads us to see at a glance that this massive revival of Burke, Comte, Disraeli, and Hegel below the Mason-Dixon line was in large measure a simple fraud, and that instead of symbolizing the appearance of something new in American life, it symbolized the impending disappearance of something very old. Fraud, alas, was the inevitable fate of Southern social thought. If the trouble with Southern slave society had merely been that it did not fit the American liberal formula, as historians have often noted, its ideologists might not have had so hard a time. But the real trouble with it was that it did not fit any formula, any basic categories of Western social theory. And so when the Garrisons of the North arose to drive the Southerners out of their own Jeffersonian world, they were released from the anguish of one contradiction only to embrace the anguish of another even worse. They exchanged a fraudulent liberalism for an even more fraudulent feudalism: they stopped being imperfect Lockes and became grossly imperfect Maistres. This is the meaning of Fitzhugh's "great conservative reaction," and once we understand it, its appearance changes enormously.

The Civil War, in other words, if it seems on the surface like a French Revolution in reverse, is really nothing of the kind. The fact that it seems like one in reverse, that fact that the "reaction" of the South is also a "revolution," ought to suggest this to us at once. For a feudalism that has once been liberal can never be really feudal, and its impact on the history of a nation is bound to be unique. A false Maistre, a Maistre who only a few years ago was a Jeffersonian democrat, confronts a set of problems entirely his own. He slaughters himself with the traditionalist logic he tries to use, he cannot terrify the men he seeks to terrify, and once he is defeated in war, he is not only likely to be forgotten but he is likely to forget himself. We can call America's great internal struggle whatever we like, a revolution, a rebellion, or a war, but if we identify the South with the feudalism it sought to imitate, we miss the significance of its social incongruity, of the ties it had to the liberalism it sought to defy, and above all of the swift disappearance of its Gothic dream. For the remarkable thing about the "great conservative reaction" of 1863, instead of being the way it scarred American political thought, was in fact the smallness of the impact it had upon it. Even our historians have pretty much forgotten the Disraelis and the Bonalds of the ante-bellum South.

148

There is a book to be written in the psychiatric vein, or at the very least a heart-rending romance, about the Southern search for a cultural code before the Civil War. In the time of Jefferson the agony of the South had been complex. Not only had John Taylor been embarrassed by slavery because of liberalism, but he had been embarrassed by liberalism because even then he had nourished a Disraelian streak. Now, in the age of Fitzhugh, when both of these problems would seem to have been solved, Taylor discovered that he could not be a real Disraeli even if given a chance to be one. He was a plantation capitalist, and in the Southwest, for all of its stratified social life, he was a very new, very raw, very fierce plantation capitalist. And so the sweat that had to go into making the South medieval was even greater than the sweat that had gone into making it modern. Henry Hughes had to twist slavery into a kind of feudal "warranteeism" when it was obviously nothing of the sort. George Frederick Holmes had to link it up historically with European serfdom when there was a gulf between the two. A thousand Southern gentlemen had to call themselves "The Chivalry" when a Northerner like Frederick Olmstead would only call them "Cotton Snobs." It is easy to understand, perhaps, why some Southerners occasionally gave up the idea of becoming imperfect feudal lords and tried the experiment of becoming imperfect ancient Greeks or imperfect Hebrew patriarchs. These roles, which just about exhausted the repertoire that Western culture offered, confused Holmes's historical pattern by shifting it back to ancient times, but the first of them had the merit at any rate of seeming to retain half of the Lockian world in which the Southerners had been accustomed to move.

149

Parrington, seizing upon the idea of "Greek democracy," has actually identified Southern thought with it.

There were good reasons, however, apart from the stratified nature of Southern white society, why the Greek idea did not become the master image of Southern political thought. Locke's scheme had been fashioned not in response to Pericles but in response to Filmer, and when the Southerners were forced to assail it, they found themselves willy-nilly drifting in Filmer's direction. There is a categorical logic to political arguments that Mannheim has brilliantly discussed. Since Garrison was using the doctrine of consent, Calhoun naturally replied with the doctrine of "Divine ordination." Since Garrison was using the concept of reason, Fitzhugh instinctively countered with the concept of human "prejudice." Since Garrison was using the idea of equality, Harper's course was clear: there was an "endless diversity in the condition of men." [2] Actually what we have here is a most remarkable twist coming out of America's odd relationship to modern political thought. A nation built in the liberal image and yet without the feudalism that liberalism destroyed, once it challenged the liberal formula, it began to reproduce the philosophy of a feudal world it had never seen. This is why, even when the Southerners do not read the European conservatives, they write uncannily as if they did. Fitzhugh, who read the English conservatives but apparently not the French, resembles the French most. A ruthless and iconoclastic reasoner, he pursued the attack on Jefferson all the way back to a belief in absolute monarchy and a hatred of the Reformation.

But at this point a question arises, which brings us to the first of the various punishments that the American liberal world imposed on the feudal dreamers of the South. How can a man be an iconoclastic "conservative"? How can Maistre breathe the spirit of Voltaire? Surely if any movement in American thought resembles the French Enlightenment in its sheer passion to shock, to tear down ancient idols, to stick pins in the national complacency, it is this sudden Burkian outburst in the South. And yet the argument of Burke is straight traditionalism. Shouldn't the Southerners, by their own reasoning, be clinging to Jefferson rather than trying to destroy him? Shouldn't they in fact be denouncing themselves?

There is no exaggerating the philosophic pain the Southerners endured as a result of this contradiction. Not to be quite genuine supporting the doctrine of Locke was one thing; not to be genuine supporting the doctrine of Disraeli was another, but to have the second doctrine constantly reaffirming one's ancient allegiance to the first was as keen a torture as the devilish brain of history could devise. How under such circumstances could John Taylor ever forget his democratic past? How could he ever hide his liberal origins? Long before, in the seventeenth century, America had laid this trap for the Southern thinkers. By being "born equal," by establishing liberalism without destroying feudalism, it had transformed the rationalist doctrine of Locke into the traditionalist reality of Burke, so that anyone who dared to use conservatism in order to refute liberalism would discover instead that he had merely refuted himself. I have said that the Southerners, simply by the logic of assailing Jefferson, were led to discover Bonald. But one thing has to be added to this: when they discovered him, they were no longer in America but in Europe. And when in triumph they tried to bring him back to America, he ceased to be Bonald and suddenly became Tom Paine. Surely Fitzhugh's attack on the Reformation, had he ever seriously extended it beyond its "political phases," would have caused a turmoil in his own Protestant South.

Under such conditions it is not surprising that Southern thought should try to stick as much as possible to the European experience. After all, in a land where liberalism had destroyed nothing, unless it was the society of the Indians, which the Southerners were hardly trying to restore, it was very hard to denounce it in good conservative terms as being explosive, "metaphysical," and utopian. In order to use the arguments of Burke or Comte, one had deliberately to twist American liberalism into the millennial molds of Europe. One had to make the same mistake about it consciously that Condorcet, observing the American revolution from Europe, had made about it accidentally. This was very distasteful. An American knew that Jefferson was really not Robespierre, that the idea of compact had been used by the soberest men in American history since the sailing of the *Mayflower*. The Southerners could scarcely wait until they could blend their discussion of Jefferson into a discussion of the French Revolution, though of course they always hid their eagerness behind straight faces. "The prophets of Utopia," Holmes soberly said, were to be found "on both sides of the Atlantic." [3] In the case of "feudal socialism" the situation was even worse, for if American liberalism had not been revolutionary, it had fulfilled itself to a remarkable degree in individual proprietorship. The Southern disciples of Carlyle and Disraeli were relieved of an awful burden when they managed to move from the miseries of the Northern worker to those of the English proletariat.

Locke, in other words, was too real, too empirical, too historical in America to attack: and the consequences of this are obvious. The God of the reactionaries was Himself on Locke's side, and the Southerners, when they assailed "metaphysicians," were committing a vigorous suicide. E. N. Elliott cherished the sociological relativism of Montesquieu, but the relative unfolding of America's culture had alas been liberal. Fitzhugh spoke of Burkian "prejudices," but the prejudices of America were alas the prejudices of liberty and equality. Indeed the "prejudice" argument was even more self-annihilating than the argument of cultural relativism. One might argue, insofar as slavery itself was concerned, that it was a historic institution, despite its sudden expansion after 1830, and that Montesquieu's lesson for the American Negroes was therefore different from his lesson for the American whites. But on the plane of "prejudice," the problem was not so simple: in its Jeffersonian youth the South itself had considered slavery bad. How then could Burke be used to assail Locke when even below the Mason-Dixon line Burke actually equaled Locke?

Few political theorists, save possibly in a nightmare dream, have ever found themselves in a predicament quite as bad as this. What it meant, of course, was that meaningful thought was practically impossible. The more consistently a man advanced the antiliberal arguments of Burke, the farther away he got from the traditionalist substance they were designed to protect. The more he cherished the traditionalist substance, the farther away he got from the antiliberal arguments. The only question was on which horn of the dilemma he wanted to impale himself. Most Southerners, unlike Fitzhugh whose logical passion usually led him to embrace only one of the horns, actually embraced both. Nor is this at all difficult to understand. It is not easy to work out a reactionary scheme of thought in twenty or thirty years, especially when it is far removed from reality. The Burkian power of America's liberal tradition manifested itself most clearly in the inability of the Southerners ever to get completely away from it. Down to the very end, to the Civil War, their theory was shot through and through with the Lockian principles they destroyed. In their glorification of "prejudice," they could not alas overcome the prejudices they had inherited.

Almost everywhere one turns one finds pathetic evidence of this. Calhoun repudiates the contractual rationalism of Locke, and yet when he assails the national tariff he advances a theory of minority rights and constitutional "compact" which carries it forward remarkably. Hammond poses as a defender of a feudal order, and yet he cannot help trying to preserve Jefferson insofar as the whites are concerned by building up a theory of race. Even Fitzhugh breaks down on one or two occasions. Denouncing Northern industrialism in the mood of the "English Tory Party," lamenting the emancipation of the serfs in Europe, he manages to smuggle into his theory a program for industrializing the South that would have delighted Henry Clay. W. J. Cash, in his remarkable portrait of the Southern mind, tells the story of one of the new Cotton Gentlemen who could not help telling his guests how much the furniture in his mansion cost. This is exactly the pathos of Southern "feudal" thought: the old liberal and the old bourgeois preoccupations keep sticking out all over it, betraying it, contradicting it. Even if the South had never been thoroughly liberal and never thoroughly bourgeois, it had been liberal and bourgeois enough to vindicate the insight of Burke by being unable to embrace him completely.

A confusion as subtle as this, a scheme of thought pitched to begin with on a half-fantastic plane and then destroying itself even there, is not designed to win political controversies. The next punishment that America imposed on the Voltairian Maistres of the South follows logically enough. They were not taken seriously by the North.

We must remember that all of the agony of the South was good fortune for the North. If the South was neither decently revolutionary nor decently conservative, the North was decently both. It had instigated the whole argument with its Garrisonian abolitionism, and hence was quite "jacobinical," but since it used the ancient arguments of the Declaration of Independence, and forced the Southerners to think up new arguments to refute them, it was quite traditionalistic as well. Having issued a violent attack, it could proceed to preserve ancient principles from the attack of others. This was the ironic replica in reverse of the whole Southern dilemma. Of course Garrison was forced to reject the Constitution, which recognized slavery, and in this sense could not play the part of a sober traditionalist. As a matter of fact he once exclaimed: "Thank God the Past is not the Present." [4] But to the extent that it recognized slavery the Constitution had itself been a historic anomaly, contradicting the larger liberal tradition in which it had been created. To reject it on this score was to purge, not to repudiate, America's political past.

Thus if Burke equaled Locke in America, the North had the moral force of both, and so why should it bother to reply to a set of philosophic actors who had the moral force of neither? Inherently, inevitably, the grandiose feudal discoveries of the South slid off the Northern mind with scarcely a trace of impact. Instead of reconstructing the Declaration of Independence in terms of the reactionary attack, as Mill for example reconstructed Bentham or Constant reconstructed Rousseau, the North simply affirmed its principles with a new and wilder fury. Instead of bothering to look at the great Gothic cathedrals that were suddenly arising in the South, the North simply stuck to the ancient liberal ground where they should have been built in the first place. Hence, ironically, the greatest moral crusade in American history produced practically no original political thought. Garrison is not a creator of political ideas; neither is Phillips. Even Channing is not. Conservatism is always unreflective, and since these men, by the weird, upside-down logic that governed the slavery argument, are revolutionary conservatives, they unite with their very passion a strange and uncritical complacency. They will argue about the Bible, they will even say a few words in defense of the condition of the Northern worker,* but insofar as the South's great "feudalist," "positivist," "corporatist" challenge to liberalism is concerned, it rarely occurs to them even to answer it. "Argu-

* See p. 196.

156

ment is demanded," Garrison once remarked, "—to prove what?" [5] *

This experience of being ignored, which every polemicist knows is the handwriting on the wall, produced a strange mixture of fury, gloom, and forced gaiety in the Southern literature. Chancellor Harper of South Carolina angrily assailed the North because it engaged in "denunciation disdaining argument," and then quietly, morosely, as if to himself, he said: "We can have no hearing before the civilized world." Fitzhugh, however, who pretended to believe in just the reverse idea, that the South was leading a world-wide revival of the principles of feudalism, would never let his anguish show. When the North paid no attention to his massive sociological proof that "free society" was a failure, he behaved happily as if he had won the argument: "The North is silent, and thus tacitly admits the charge." [6] Fitzhugh was not naive: he knew that silence can be a sign of intellectual security as well as of intellectual bankruptcy. But what else could he say? If the liberal formula was hopelessly entrenched in the mind of the nation, even in the mind of the South, he had nothing to gain by pointing that fact out.

As a world revolutionary, then, Fitzhugh was in an odd position: his message was ignored by half of the country in which he lived. He was a Calvin not taken seriously by half of Geneva, a Lenin not taken seriously by half of Russia. This was a harsh fate, but it was hardly more than he had a right to expect. Even in 1776 America had not issued an apocalyptic clarion call to the liberals of the

---

* I do not mean here to deny that Northern politicians occasionally used the theory of the South to frighten free workingmen. I am concerned with the efforts made to refute philosophically the Southern case.

world, largely because the "canon and feudal law" was not present here to inspire the inverted Christianity, the crusading secular visions of Rousseau and Condorcet. Was it reasonable to assume that America, nearly a hundred years later, would take a man seriously who issued such a call in defense of that law itself? The anguished fantasy of the Reactionary Enlightenment, its incredible contradictions, and its failure to impress anyone, all come out most vividly in the claim that it is going to sweep the world.

2. *The Constitution: Calhoun and Fitzhugh*

When we examine more closely the inner tensions of Southern thought, the inability of the Southerners to emancipate themselves from the liberal ideas they were in the process of destroying we find a record of turmoil as vivid as one might expect. It is not easy to live at the same time in the dark world of Sir Walter Scott and the brightly lit world of John Locke. The contrasts are blinding, confusing, and in the end they drive a thinker mad. Calhoun, it seems to me, is our clearest proof of this.*

One makes such a remark about Calhoun with some trepidation, for he is the philosophic darling of students of American political thought, the man who is almost invariably advanced when a thinker of European stature is asked for in the American tradition. And yet, despite the outward literary appearance of "rigor" and "consistency" in Calhoun's work, one is bound to affirm that the man

---

* The interpretation of Calhoun which follows is essentially a much abbreviated version of one that I have developed in an essay on the Nullification Act of 1832 in *Crisis in American History*, ed. Daniel Aaron (New York, 1952), pp. 73-89.

is a profoundly disintegrated political theorist. What is "rigorous" about grounding the state in force and Providence after the fashion of Maistre and then creating a set of constitutional gadgets that would have staggered even Sieyès? What is "consistent" about destroying Locke's state of nature and then evolving a theory of minority rights that actually brings one back there for good? There are more impressive thinkers to whom the American historian can point. Fitzhugh, as I have suggested, must be ranked as one of these, for if on the surface he seems like a cracker-barrel commentator, at bottom he has a touch of the Hobbesian lucidity of mind. He, more than anyone else, sensed the awful way Calhoun betrayed the Reactionary Enlightenment when he based the sectional defense of the South on the ancient liberalism it tried to destroy. He fought continuously to substitute the concept of "organic nationality" for the concept of state "sovereignty," and there was the keenest logic to this substitution. By extracting a traditionalist type of Southern nationalism from the conservative theory of slavery itself, he was able to give up all of the compacts and all of the checks on which Calhoun relied.

We have to concede, however, that without this approach there was really no alternative to riding the two horses Calhoun tried to ride. For the theory of the reaction grounds itself on the divinity of existing coercions, and while this may serve a purpose for the defense of Negro slavery, it hardly serves a purpose for the liberation of the South from regional "slavery" to the North. The second type of slavery, if we take the Southerners at their word, was just as existent as the first, and if Calhoun's God ordained the one, how could he have failed to ordain the other? The irony of the Burkian position, even in Europe, was that it became articulate at precisely the moment it became untenable, at the moment when God had introduced a new reality to challenge his old one, which meant that when Burke denounced the French Revolution he had to become something of a rationalist himself. Under these circumstances, lacking Fitzhugh's faith in the South's romantic nationalism, it is not hard to see why Calhoun in his battle against the North kept applying the ethos of the Kentucky-Virginia Resolutions. After all an inconsistency is better than a logical surrender.

But let us make no mistake about the fact of inconsistency: it is not merely striking, it is doubly and triply striking. Had Calhoun merely maintained an ordinary faith in the mechanics of the American Constitution at the same moment that he grounded government in force and tradition, this would have been one thing. But his faith is not an ordinary one. There is weird quality about Calhoun: he has a wild passion for the conclusions his premises nullify, as if a pang of guilt made him redouble his affection for the things that he destroyed. The idea of state "sovereignty" shatters a meaningful American union, and yet he insists with the most anguished repetition that this alone can serve as a national "preservative." The idea of a fixed Southern minority and a fixed Northern majority amounts to civil war, and yet the scheme of the "concurrent majority" he builds upon it he describes in terms of compromise that are nothing short of idyllic.* The best

* Note the words in the *Disquisition:* "And hence, instead of faction, strife, and struggle for party ascendency, there would be patriotism, nationality, harmony, and a struggle only for supremacy in promoting the common good of the whole." Ed. Cralle (New York, 1943) p. 49.

example of this mounting love in the midst of murder is the one that I have mentioned: the attempt to ground both of these mechanical schemes on the organic naturalism that his social defense of slavery inspired.

For surely the idea that the Constitution is a "compact" among "sovereign" states, that states may therefore nullify federal legislation, and that the proof of this is to be found in a diligent study of ratification procedures in 1787, is about as far away as you can get from the spirit of "Divine ordination." This not only makes the American system of government a rationalistic instrument of extreme delicacy but it pins its origin to a decisive moment in historical time just as Condorcet, misunderstanding American constitutionalism, pinned it in the eighteenth century. If the Southerners usually had to distort American liberalism in order to denounce it as "metaphysical," they would not, ironically enough, have had to distort Calhoun's version of its constitutional embodiment in order to denounce it in that way. That version met all of the "metaphysical" standards. It left nothing to tradition, nothing to force, and nothing to God. Nor is it the only thing we have to consider. There is also Calhoun's theory of the "concurrent majority," which supplemented state nullification with the nullification of individual "interests." When we pile the one on top of the other, we have a scheme of man-made political instruments which the French Enlightenment in its palmiest days never dared to develop.

It is here, in his passionate defense of the minority interest, that Calhoun goes back to Locke's state of nature after having destroyed it in a blaze of organic glory. For there are of course minorities within minorities—as Unionists like Hugh Swinton Legaré did not fail to remind Cal-

houn in South Carolina in 1832—and since Calhoun offers
no reason why these should not be given a policy veto
too, the idea of the "concurrent majority" quickly unravels
itself into separate individuals executing the law of nature
for themselves. When Locke accepted majority rule, in
other words, he accepted more force in politics than Calhoun, the great theorist of force and slavery, was ready
to accept. When Locke accepted majority rule, he was
more pessimistic than Calhoun, the great pessimist, would
permit himself to be. What could be worse for the logic
of the Southern position? Here are grim traditionalists denouncing Northern liberalism as a code of "anarchy," and
Calhoun supplies them with a political theory that even
Daniel Webster can denounce as a theory to "anarchy."
Here are ardent corporatists denying that a natural harmony of interests can ever exist—and Calhoun advances a
logic of harmony that one would have to go to Godwin
to duplicate.

Since Calhoun's mechanical suggestions were a failure,
it is interesting that his new-found organic philosophy did
not suggest the nature of their failure to him. One might
say, as has often been said, that Calhoun was here merely
extending the checking-and-balancing ethos of the Founding Fathers. If this is true, then his wild rationalism has
a curious logic to it. Adams and Morris, instead of grounding their hope for America on a liberal unity that could
support even their clumsy scheme of checks and balances,
grounded it on the capacity of those checks and balances
to contain and control frightful social conflicts that did
not exist. In the only time in American history when such
conflicts did appear, what was more reasonable than for
a disciple of theirs to multiply passionately all of the

checks and balances that were about to be exploded? But in his role as an antagonist of American liberalism, why didn't Calhoun see the futility of this reasoning? Why didn't his organic sense for the importance of social solidarity make him realize that however much you compounded "interest" checks with other checks none of them would work if the social fabric was actually torn apart? There was at least this relevance of traditionalism to the liberal cement of American life: that by concentrating on the solidarity that comes from "prejudice" it might have exposed the liberal prejudices that had held the country together to the view of "realistic" thinkers who had managed not to see them. Some Southern organicists actually caught this point, but Calhoun himself did not: the lesson of Adams ran too deep for a sudden correction by Burke.

And yet it would be unfair, after all of this has been said, not to notice that Calhoun was aware of the basic contradiction he faced. In his famous *Disquisition* he drew a distinction between "government" and "constitution." Governments were rooted in force and inspired by God even as Negro slavery was, but constitutions were a different thing entirely. They controlled government, and being the product of a later age, when "invention" replaced "superstition," they could be used to abolish the South's regional enslavement to the North.[7] Here was a straightforward effort to deal with the problem of Maistre and Sieyès. But it reminds us alas, for all of its ingenuity, of a man carefully placing a match on top of a stick of dynamite. For clearly if "constitution" and "government" ever come together at any point, if it is ever established that the one has any of the characteristics of the other, an explosion is bound to occur which wipes the Southern position off the face of the philosophic earth. Not only does the South become validly enslaved to the North, but the whole structure of "compact" and "concurrent majority" is swept away in a fierce tide of irrationalism. What difference then does it make whether a genuinely "American people" did or did not exist in 1787? God could have created one in the interval. What difference does it make whether minorities are coerced? Coercion is a law of life. What difference does it make whether the Southern "interest" is consulted? Interests can never work together freely and harmoniously anyway. This was a great deal to stake on a tenuous distinction between "constitution" and "government." And to say that the distinction was tenuous is putting the matter mildly. There are some who would argue that the control of government is actually the highest form of the governmental task.

Fitzhugh, then, was rightly terrified at the doctrines of the "Calhoun school." His theory of blood and solid nationalism, of "organic nationality," avoided all of the inner turmoil and the brink-of-destruction gyrations that the Calhounian position involved. Romantic, grounded in the claim of slave culture itself, it could never be assailed by the conservative theory that slavery produced. Nor should we assume that Fitzhugh was here a voice crying in the wilderness. Many Southerners, as the sense of their separateness was forced upon them and as the appeal of Scott and Disraeli grew, became attached to the principle of traditionalist nationalism with a genuine and ardent feeling. Of course, few of them became attached to it so much that they were ready to give up constitutional apologetics entirely, which meant that their original dualism of Burke and Locke was simply duplicated again on the plane of nationalism. But under the circumstances what is striking is not how little romantic nationalism there was in the political thought of the South but how little there was of it in the political thought of the "nationalistic" North. Daniel Webster remained as legalistic as Marshall, despite the fact that had he adopted some form of romantic nationalism (it would, of course, have to be a Rousseauan or a Mazzinian type in his case), he would have been able to explode against Calhoun much of the dynamite that he was playing with. There was much romanticism in the North, but with the exception of a few men like Barlow and Emerson, it spent itself in a Thoreauan individualism or a Garrisonian cosmopolitanism. Garrison denounced constitutional lawyers as fervently as Fitzhugh did, but he put on the masthead of the Liberator, "Our country is the world."

Thus, oddly, the South, the "sectionalist" South, became the real originator of romantic nationalism in American political theory. But one thing has to be said about that nationalism: it radicalized the whole Southern position. For it is hard to control the claim of nationalism, and especially the claim of Scott's nationalism, with its love of chivalry, its faith in force, its ethos of blood and soil. Implicitly the solution that Fitzhugh offered called for independence and beat the drums of war. And here the "Calhoun school," at least until 1860, might have offered a reply: it did not want independence and it did not want war. If it clung to Enlightenment contractualism because it wanted to defend the South against the North, it clung to it also because it wanted them both to live together.

Its inconsistency pointed in two directions. This is the larger secret of Calhoun's intellectual madness: he appears at a moment when the South's fear of the North and its love of the Union hold each other in perfect balance, so that starting with explosive premises like sovereignty and conflict and force he drives himself somehow to avert the explosion with conclusions like nullification and the "concurrent majority." He was caught in the classic agony of the brink-of-war philosopher.

But the main point I want to emphasize is the coexistence in the Southern mind of its new Burkian traditionalism and its old Jeffersonian rationalism. Calhoun exemplifies it perfectly, a man whose thought is cut in two by the tug of the liberal past and the pull of the reactionary present. He slays Jefferson only to embrace him with a passion in the end, he destroys the Founding Fathers only to carry their work forward. Under such circumstances why should Garrison bother to reply to the elaborate Providential organicism of the South? The South was doing a good enough job of replying to it itself. The point illustrates again the basic dilemma the Southerners faced: their liberalism was so traditional that even they could not get away from it: Garrison the "jacobin" had the power of their own historic irrationalism on his side, and they, the historic irrationalists, could not even be decent "jacobins." They were, in a sense, outside of time and space, carrying on a reactionary conversation with themselves in a kind of Alice-in-Wonderland world where nothing was what it seemed to be, where nothing was what it ought to be, where liberalism was oddly conservatized and conservatism oddly liberalized. Or, if one prefers Stevenson to Carroll, they were a set of Dr. Jekylls constantly becoming Mr. Hydes—their own worst enemies and their own executioners.

3. *Race, Religion, and the Greek Ideal*

The effort to save half of Locke by evolving a theory of Greek democracy presents us with the same problem. If it was hard to forget the Kentucky and Virginia Resolutions, it was even harder to forget the simple prejudice in behalf of human freedom and human equality. There was a strange compulsion here. For in order to keep democracy for the whites, it was essential to develop a theory of separate races for the blacks, and so the retention of a part of liberalism grounded itself on one of the most vicious and antiliberal doctrines of modern times. This meant that when a stunted fragment of Locke reappeared to challenge the new Filmerians who had shattered him what was actually at stake was a principle of racial inferiority that Filmer had never seen. The battle between the South's feudal image and its old liberal image was here fought out, curiously enough, on a plane that was alien to liberalism and feudalism alike.

There was an important strategic reason behind the racialist challenge to the South's Burkian social dream. Unlike the federal struggle, which accounted for the persistence of Calhoun's contractual rationalism, that reason arose out of a tension in Southern society itself, but it was certainly no less real. The democratic age in which the "small proprietor" side of John Taylor's personality had dominated its "aristocratic" side could not quite be forgotten during the "feudal" age when the situation was reversed. Many of the poor whites who lived in the South, instead of feeling that the presence of slaves put them in the position of a privileged peasantry, actually had the audacity to feel that it put them on a kind of par with the "aristocrats" who led them. Burke himself, long before, had recognized that the effect of the "multitude of slaves" in Virginia and the Carolinas had been to give all the whites there a sense of common "rank and privilege." [8] Even Hinton Helper, who cried out against the unity of the "poor whites" with the Southern "lords of the lash," betrayed in the wild intensity of his own racial theories the sentiment of common whitehood that had helped to produce it. Whatever the assailants of Locke might say, passionately as they might identify the stratified society of the South with the world of Sir Walter Scott, vigorously as they might insist on the principle of "feudal socialism" for all mankind, there was no avoiding the fact that one of the crucial factors in the solidarity of the South was a democratic spirit enhanced by the slavery on which it rested.

The religious issue played a two-sided role in this respect. Since a literal reading of scripture supported the ownership of slaves, many Southerners began to think in terms of Hebrew patriarchy, while the North became increasingly liberal as regards the Bible, with Garrison giving it up completely. But there was a rub here. Biblical slavery had not been confined to the Negro, and Genesis, moreover, asserted the common origin of man. This was the point at which Fitzhugh, determined to extend a feudalized concept of slavery to whites as well as blacks, began to level his attack. Confusion necessarily reigned. Dr. George Armstrong could say that though in the first instance the Negro came from Adam in the second instance he came from Ham, and Josiah Nott, departing from the

168

Bible for an entirely different reason from the one that Garrison had, could develop an anthropology of different races. But these arguments tended to cancel each other out, further confusing the issue with a Darwin-like struggle between science and religion before the arrival of Darwin. Fitzhugh, adopting a razor-edge fundamentalism, lashed out at the entire "argument about races" as an "infidel procedure" and insisted that since the Bible "expressly authorized" the enslavement of whites, the matter was closed.[9] Here was a case, in other words, where being a Hebrew patriarch was a prerequisite to being a feudal lord. It was a strange situation, but it did not seem to bother Fitzhugh much. Even he, alas, could work within the madhouse of Southern thought before the Civil War.

The truth is, the racial theory was bound to pose difficulties so long as any human attribute was permitted to remain with the slave. And to take all humanity away from a human being was, even in pre-Christian Greece, more than the philosophic conscience could successfully accomplish. Aristotle, defining the slave as a "living tool" and nothing more, conceded at one point that the slave had a capacity for "friendship," which was an intolerable admission, since the whole of the human community from which he was excluded was built around that capacity. In a Christian and a humanitarian age the closest the Southerners could come to the Aristotelian definition was their legal concept of the slave as "property," and this concept, as Channing shrewdly observed, they immediately reversed with restrictions on slaveholders which implicitly conceded that he was a human being. Outside of the law their admissions were vaster still. Not only did

169

they make the Aristotelian concession, they embroidered it. The "affection" between slave and master was one of the finest things about Southern life. Not only did they agree that the slave had a soul, they were happy about it. They had saved his soul through giving him Christianity. Albert Bledsoe hastened to say that only the right to labor as a free man had been taken away from the slave. His "human character" had been impaired "in no part whatever." [10]

Thus if the racial theory tried to save the whites from the attack on Locke, an inescapable reality kept pulling them into its orbit, since their common humanity with the Negro could not easily be denied. Indeed the very compulsion they felt to attack Locke betrayed them on this score, since Locke had been concerned with men in general, not with Negroes in particular. If the Negro was not a Lockian "man," why bother to attack Locke? If the Negro was a parcel of property rather than a human being, why bother to attack Jefferson? Certainly Jefferson had believed in property rights. The Southerners could not remove the Negro from the human category, and, not being able to do so, their logic of inequality was bound to backfire on themselves. Again we are confronted with that strange intellectual rationale whereby the South, assailing Locke, found itself going back to the hierarchical world that the theories of Locke had destroyed.

But of course this was, with half of its mind, exactly what it wanted to do. Fitzhugh, who always represented that half in a highly integrated form, lashed out at the other half with all the vigor he had. He asked the racialists what they were going to do about the "mulattoes, quadroons, and men with as white skins as any of us" who were in slavery everywhere. He asked them how they could reconcile the historic novelty of Negro slavery with their appeal to the "universal usages of civilized men." But it was when he came to the whole feudal scheme of Southern thought, its Tory socialist attack on the North, that his logical passion reached its peak. "We are all in the habit of maintaining that our slaves are far better than the common laborers of Europe, and that those laborers were infinitely better situated as feudal serfs or slaves than as freemen. . . ." How then can the slavery argument be confined to the Negro? The racial thesis, he cried, "has involved us in a thousand absurdities and contradictions." [11] *

The theme by now is a familiar one: Fitzhugh trying to be a good reactionary, the South as a whole not quite having the courage to do so. Different as the issues seem to be on the surface, Fitzhugh's attack on the racial idea on which the halfway retention of Locke rested was cut from the same cloth as his attack on the "compact" theory of Calhoun. Fitzhugh wanted the Reactionary Enlightenment to come to full bloom, but the South, wedded still to ancient liberal notions, was frightened of its appearance if it did. But if the South itself was frightened of the Reactionary Enlightenment, why should Wendell Phillips be frightened of the South? If Fitzhugh's "feudalism" was being slaughtered by his own comrades because of their love of Locke, why should Garrison take the trouble to slaughter it? Another theme appears, the basic theme: The Southerners were too conservative to be "conservative," which meant that the hotheads of the North could

* In 1861, however, Fitzhugh himself became a convert to racialism. See Harvey Wish, *George Fitzhugh* (Baton Rouge, 1943), p. 298.

be as complacent as real conservatives. The whole thing is fantastic of course, but it is fantasy we are dealing with. And the origin of that fantasy, the frantic search of an incongruous Southern culture for some sort of social identity, comes out as plainly as one might ask in the Southern discussion that we have just examined as to whether the South, instead of being feudal, or perhaps at the same time that it was feudal, might not be Biblical or Greek.

4. *Oblivion and Defeat*

We are now prepared for the final punishment that the American liberal community imposed on the feudal dreamers of the South for daring to attempt an escape from its confines: after the Civil War they were soon forgotten and they all but forgot themselves.

Here the difference between the Civil War and a French Revolution becomes most apparent. For if the former had been the latter, military defeat would never have been able to annihilate the Tory philosophy it produced. That philosophy would have clung to the conscience of the nation, providing a new dimension to its political thought, serving as a point of departure for a whole set of subsequent conservatives. But who in America would be reading Fitzhugh in twenty years? Who would be going back to Tucker, as Englishmen still go back to the Burke that he loved, for a lesson in political wisdom? The point is clear enough. The fact that the Southerners were false Burkes, halfway Burkes even in the time of their prime insured a sorry fate for them after that prime was over. When the guns of the Civil War were stilled the liberal self that the South could not sublimate even in the age of its great "reaction" would gradually come to the fore again and, as in the days of Jefferson, would unite it to the North. The logical agonies of Fitzhugh were a prelude to the emergence of Benjamin Hill.

The new age would not of course solve the philosophic problem of the South. Locke had been imperfect there to begin with, and the brute emancipation of the slaves was hardly enough to make him perfect when he returned on the scene again. The truth is, there was no solution to the philosophic problem of the South: its stark social incongruity was bound to remain, its search for a social identity bound to continue, inspiring as always a mixture of pain and wild hyperbole. But all of this would fester beneath the mainstream of American political thought, never resurrecting the Fitzhughs and the Holmeses of the ante-bellum era. If we ask ourselves what we have remembered of the South's "feudal reaction," the answer we must give is ironic. We have remembered the very liberal rationalism its philosophers could not destroy in formulating it. It is Calhoun whom we are constantly rediscovering, and not because of the lush organicism that he shared with the philosophers of slavery. We rediscover him because of his defense of minorities, because of his Adams-like theory of the "concurrent majority," and so far are we from bothering to cherish his organic theories that we scarcely realize that they make a logical farce out of his whole Enlightenment structure. Indeed we do not find it incongruous for this great reactionary to be hailed as the chief philosopher of America's free and easy pressure group system of politics, a system which, if it does anything, denies the principle of a "controlling power." What could be a more vivid commentary on the destiny of the Reactionary Enlightenment: that it should be remembered for its defects, for the traditional liberalism it could not overcome?

The grim fate of the Southern reaction is reflected too in its treatment by historians. I do not have in mind now the neglect into which its grandiose social theory fell when it began to be listed in textbooks as merely the "theory of slavery," a neglect which is happily being repaired by the excellent researches of men like Joseph Dorfman, Rol lin Osterweiss, and Harvey Wish. What I have in mind is something else, something even more devastating: the fact that our familiar historical categories leave no room whatever for the feudalists of the ante-bellum South. Calling "conservative" men who are actually liberal, those categories shove out into the cold the only Western conservatives America has ever had. If John Winthrop is a "conservative," how should Fitzhugh be classified, who denied the right of individual conscience altogether? If Daniel Webster is a "conservative," what are we to say about Hughes who wanted a system of authoritarian industry organized around seven different "sovereignties"? If William McKinley and Herbert Hoover are "conservatives," surely there is no place save in heaven or hell for a man like Holmes who cried over the death of feudalism.

But this is logical enough. Our current historical categories reflect but they do not analyze the American political tradition, and if America was destined to forget the Reactionary Enlightenment, those categories were destined to forget it too. Since after the Civil War Bryan and McKinley would pick up the classic battle between American democracy and American Whiggery where Jackson and Webster left off, since Fitzhugh would look as his beloved Disraeli might look if he had suddenly appeared for a moment in a tradition exhausted by the difference between Brougham and Cobbett, his fate was practically predetermined. The "conservative" label that he cherished more than anything else would be taken away from him, it would be given to William McKinley whom he would have hated with a violent passion, and he himself would be left nameless. History has been cruel to many thinkers after they have died, and historians have conspired in its cruelty, but there are few parallels for this.

But it might be asked, Why worry about the fate of the Reactionary Enlightenment?—either when it slaughtered itself, or when Garrison ignored it, or when history forgot it, which of course are all parts of the same problem. If the episode was fantastic, why worry about fantasy? If behind its elaborate feudal façade lay the vicious institution of slavery, why lament the fate of the façade?

The answer, it seems to me, is this: fantasy may serve a curious purpose for the American political mind, for it may well be the only technique whereby it can seize any kind of perspective other than the liberal perspective which has governed it throughout its history. Even a good idea can be a little frightening when it is the only idea a man has ever had. A genuine feudal ideology could not by definition emerge in a world that had always been liberal, and there is some doubt whether a genuine socialist ideology can ever appear in such a world, for there is a relationship between the Bourbons and Babeuf that the work of Rousseau exemplifies and that America has missed. It is no defense of these ideas to say that a nation ought to know what they mean, and it is not to disparage liberalism to say that a knowledge of it and nothing else can produce an absolute temper of mind that in the end is self-defeating. The Reactionary Enlightenment deserves evaluation in these terms.

For this was the great imaginative moment in American political thought, the moment when America almost got out of itself, as it were, and looked with some objectivity on the liberal formula it has known since birth. Here was a time when a group of major thinkers, not men at the fringes of the American scene but men at its very center, dared to insist that life can be lived in an utterly different way from the way that Hamilton and Jefferson both agreed to live it. America's rejection of their philosophy was proper, but the way it rejected it was, I submit, not. For America rejected it in the purest mood of its liberal absolutism, of the "opinion" that Sumner assailed in the colonial era, that Tocqueville noted in the Jacksonian era, and that has been a part of our national temper ever since: not through controversy, not after consideration, but by a vast and unbelieving neglect. Where in the whole history of American thought is the sublime assurance of that "opinion" better expressed than in the words of Garrison: "Argument is demanded— to prove what?" Reading these words on the part of a leading American philosopher in time of civil war, it is not hard to understand why America has not produced a great philosophic tradition in politics in time of peace. But these are the words of a powerful perspective as well as of a limited one, and perhaps it is asking too much that America have all the liberal virtues of a triumphant liberalism and all the liberal virtues too of one that is not so triumphant. The American experience remains, in this sense, forever paradoxical.

One thing in any case is clear. The political thought of the Civil War symbolizes not the weakness of the American liberal idea but its strength, its vitality, and its utter dominion over the American mind. The strange agonies the Southerners endured trying to break out of the grip of Locke and the way the nation greeted their effort, stand as a permanent testimony to the power of that idea. It is not every day in Western history that a "great conservative reaction," dies without impact on the mind of a nation.

CHAPTER SEVEN

The Crusade Against "Free Society"

1. *Feudal Paternalism and Social Science*

Marx and Engels, attacking the "feudal socialists" of Europe in 1848, said that they displayed a "total incapacity to understand the march of modern history," since it was in the nature of things that capitalist society could not be reabsorbed into the feudal structure it had destroyed.[1] In general, events have proved them right, which gives us a clue to the failure of the Southern attack on the "free society" of Northern capitalism before the Civil War. For if the Young England movement was historically futile even in England, how much more futile was it destined to be in the United States? Instead of defending an ancient society of status, the worshipers of Disraeli and Carlyle in the South, were defending a mixture of slavery and capitalism that the South itself had once considered bad. Instead of confronting the ruthless class oppressions of a capitalism that was rapidly reaching its peak, they confronted the easy early stages of a capitalism whose longevity was to be the marvel of the world. Marx derided Europe's Tory "socialists" as being "half echo of the past, half menace of the future." The tragedy of their Southern imitators was that they were not even this—

neither an echo of the American past nor, shrewd as their capitalist criticism was, a menace of the American future. They did not look backward to feudalism and they did not look forward to socialism, which means that, instead of trying to combine uncombinable parts of history, they had removed themselves from history entirely.

As the Reactionary Enlightenment enters upon its offensive phase, as it tries to carry its polemical war into the camp of the Northern enemy, the pathos of its unreality becomes more apparent than ever. It is hard enough for the plantation capitalists of the South to pose as Sir Walter Scott aristocrats when presiding over their slaves, but when they argue that they or their counterparts ought to preside over the free workers of New York and Philadelphia as well, they put a strain on the imagination which is hard to bear. The mixture of "sociology" with Southern Tory socialism did not improve the situation much. There was, to be sure, nothing illogical about the mixture in and of itself. The European matrix of Comte is in large part Bonald and the French reaction, the effort to challenge the libertarian apriorism of the Enlightenment with a social empiricism that denies the Enlightenment values,* and if Holmes worshiped Dis-

---

* This correlation has been badly neglected in European intellectual history. While Comte cannot of course be categorically identified with the reaction, his substitution of "positive" for "metaphysical" thought is logically bound up with the effort of the reaction to reinterpret natural law in empirical terms. In the social science of Bonald this meant the reintroduction of the whole content of society, from religion to economic coercions, which the Enlightenment had reasoned down the drain through the use of an atomism claiming to be factual as well as normative by a reliance on the concept of nature. Methodologically, of course, the reactionary argument which sought to justify institutions because they existed was no sounder than the Enlightenment argument which sought to empiricize norms. But it did at any rate lead in the direction of "so-

raeli, he could, up to a point, worship Comte as well. Certainly Henry Hughes, who met Comte in Paris and who turned out a scheme of authoritarian industry not unlike that of the French thinker himself, was never ill at ease amid the Disraelian passions of the South. But even though this is true, "sociology" confounded the Southern dilemma. For like the "prescription" and "prejudice" of Burke, it turned the Southern argument against itself since the "positive" reality of America had in fact been largely Lockian. In America it was just as embarrassing to say that liberal capitalism violated the laws of social science as it was to say that liberal capitalism violated the laws of God.

Here, as in the case of Calhoun's "compact" theory and Hammond's effort to save Locke through the medium of Greek democracy, the Southerners gave themselves away again and again by being unable to transcend entirely the liberal past out of which they came. They were aristocratic agrarians bemoaning the wage-slavery of Northern towns, but many of them, following the leadership of Dew and De Bow, wanted to industrialize the South. They were the "Chivalry" holding in contempt the Yankee's love of money, and yet the profitability of slavery was something they could not resist discussing. They were grim social empiricists undermining the school of Adam Smith, but the principle of free trade was itself one of the dog-

ciology." What is interesting here, however, is the confirmation which this fusion of sociological empiricism and Tory thought in the South gives to the point made earlier that, in the very process of assailing Locke, the Southerners were driven to duplicate European patterns of thought. Quite apart from Old World intellectual influences, the thinkers below the Mason-Dixon line were naturally led to discover for themselves the link between Bonald and Comte.

mas by which they lived. When one piles these contradictions on top of the others, one gets an almost frightening sense of how hard it was to be reactionary in the
South. We can hardly blame Fitzhugh if he ultimately
broke down. He repudiated free trade as ardently as he
repudiated contractualism and racism, but when it came
to promoting Southern industry, he fell for the dream of
De Bow.

The situation gets worse also in terms of the variety
of poses the Southerners are forced to adopt. Simply defending slavery, they can divide their energies among the
roles of feudal lord, Hebrew patriarch, and Greek democrat. As Tory critics of capitalism, they are inspired to
branch out in a number of additional directions. First of
all, of course, they are traditional Tory socialists, offering
Northern workers the benefits of corporate discipline for
the impersonal miseries of wage-slavery. But since their
obvious purpose is to belabor the North rather than to
redeem it, they do not hesitate to try other gambits as
well. They become Tory petit-bourgeois liberals like Edward Elliott, offering workers of the North free home-
steads as well as the principle of "domestic affection."
They become Tory anarchists like Hammond, threatening
to light the fires of revolution in the North simply in re-
taliation for abolitionism. They even become, alas, Tory
capitalists like Calhoun, pleading for an alliance with the
wage-masters of the North in order to keep both the
slaves and free labor down.[2] Considering all these roles,
one can reasonably say of the Southern Tories that they
lacked one of the greatest of all the virtues of their beloved Carlyle: namely, sincerity. Even if Carlyle had never
written to Beverly Tucker saying that he did not approve

of the American system of slavery, surely a heart-breaking message, the gap between Tucker and himself would still be evident enough.

Fitzhugh, in an off moment, admitted that the Southerners were not real Tory humanitarians. Echoing the lament of Orestes Brownson at an earlier time, he complained that Europe's "natural friends of the poor," the feudal and clerical classes, did not exist in America to stave off the miseries of capitalist oppression.[3] And, of course, if the most logical reactionary in the South could, even for a moment, let his guard down, the North had little to worry about philosophically. Here again the Northern evasion of the Southern argument took place according to schedule. The South blasted Northern capitalism with a new Tory moralism that it could not itself quite entirely believe, the North ignored the blast and hammered at the South with an ancient natural rights moralism that everyone really believed, and Fitzhugh was left complaining that no one in the North paid any attention to him. Indeed on the score of capitalism it was doubly inevitable that the North would say little or nothing. With moralists like Channing and Emerson at the heads of its philosophic armies, was it going to advance a set of Jeremy Benthams to justify its own materialism? American liberalism, unchallenged by feudalism, had never become thoroughly utilitarian, and the revolutionary feudal dream of the South, inspired to begin with by the conservative natural rights radicalism of the North, was hardly designed to make it become so. Confronted with the greatest moral crusade in American history, the Reactionary Enlightenment had a small chance indeed of driving the North into a frenzied defense of its materialistic behavior. Though Channing on occasion did concede that the acquisitive spirit of the Yankees had to be remedied, the technique of "disdaining argument" that Hammond complained about was used more widely here than anywhere else.

Thus if the Southern Tories did not look backward to a real feudalism and did not look forward to a real socialism, one thing that Marx said about their European counterparts can be said of them in a superlative degree: that they were fighting a "literary battle." The battle of the Southerners was so literary that historians have only just begun to unearth it from the dust-ridden books in which it is buried. The final comment on the South's Tory attack on the North, as on the whole of the Reactionary Enlightenment, follows automatically. It was forgotten, and with a vengeance that few intellectual movements have ever experienced. Both Fitzhugh and Holmes made slashing attacks on Herbert Spencer in the course of their Tory crusade, but when Sumner discovered him after the Civil War he wrote as if they had never been alive. The tradition of Disraeli and Carlyle went at least into British socialism and conservatism, the tradition of Berryer into the corporatism of France. But the tradition of Hammond and Tucker went, to put the matter bluntly, nowhere. Even our contemporary Southern agrarians, men like John Crowe Ransome and Herbert Agar, do not build on their work. And our historical categories, if they leave no room for the Tories of the South, leave no room also for their Tory radicalism. American "conservatism," the "conservatism" of Hamilton in one era and of Horatio Alger in another, being Whig in character, has never dabbled with socialism.

2. *Comte in America: Positive Metaphysics*

The irony of the Southern sociologists is that, for all of their sad American fate, they had gotten hold of a relevant point: the real nature of social oppression. Considering the superficiality of the Jeffersonian and Jacksonian traditions on this score, their achievement can hardly be dismissed. These traditions, confounded by the promotional program that Whiggery was forced to advance in the primitive setting of American economic life, had traced the origin of social inequality to the action of the state—an idea which, as Beard himself noted, put the cart before the horse. When men like Fitzhugh, Holmes, and Hughes began to go behind the action of legislatures to the nature of society itself, to the drive within it for hierarchy and subordination, they were bound to produce a set of new and fruitful insights. What undid them was this: Jefferson's governmental obsession had been inspired by the remarkable freedom of American life, a situation which naturally tilted all attention toward the political conclusions of Locke rather than toward his social premises, and that freedom had by no means disappeared. Thus their social insights were injected into an atmosphere that was still unprepared to appreciate them, and being vastly overdrawn, were bound to fall flat. It was one thing to say that Locke's individualism was technically a dream, and it was quite another to say that it had no meaning at all in the North and was nothing but a façade for the erection of tyrannies even greater than those that existed in the South. Fitzhugh substituted for the social blindness of Jefferson a hopeless exaggeration of the truth. The South exchanged a superficial thinker for a mad genius.

This is exactly the impression that the Southern sociologists communicate: the impression of brilliant men gone haywire. No one who reads the beginning of their argument can fail to find it refreshing and no one who reads its conclusion can fail to find it fantastic. The basic idea is the one that Henry Hughes worked out in his theory of "association": that all human activity requires some degree of organization and that this in turn requires leadership by some and subordination by others. Surely a concept of this sort goes deeper than the cry of William Leggett that all will be well in a Lockian way once the system of charter "monopoly" is abolished. On top of this concept Fitzhugh builds the historical theory that the growing complexity of economic life, in labor unions no less than in corporations, is binding the individual down more and more to the coercions and hierarchies inherent in social organization. Again one is bound to voice approval. This is a problem that Marxism never solved, and it is one that did not occur at all to the men of the Jacksonian era, save possibly for a few stray spirits like Emerson. The sense the Southerners had of the frustration that liberalism could produce in a socially coercive setting is also something one has to admire. Chancellor Harper, not himself, so far as I know, a devotee of Comte or sociology, expressed it beautifully when he said that individuals were "tantalized, baffled, and tortured" by the quest for wealth they could not attain.[4]

But what is the upshot of this penetrating analysis, reminiscent of Comte, Le Play, and Veblen all at once? It is that the only solution to the problem of the actual slavery that exists in the North is the adoption of the outright, formalized slavery that exists in the South. This,

185

surely, is stretching things a bit too far. Everything that the Southerners had said was superlatively a matter of degree, and in the North, of all places in Western culture, of small degree. If the free world of Jefferson was part dream, it was part reality also. Association did exist in the North, but it was remarkably fluid. Labor unions were coercive but the chief problem they had was holding themselves together. Men were frustrated by the capitalist goal but hardly to the point of hysteria. The Southerners, in a word, carried their insights to the point of self-annihilation. Starting out as positivists, they ended up as metaphysicians.

Hence their rush to save the North by redefining freedom in terms of status—in terms of "orderers" and "orderees," as Henry Hughes put it—was, to say the least, premature.[5] The German concept of duty, which they got through Carlyle as well as through Hegel, had already invaded the North, but the Northern romantics had found a Kantian, individualistic version of it suitable enough for their purpose. Indeed this revivified individualism, at the hands of Channing and Parker and Emerson, was one of the great weapons of the antislavery movement. The slave must be free, insisted Channing, because he experiences that "sense of Duty" which is the core of human nature, because he is an "End in Himself."[6] When the Southerners defined freedom in terms of duty, they were telling the North nothing new, and when they defined duty in terms of external coercion, they were telling it nothing it cared to hear. Certainly Fitzhugh's concept of "domestic affection," which romanticized the status relationship between slave and master, which was grounded in the notion that only a "property" right in another man can make one truly care for him, was not designed to appeal to the North. This weird extension of Locke in order to fill the utopian vacuum his theory had left was fantastic. Of all the real Lockian sensations the Northern worker experienced, the most authentic was surely the fact that he had a property right in himself.

But the attack of the Southern sociologists upon Northern liberalism was not of course confined to the charge that it created heartless coercions under the utopian guise of individual liberty. Being utopian, as George Frederick Holmes sadly pointed out, it was constantly generating a "succession" of new utopias which threatened to destroy the organization it did produce.[7] "Socialism," with its strikes and its riots, was the great bogey here, although there was not a shred of social unrest in the North, from crime to marital infidelity, that the Southern writers omitted to mention. The fact that abolitionists like Garrison and Greeley were themselves social reformers was seized upon as a pure giveaway of the Northern case. Not only did it prove that "free society" was a failure, but it proved that the anarchistic impulse implicit in it was practically without limit. Fitzhugh, in *Cannibals All!*, described the argument as his "trump card."[8]

Again the Southerners were badly off base. The outstanding thing about socialism in America was not its presence but its absence. The outstanding thing about the Simpsons and Owens who bubbled at the peripheries of American political thought was that they were in fact peripheral. The truth is, when the Southern positivists opened up the question of the generative force of the original "metaphysical" idea, they revealed without knowing it one of the central weaknesses of their whole position. For quite apart from the objective reality of the liberal experience in America, one of the reasons that American liberalism had not rapidly turned socialist was precisely that it had not originally been "metaphysical," that is to say revolutionary in the Holmesian or Comtian sense. James Otis and Patrick Henry, because they did not live in French society, did not develop the millennial passions of Condorcet, and the significance for the future this was going to have had already been mirrored in the difference between a Daniel Shays and a Gracchus Babeuf.* Holmes's insight into the tendency of the liberal mood to perpetuate itself was a good one but unfortunately it cut the wrong way in America.

The Southerners, however, were not entirely taken in by their own distortions. They sensed most of what I have been saying, which is why here as elsewhere we find them hastily turning to Europe for much of the evidence they need. Louis Blanc was a much more important "anarchist" than Stephen Pearl Andrews, even the Chartists were more vivid than anything the North provided. Pointing out that Enlightenment utopianism was not "a theory of indigenous growth on the Western Continent," [9] the Southerners seized upon the European revolutions of 1848 with an eagerness that was all too apparent. This to be sure was not an American way to greet revolutions abroad: to hail them as proof that "free society" was a "failure." America had on the whole been receptive to European revolutions, and in 1830 Southern slaveholders had lit bonfires to celebrate the flight of Charles X. But in the new age of Burke and Carlyle and

* See pp. 76-8.

Comte, the Southerners had seen the error of their liberal sympathies, and while many of them instinctively responded in the old way, applauding 1848, without realizing that they ought not to do so, the sociologists of the South utilized with a vengeance the missing American evidence of social "anarchy" that it provided. Much too gloomy for an America that was on the verge of the greatest age of capitalist expansion in history, they flourished amid what Fitzhugh happily called the "social revolutions" of Western Europe.[10]

In light of the exaggerated social truths the Southern sociologists had seized upon, one might be tempted to say of them that they were "ahead of their time." Certainly in a mass production age the organizational and psychological insights of Fitzhugh and his friends carry more meaning than they did on the eve of the Civil War. And yet we cannot really say of these men that they were prophets in the American wilderness. What ruined their argument before ruins it still today: there has been no flight to slavery in the United States. If the liberal formula is imperfect, its viability has been impressive, and the Southern sociological analysis has about it even now a reckless quality. Here as elsewhere, alas, the Southerners were not even a Marxian "menace of the future."

3. *Tory Socialism and Capitalist Promotionalism*

Betraying Southern "sociology" all along of course was not only the liberal reality of the North but the liberal reality of the South, the bourgeois prejudices the Southerners could never completely destroy. But it is when we turn to their Tory socialism that these become most shockingly apparent. As disciples of Comte, the Southerners can speak in solemn abstractions that are not immediately exposed by their liberal capitalist selves. But as feudal opponents of Yankee moneymaking, as assailants of the Smithian laws of economic competition, as agrarian haters of industry, the workaday convictions they share with everyone else in America stick out in quite an appalling way. Here, as I have said, Fitzhugh himself collapses, giving way to a capitalist dream that leaves the spirit of Sir Walter Scott far behind.

There is, however, a curiously misleading issue here. Within the Southern scheme of capitalist thought which clashed with the Southern scheme of Tory thought there was a secondary struggle: the struggle between free trade and promotionalism. Now the theory of free trade, which at the hands of men like Dew and Hugh Swinton Legaré was a pure Manchesterian proposition, represented the clearest and most pronounced contradiction to the Disraelian ethos. The theory of state promotion, on the other hand, controlling the free operation of economic laws, seemed on the surface to harmonize with the Tory paternalism of the South, and this is the theory that Fitzhugh, together with J. B. De Bow and others, was inspired to advance. Consequently Fitzhugh appears for a moment in much the same role that he had when he lashed out at the compact rationalism of Calhoun and the racial theory of Hammond: as a logical reactionary. Indeed on the score of free trade the situation was much the same as it was on that of the "concurrent majority," for the Southern Manchesterians expanded the purity of the Enlightenment, just as Calhoun did, at the very moment the reactionary drift of Southern thought was destroying it. Even the "capitalistic" North had never advanced anything like the premise of unrestrained competition that lay at the base of the Southern attack on the tariff. The "capitalism" of the Yankees had been Hamiltonian, their "wage-slavery" more paternalistic, in other words, than the free-tradism that many of the Southern paternalists were advancing. Fitzhugh rose to his normal pitch of logical anger. How could a good Carlylian denounce Manchester when the South was more Manchesterian than the North? How could the theory of "let alone" be identified with the "anarchy" of abolitionism when the South itself advanced it? How could the Christian law of "domestic affection" be espoused when the Southerners were advancing the middle class theory that destroyed it? How indeed could the "organic nationality," the "patriotism" of the South flourish when the South displayed the cosmopolitan leanings of Adam Smith? [11]

But Fitzhugh's anger here does not quite convince us. What about his own capitalist promotionalism? True, it was a species of paternalism. True, too, it was the sort of paternalism that, having invaded the ethos of the free market, could be geared philosophically to a Tory scheme of thought. There is the striking case of Stephen Colwell, a Philadelphia economist so close to the promotionalist Whiggery of Henry Carey that the latter once said there had never been any essential difference between them, who moved from Carey's attack on Manchester to a medieval theory of status and social discipline that even George Frederick Holmes could not resist.[12] But what was it, after all, that Fitzhugh, De Bow, and the other promotionalists of the South wanted to promote? It was industry, cities, manufactures—precisely the things that their Disraelian criticism lamented in the North, the things that had there produced "wage-slavery," class conflict, "socialism," crime, riots, mobs. This surely was not an easy contradiction to swallow. De Bow himself fearfully admitted that a great "upbearing of our masses" might come about as a result of industrializing the poor whites.[13] And anyone who studies the commercial conventions of the thirties and the fifties in the South can hardly fail to see that they are governed by a jealousy of Northern industrialism rather than a Tory hatred of it. The truth is, the South was caught here in another one of its thousand contradictions. Laissez faire threw it into the social theory of Manchester, Whig promotionalism threw it into the social reality of Manchester. In either case the medieval dream was betrayed.

These persistent bourgeois giveaways, however, damaged the Southern argument against Northern "wage-slavery" less than the brute reality of economic freedom that prevailed above the Mason-Dixon line. A Disraeli is merely embarrassed by the presence of a Manchesterian impulse, but his entire reason for being is impaired if the two Englands he worries about do not in fact exist. Here we come back to the familiar dilemma of Southern sociology: a realistic insight carried to utopian lengths, a "positive" observation going up in the flames of "metaphysics." There can be no doubt that the Ricardo-Malthus analysis of Edmund Ruffin cuts behind Jefferson's political obsession just as cleanly as the Comtian analysis of George Frederick Holmes. It is a refreshing experience to move from the badness of Hamiltonian legislatures to the economic world which inspires it, from a repetition of the limited-government conclusions of Locke to an inquiry into the reality of his individualistic premises. But in this case, as in the other, enough American reality remained in those premises to make the "wage-slavery" indictment a grotesque exaggeration. The obvious facts of economic history show that this is true. The Ricardian theory was a theory of industrial society but, quite apart from everything else, America was just emerging from mercantile capitalism at the time the Tory socialists of the South tried to turn that argument against itself. The idyllic contrast between the joys of chattel-slavery and the miseries of wage-slavery, the sort of thing we find in the poetry of Grayson, undoubtedly represents a high point in the conscious twisting of the Southern imagination.

Even here, however, we are not always sure what the Southern argument is. At one point Edmund Ruffin and Henry Hughes seem to insist that slave labor is cheaper than free labor, since self-interest is an insufficient spur to activity, and at another they seem to insist that just the reverse is true, which presumably shows that the slave is better cared for than the worker of the North.[14] The latter point was, of course, at the heart of the "wage-slavery" indictment, and ironically enough, it was a Northern point to begin with. The superior profitability of free labor had been stressed by the Northern publicists. Overlooking the fact that free labor could be economically advantageous without involving a corresponding degradation of the worker, overlooking the whole question of types of industry which this involved, and overlooking also the moral case for individual responsibility, the Southerners seized upon the Northern argument as an admission that more "exploitation" was going on above the Mason-Dixon line than below it.

This, too, was the point at which various theories of surplus value were introduced. "My chief aim," wrote Fitzhugh in *Cannibals All!*, "has been to show that Labor makes values, and Wit exploitates and accumulates them. . . ." [15] The fact that the profits of the Southern slaveholder were less than those of the Northern capitalist proved conclusively that a smaller share of surplus value was extracted by the former. Indeed Fitzhugh's theory, which his biographer Harvey Wish has compared with that of Marx, goes beyond the Ricardian labor theory of value and premises the increasing concentration of capital until a revolution in behalf of slavery takes place. The fact that the revolution is in favor of slavery rather than a classless society is really fairly marginal. Socialism was for Fitzhugh, as it was for Ruffin and many others, the clearest evidence of the world's drift toward the Southern system, since it demanded a guarantee of human subsistence which only slavery could in the end provide. It was at once evidence of the "anarchical" tendency of the Enlightenment and evidence that it was doomed to failure.

But regardless of which way one looked at socialism, did not the fact of its insignificance remain the same? If that fact turned Holmes's theory of multiplying utopias against itself, actually exposing the truth that American liberalism had not originally been utopian, did it not also undermine the objective charge of wage-slavery based on the Ricardian analysis?

At this point the historian of the Reactionary Enlightenment, having recorded a mass of agonies and contradictions in the dream world of Southern thought, must record something even worse: a total confession of bankruptcy. For now the Southerners do not merely shift with

haste to Europe, where better evidence for their indictment of the North is available, but many of them actually
admit outright that the indictment is a false one. What
brings about this breakdown is the nature of the Ricardo-
Malthus argument itself: the argument that a progressive increase of population vis-à-vis resources pushes the
wage level down to subsistence and below. In America,
with half a continent still undeveloped, it was simply impossible to advance this argument with a straight face.
Henry Carey and Alexander Everett had already used the
American experience to attack the Malthusian proposition. Franklin, who in some sense anticipated Malthus,
had done much the same thing. Indeed Malthus himself
had pointed to America as a land where population pressure was uniquely at a minimum, just as Locke, earlier,
had used America as an empirical instance of the state
of nature proposition. The Southerners, though geniuses
in the art of evading reality, confronted here something
they could not evade.

And so, after all of their Tory lamentations about Northern wage-slavery and the socialism it was producing, a
number of them admitted that it had not in fact mate-
rialized. An admission of this sort was such a stupendous
anticlimax that we need not be surprised if it drove them
well-nigh berserk. Like Frederick Jackson Turner, whom
they clearly anticipated, they actually exaggerated the
power of America's material resources, overlooking the
weakness of their utopian theory of American liberalism
which, insofar as the absence of class war was concerned,
was fully as important. Dew said that the miseries of Europe could come to America only when "the great safety
valve of the West will be closed." [16] But it was Fitzhugh

who really went wild on this point. Rushing from a false view of Northern slavery to a false view of Northern social fluidity, he announced that "in forty-eight hours, laborers may escape to the West, and become proprietors." [17] This was a good deal more than he ever needed to admit. Even Daniel Webster, who replied to the Southern argument by insisting that small capitalists were constantly being created out of wages, did not go as far as this. Even Channing, who made the same point, did not go as far. Fitzhugh, coming out into the fresh liberal air of American life, simply lost control of himself.

Once a concession of this sort had been beaten out of the Southerners, what could be salvaged from their great offensive on "free society"? It was essential at once to change the mood of the whole attack. The North had to be warned that if it had escaped the proletarian evils of Europe, this was because its condition—to use the capital letters of Fitzhugh—was "ABNORMAL AND ANOMALOUS." [18] But alas, what difference did this make? Was American society any less free because other societies were not? Did Tory socialism make any more sense because America was the only community in which it could not reasonably be advanced? Social struggles are not a matter of abstract theory. If they happen to take place within the exception to the rule, that exception becomes the rule. Of course, the Southerners could point a grim finger to the future, and begin to worry about the "wage-slaves" who would appear when the Western safety valve was gone. But the sympathies of men need immediate stimuli, and the passion of a Carlyle is not likely to be aroused by the thought of a time a hundred years hence. In any case the American future, in economics as in "sociology," has failed to vindicate the Southern "feudal socialists." There has been no apocalyptic outburst in behalf of slavery on the part of an American proletariat, just as the bureaucratization of American life has not yet made the memory of Henry Hughes's "warranteeism" a very attractive one.

When Fitzhugh shouted in desperation that America was "ABNORMAL AND ANOMALOUS," he described of course the situation which ruined the whole of the Reactionary Enlightenment, with its anguished contradictions, its hundred false fronts, and its certain doom as an intellectual movement after the Civil War. It was abnormal for a nation always to have been liberal, and it was anomalous for a group of thinkers suddenly to appear in the midst of its history and try to be feudal. Only a serious incongruity within such a nation, the incongruity of a slave culture which was suddenly driven out of the liberal camp by the rise of a new humanitarianism, could possibly inspire America's "great conservative reaction." But if Fitzhugh's words were applicable to the whole of the Reactionary Enlightenment, they were still most vividly applicable to the theory he was discussing when he uttered them: the theory of Tory paternalism and capitalist collapse. The final clue to the Southern ideology is the way America managed to forget it, and who can deny that the rejection of capitalism has been forgotten as much as any part of it has? An abnormally capitalist nation has buried the anomaly of a Tory attack on "wage-slavery" with a fine and uncompromising vengeance. Which brings us to the historical mechanism by which the Reactionary Enlightenment gave way to the movement that followed it.

4. The Reactionary Enlightenment, Whiggery, and the Theory of Democratic Capitalism

As we watch the American liberal community tripping up the Southerners in their attempt to follow the European path of Comte and Disraeli, we are reminded almost inevitably, of the way it tripped up the American Whigs in the attempt to follow the European path of Macaulay and Guizot. Fisher Ames robbed of the chance to fight a Wellington is hardly less pathetic than Fitzhugh trying to behave like one, Hamilton robbed of the chance to ally with an aristocracy is hardly less pathetic than Hammond trying to create one; and surely, on the score of denouncing a nonexistent proletarian mob, the Whigs and the Southerners are practically alike in the pain that they experience. The American liberal world had no room either for a feudal reaction or an elitist Whiggery: it has always been hard on the men who have not been "American."

But beneath the common anguish of Fitzhugh and Fisher Ames there lies an ironic contrast: the defeat of the one was the instrument by which the other was democratized and Americanized. By 1840 the Whigs had already given up their elitist strategies for a theory of democratic capitalism. But it took their immersion in the democratic idealism of the Civil War, which allied them with the Western farmer, to complete the process that Harrison had begun. It was not until Lincoln appeared that the memory of Fisher Ames was entirely forgotten, that the taking over by Whiggery of the whole of the Jeffersonian ethos was finally achieved. Lincoln is thus a powerfully "American" figure. He Americanizes Whiggery and

he shatters the "un-Americanism" of the Reactionary Enlightenment. He transforms Hamilton in the process of
destroying George Frederick Holmes. He democratizes an
elitist liberalism in the process of abolishing a "feudal reaction." After Lincoln there are no more frustrated Gui-
zots, frustrated Disraelis (or at least no more important
ones) in the history of American political thought. The
slate is wiped clean for the triumph of a theory of democratic capitalism implicit from the outset in the American liberal world.

Here surely is the final irony in the fate of the South's
feudal Enlightenment. It was not even buried by an elitist
liberalism; it was buried by a democratic liberalism. It
was not even put to rest by a man as sympathetic as
Hamilton; it was put to rest by Andrew Carnegie and
Horatio Alger, the children of Lincoln's achievement. If
political theorists turn in their graves, Fitzhugh has turned
many times, but could anything have bothered him so
much as the sight of Jed the Newsboy walking unconsciously over his corpse? The post-Civil War theory of
democratic capitalism was a pure and absolute antithesis
to the philosophy of the Reactionary Enlightenment, and
the dreamlike nature of the Southern argument could
hardly be better confirmed than by the fact that this
philosophy should succeed it and should ultimately influence even the South. Consider the contrasts: Carnegie
emerging to glory in the absence of the English class system in America, Alger emerging to promise every individual a chance of wealth, Sumner emerging to lay down
the law of the most rigorous social atomism. Where amid
this great and almost frenetic energizing of the Lockian
formula could there be a place for the "Chivalry," for the

sociology which held the liberal formula to be a myth, for the Tory socialism which prepared to take over America in the face of capitalist collapse? America did not merely forget the Reactionary Enlightenment, it forgot it amid the extravagant enthusiasms of the worst of its enemies. Its punishment of the South left nothing out.

PART FIVE

The American World
of Horatio Alger

CHAPTER EIGHT

The New Whiggery: Democratic Capitalism

1. The "Discovery of America": Charm and Terror

Unfurling the golden banner of Horatio Alger, American Whiggery marched into the Promised Land after the Civil War and did not really leave it until the crash of 1929. The contrast with Europe is ironic and precipitous. While the disciples of Hamilton enchanted a nation with the dream of wealth, and were assailed only by a sporadic Progressivism, the disciples of Guizot and Macaulay, of the big property of Europe, were confronted not only by a lingering Toryism on the right but, more significantly, by a rising tide of Liberal Reform and socialism on the left. They still used their old techniques, the techniques that Hamiltonian Whiggery had tried in America before but had found impossible here. They engaged in anti-aristocratic crusades, especially in France. They allied with the aristocracy, especially in England with the drift of big business into the Tory party. And, to frighten the Liberal reformers, the European counterparts of American Progressivism, if any can technically be said to exist, they pointed to the Marxian menace on the left. But for all this, as the "social question" rose to a position of burning importance, they fought an ever more difficult battle. Lloyd George and Clemenceau came to power in western Europe at the turn of the century, and before long a huge controversy flared up between these Liberal reformers and the socialists, so that the issue of the time gradually became not radicalism but how much of it.

The victory of American Whiggery under the Horatio Alger dispensation was thus not due in the first instance to the spectacular growth of American capitalism after the Civil War, to "America's Economic Supremacy," as Brooks Adams put it, though a crash would end its reign and bring the American democrat to power with a distinctive New Deal. Actually capitalism was advancing in European countries as well during this era, most of all in Germany where, needless to say, Alger was an ever more alien figure than he was in England or France. The triumph of the new Whiggery came from the effect of an economic boom within the confines of the American liberal world, or more specifically, the effect of a boom on the peculiar mentality of that "petit-bourgeois" giant who was its distinguishing product: the American democrat absorbing both peasantry and proletariat. If he was able to smash Whiggery in the age of Hamilton when it tried to use the European techniques, he was a pushover for its democratic capitalism, its pot of American gold, when it gave those techniques up. The line of Whig development from Edward Everett through Abraham Lincoln to Andrew Carnegie was the clue to his undoing.

And yet now, as socialism becomes a crucial challenge in Western politics both to Whiggery and Liberal Reform, we must repeat that this "petit-bourgeois" giant, because he had never contrasted his liberal creed with an opposing set of values, had never infected it with the European ethos of class and revolution, was impervious to that ethos when the disciples of Marx advanced it to him. His Lockianism was absolute and irrational. Actually we do not need to go into the familiar and bitter isolation of Socialists like De Leon and Spargo in order to establish this. We see it even more vividly in the classless way in which, when he rose to a pitch of independence and anger as during the Progressive era, he rationalized his own liberal reformist objectives. He did not speak of Hobhouse's "Liberal Socialism" or Bourgeois' "social debt." He spoke of achieving a Horatio Alger world himself by smashing trusts and bosses. Thus while it was possible for a European liberal reformer to drift into socialism, since this was merely a matter of using language a bit more radical than he used in the first place, it was extremely difficult for a Wilsonian Progressive to do the same thing. The language of De Leon was just about as different from the language of Wilson as it was from the language of McKinley, and if anyone believes that this was due to economic boom, all he needs to do is look at the New Deal: even when Franklin Roosevelt adopted many of the quasi-collectivist measures of the European Liberal reformers, he did not use their language of class but submerged his liberalism and spoke pragmatically of solving "problems," which meant that no larger number of New Dealers drifted into socialism than did Progressives. The root of the matter was the dogmatic bourgeois orientation of a nation "born equal."

Thus American Whiggery, when it gave up the aristocratic frustrations of Hamilton and catered openly to the acquisitive dreams of the American democrat, uncovered by a strategic accident the historic ethos of American life: its bourgeois hungers, its classlessness, the spirit of equality that pervaded it even when Taylor and Hamilton hurled the charges of "aristocracy" and "mob" at each other during the vivid days of the earlier time. This is why, when you think of it, a strange resemblance at once appears between the new Whig ideologists and Europeans like Tocqueville or Americans like Jefferson pondering Old World contrasts. It is as if a thousand chamber of commerce epigoni suddenly appeared in the great tradition of American criticism, reducing insight to platitude, transforming philosophy into the complacent after-dinner speech. And in the case of a man like Carnegie, who fled from the class "stigma" of England as he called it, and flowered into an American millionaire, both the Old and the New Worlds meet in their worship of American opportunity. Whiggery, in other words, "discovers America" in its use of America, and transforms into a conscious ideology the very conditions of its success: the death of Toryism, the peculiar language of Progressivism, and the isolation of Marx.

There is one proof of this so obvious that it has gone almost completely unnoticed: the fact that the new Whiggery was able to attach to the Horatio Alger cosmos the grand and glorious label of "Americanism." The Progressive scholars, of course, have contemptuously dismissed this label as a fraud, but is it? Can frauds of such magnitude ever be perpetrated in the realm of popular ideology? Actually it is the true egalitarian insight of Tocqueville shining through the platitudes of Alger which accounts for the latter's grip on "Americanism." And if those platitudes unite Hamilton and Jefferson, making it possible to use a genuinely national label, was not that unity in fact the very point Tocqueville made? Were not the large Hamiltonian prizes of the American community always being won by small Jeffersonian men pushing upward to attain them? Even the Spencerian version of liberalism, so popular with the new Whig theorists, was peculiarly "American," since long before the Civil War the competitive spirit of American life had gone beyond the comparatively static individualism that Locke had formulated in the seventeenth century. But the Progressive historians, in their doctrine of betrayal, overlook an even more embarrassing fact. Their own heroes, Brandeis and Wilson, themselves conceded the "Americanism" of the Horatio Alger theme, arguing only that it was disappearing as a result of trusts and bosses. Surely when a Progressive agrees with a Whig some attention ought to be paid to the common judgment. The truth is, once Whiggery "discovered America," the whole of American thought shook down almost automatically into a kind of nationalism found nowhere else on earth, exploding the familiar categories of Carleton Hayes: a "traditionalist nationalism" that was liberal, a Burkian nationalism that was Lockian.

But this is only the beginning of a highly subtle tale. If the nationalism of the new Whig doctrine reveals that it uncovered America's liberal mind, it reveals as well that it uncovered the historic absolutism which characterized it. For nationalism is not an argument but an emotion: one of the most powerful social emotions of modern times. Hence what was really being expressed in the "Americanist" theme was that Lockian dogmatism which had tormented Cooper in the Jacksonian era, had consigned to oblivion the "feudalism" of Fitzhugh, and which now, whatever economic conditions might be, not only isolated De Leon but made it unthinkable for the Progressives to use even a trace of his class-conscious language. And yet, of course, Whiggery hurled this very "Americanism" at the American Progressive himself. Which shows us that in addition to the golden charm of Horatio Alger, it was able to use a second weapon: terror. It tried to frighten the American democrat with his own absolute liberalism, tried to precipitate, as it were, an internal moral crisis whenever he turned to the instrument of the state. And the best way of doing this was to call him a "socialist" which, of course, was to make him perfectly "un-American." To be sure, he responded with his own Brandeisian "Americanism," but since he was the man who sought change, "traditionalist nationalism" was curiously stacked against him—stacked against him even though he blasted the trusts for changing America and tried to be more traditional than the Whigs. We see here how ironically the new era has turned the tables on the American democrat. In the time of Jefferson he was able to isolate the Whig from the American world: now having "discovered America," they are able to isolate him.

Two moods then run through the new Whig doctrine: one rational, the other irrational; one liberal, the other "Americanistic." The difference between them is the difference between William Graham Sumner and the American Legion: the latter is the former boiled down to a nationalist essence. Somewhere in the middle lies the spirit of Mr. Justice Field not quite as philosophic as a disciple of Spencer nor quite as obscurantist as a disciple of Harding. And this is reasonable enough, for the Supreme Court had always been the Hebraic expositor of the American general will, building on the irrational acceptance of Locke the Talmudic rationality involved in his application to specific cases. Nor did the two moods, different though they were, ever really clash. They moved through the age of Carnegie and Coolidge in a happy reliance upon each other, the American flag wrapped around the Alger dream. They reached their climax in perfect unison after the First World War when the stock market boom made a giant out of Alger and the Bolshevik Revolution transformed irrational "Americanism" into pure hysteria. Together during this era they disenchanted and terrified the American democrat so completely that in 1924, while big business in England was living under a Socialist government and in France under a Radical government, La Follette was about all that remained of the high enthusiasm of the Progressive movement.

Even in connection with the issue of state economic policy, where its distortions were clearly wildest, Whiggery "discovered America." There was this much truth to Hoover's "American Individualism": that America had indeed never had the stuffy economic restrictions of the feudal world, that it had been a land of comparatively free entrepreneurial activity.* True, even in a liberal world

---

* In light of the current researches into early economic policy being published under the sponsorship of the Committee on Research in Economic History, which reveal a remarkable acceptance of state action in economic life prior to the Civil War, it is easy to fall into the mistake of assuming that the early period was not one of very considerable economic freedom. But the pragmatic acceptance of so much state action stemmed precisely from the fact that, lacking most of the corporate economic restraints of the Old World, Americans did not develop the laissez-faire biases of Europe which Whiggery after the Civil War sought to make a part of the American legend. A lot of freedom, in other words, reduced the frenzy for attaining it. In recovering from the laissez-faire myth of the American past which Whiggery advanced, it would be un-

there is a note of chamber of commerce hypocrisy about the equal opportunity that Hoover portrayed, especially as trusts are springing up, which only the most sympathetic observer can overlook. True, too, and more significant, the freedom of American economic life, instead of producing the laissez-faire fetish, had produced a pragmatic outlook toward economic policy before the Civil War which had inspired a whole series of public enterprises and controls. One of the most devious twists of the new Whig "Americanism" was to make a Ricardo grow where a Carey had grown before. But if America's rugged individualism had not been so rugged as Hoover made it out to be, it was still rugged enough, and if the charge of "socialism" when leveled against Progressive economic policy was fantastic, its effectiveness oddly enough stemmed from this very fact. Here, as elsewhere, it was the irrational liberalism of the national experience which made the redscare tactic possible.

This is why we are indebted to the new Whig theory for a classic betrayal of the social tensions of the American world. Of course, the Whig ideologists did not speak directly of these, preoccupied as they were with the strategies of charm and terror. But those tensions are there, practically on the surface of their thought, for any analyst to see. First of all, we find the issue of status in a society that compulsively and irrationally cannot recognize its existence. For stripped of the feudal ethos on the right and the socialist ethos on the left, and with Progressivism

fortunate if a corporate or collectivist myth were substituted for it which would make the actual reality of the situation impossible to understand. For this same point during the revolutionary and Jacksonian eras, see pp. 53-4; and for a fuller development of it after the Civil War, pp 99-100.

itself collaborating in the Alger movement, there was literally no escape in America from the frightful psychic impact of the bourgeois competition. "In England," Stuart Chase once said, "the wealthy soap maker can buy a peerage through a contribution to the party funds, and so seek to get meaning into his life by association with a feudal tradition." [1] If this was impossible here, so also, and for the same reason, was entry into a socialist party for the worker the capitalist employed. No comfortable aristocracy, in other words, awaited the millionaire "success," and no apocalyptic dream of revolution functioned as solace for the proletarian "failure." But even more significant than these denied satisfactions was the simple fact of denial itself: the compulsive impact of a single creed. In the end this was what came to the surface when Whiggery, giving up its Hamiltonian trappings, "discovered America."

2. Rugged Individualism and State Power

The approach of the new Whigs to state economic action displays the usual pattern of American substitutions and compensations. Had McKinley been in Europe he would have denounced Liberal Reform and socialist legislation as the "New Toryism," as Spencer did, or he would have surrounded property rights with the irrational Tory ethos, as Lord Hugh Cecil did. But being in America he denounced it in terms of irrational liberalism, that is to say, "Americanism," which meant that when he accused the Progressives of being "socialistic," a technique he would also have used against the Lloyd Georges of Europe, his accusation though much less legitimate was far more devastating since socialism was of course a national heresy.

All in all, what with capitalist expansion to keep the charm of his theory going along with its terror, he did better than he ever could have done in Europe.

Certainly little was lost by being unable to argue that the Progressives were attempting to revive an earlier American set of feudal restraints on trade—the "old sumptuary laws," as Wordsworth Donisthorpe of the Liberty and Property Defence League in England put it in the eighteen eighties. By then, even in France, the specter of the *ancien régime* insofar as economic restrictions were concerned had been pretty well forgotten. One would not even quarrel with the propensity of American students of Spencer to neglect the remarkable omission of the "New Toryism" theme on the part of his New World disciples, were it not that this omission reflects the whole of Spencer's peculiar role in America, another aspect of which was the fact that he flowered here at the very moment that he was smothered abroad by the liberal and socialist collectivism of T. H. Green and Jaurès. Moreover American men of property were not without their own "New Toryism" twist, as Attorney Campbell revealed in the Slaughterhouse Cases when into the sympathetic ears of Field he poured the idea that the whole purpose of the "settlement of this continent" lay in the effort to escape European trade regulation.[2] Whiggery in a liberal community, if it could not frighten men with the vision of Bourbon France, could at any rate frighten them with the idea of betraying their ancestors who fled it which, needless to say, was the beginning of "Americanist" wisdom.

This meant, however, no substitute whatever for the Lord Hugh Cecil argument: the cloaking of property rights in the Burkian ethos of prescription, which proceeded apace as big business drifted into the Conservative party in England. Prescription and inheritance, instead of being anything the idea of democratic capitalism could rely upon, were indeed the chief monsters with which it struggled, for of course its essential premise was, to use the words of Harding, that "there is no reward except as it is merited." [3] Rather than glorifying the family, it was compelled, almost after the fashion of social revolutionaries, to minimize its significance, which accounts for its obsession with the log-cabin myth of Lincoln and for Elbert Hubbard's curious interest in millionaires whose fathers were poverty-stricken or alcoholic: George Peabody was "another example of a boy who succeeded in spite of his parents." [4] This, too, was the clue to Carnegie's doctrine of "trusteeship," of philanthropy rather than personal bequest, and it is not surprising that in England even Gladstone, who hailed Carnegie as a fellow liberal, would not go along with it. Gladstone, to be sure, had a singular passion for the family concept, but English liberalism as a whole was sufficiently infected with the feudal ethos to find the wholesale denial of family more than a bit appalling. The American Whigs in their Lincolnian phase, instead of being able to rely upon the growing European synthesis of Locke and Burke in the defense of property, were driven to a devotion to Locke of the wildest kind.

But these deprivations merely set the stage for their own peculiar tactic: the hurling of the whole absolute American liberal ethos against their opponents. It is an odd pity, looked at from the logical point of view, that Whiggery should have been tripped up here by the fact that the rugged individualism it glorified had inspired a pragmatic approach to public policy during the earlier era. If this did not alter its basic point, that America had been a land distinguished by free entrepreneurial activity, it compelled it nevertheless to engage in some curious twisting and turning. It had to join the reality of a successful Locke with the doctrinaire passion of a frustrated Locke, or, to put the matter differently, European liberal thought with American liberal reality. This accounts for the sudden popularity in America after the Civil War of the laissez-faire economists of early nineteenth century Europe, a curious business which Charles Merriam and others have noted. But in the popular symbolism of "Americanism" this was not so bad a distortion after all: for the average man one sort of Locke was just as good as another, and if it was rather howling to argue that equal opportunity had always been perfect in America and that Americans at the same time had been passionately concerned with achieving it, even many scholars managed to miss the contradiction.

The tangled and deceptive nature of this issue becomes apparent when one studies the passion of the new Whiggery to stress the fact that America had never had a concept of absolute legislative sovereignty, that it had, as President Phelps of the American Bar Association said in 1880, a "different theory" from the one that prevailed in England.[5] Actually the absence of the concept of sovereignty, which was supposed to fortify the laissez-faire view of the American past, tended to fortify a concept just the reverse of that, for sovereignty, as we have seen earlier, flowed in considerable measure from the very drive against feudal restrictions which produced the laissez-faire fetish itself. The same mistake was made by Dicey who lamented the fact that the Benthamites had, in their theory of sovereignty and their destruction of natural rights, laid the basis for positive social legislation later. True, the American tradition of natural rights did, as Dicey said, play into the hands of the laissez-faire idea. Sumner was wrong when he held that the idea of natural right was a "sentimental" doctrine which, socialistically, justified state action by guaranteeing a subsistence right for all individuals. Actually, as the record of Field and others showed, it was an admirable technique for restraining the state, guaranteeing not happiness, as Carnegie said, but merely the "freedom to pursue it." [6] But Dicey nevertheless overlooked the fact that along with Bentham in England had gone Ricardo, and that the American liberals now had to import the latter fifty years late into their own milieu.

Moreover, American Whiggery had itself been largely responsible for the tradition of economic policy it now proceeded to bury and destroy. It had been the American democrat, with Jefferson, who in theory at least had opposed it and had developed the closest thing to a laissez-faire dogma that the country had produced. The principle at work here was obvious enough: big capitalism was able now, with the major exception of the tariff, to dispense with the Hamiltonian promotionalism on which it had relied in the days of its weakness, especially since the corporate technique had become established and important. And so, if in the age of Jackson the American Whigs looked like the Corn Law "monopolists" of England, in the age of Carnegie they were prepared to look like the John Brights who had assailed those "monopolists." One can trace this process of spiritual conversion and dramatic flip-flop with a brilliant clarity within the American states where on the eve of the Civil War the Hamiltonian interests who had originally demanded many public investments, especially in banking and transportation, proceeded to deride them, producing precedent after precedent for the laissez-faire constitutional law so famous in the later time.

What made the matter even more complicated, however, was that when Whiggery shifted from Carey to Carnegie it proceeded to use the ancient arguments of the American democrat himself, thus gravely confounding this figure. He, of course, in assailing state action, had opposed "monopoly," which meant particularly the corporate charter. Indeed, lacking any real understanding of social oppression, he had defined all nonpolitical tyranny in terms of inequitable political decisions. Now, with the corporate charter universally accepted, due in part to his own ultimate drive for general incorporation, and with a huge trust growth being built upon it, he found himself confronted in his effort to solve a real social problem with the very symbols he had used. Sumner sounded "Jeffersonian" indeed: state action was the root of inequity, it took away from one man and gave to another. If a massive confusion of political traditions took place in general when Hamilton absorbed Jefferson and Horatio Alger emerged, this was its most vital spot, the issue of economic policy. Who was the real disciple of Jefferson, the man who wanted the Anti-Trust Act or the man who opposed it? Surely there was plenty in the Jeffersonian tradition that the new Whiggery could twist to the uses of its new "Americanism." The historic dissent of Mr. Justice Field in the Slaughterhouse Cases, where the issue dealing with a slaughterhouse monopoly was beautifully constructed for the purpose of absorbing Jefferson into the new Whig theory, reads in many passages like the pure essence of ancient radical dogma. What better way of terrifying the American democrat: not merely to cite Locke, not merely to cite "Americanism," but to cite his own ancient contribution to both?

The climax of the "Americanist" argument, however, came when Progressive economic policy was denounced as "socialistic" and "communistic," a technique Joseph Choate made famous from a legal point of view in the Pollock Case of 1895. To be sure, if Progressivism spoke in classless terms and yet was blasted more effectively by the Bolshevik epithet than the Liberal Reform of Europe, there was still one technique that American Whiggery could not easily use against it: the contemptuous charge that its economic policy was piecemeal, that it was trying to build an impossible halfway house between capitalism and socialism. Since the idea of nationalizing production was such an insignificant one in America, the ridicule that both right and left ultimately began to pour on the mild socialism of the leftwing English Liberals and the French neo-Jacobins hardly made sense here. But if the weapon of contempt was out, the weapons of fear and anger were clearly in, for where capitalism is an essential principle of life the man who seeks to regulate it is peculiarly vulnerable to the waving of the red flag. Nor ought we to be misled here by the fact that we cannot find, save possibly in Sumner, a reasoned identification of Progressivism with Marxism. The absence of reason is the very clue to the matter, for if "socialism" is to be a technique of nationalist slander, it cannot also be a philosophic issue. Which reminds us again that the root of Europe's rational attack on Liberal Reform as "socialistic," lay in the nature of its own Toryism and liberalism. How could English conservatism charge the "New Liberals" with fomenting an un-British sense of class when it founded its own theory on that very sense also? How could it blast them for using an "alien" concept of the proletariat when it had spoken itself of the glories of the middle class. Wordsworth Donisthorpe, that ardent apostle of the Liberty and Property Defence League, quite frankly acknowledged that he was afraid the English masses would take a leaf out of the liberal book.

The effect of the redscare technique as used against Progressivism flowers slowly. Justice Holmes dated the "vague terror" inspired by socialism in America at the turn of the century, but anyone who reads American editorial reaction to the Paris Commune will soon see that the historic American attitude toward European revolutions has been reversed. Wendell Phillips was one of the few who carried over into the Commune response the same enthusiasm that characterized the national response to the earlier revolutions for independence and political democracy. Still it is a fact that the impact on Progressivism itself comes most vividly later, and especially of course after the Russian Revolution, which took the earlier response to the Commune and not only expanded it but sharpened it into an effective political weapon. The repeal of much of Progressive social legislation, put on the books both by Democrats and Republicans, during the era beginning with Harding and A. Mitchell Palmer is not far removed in its meaning from the cry of "Americanism" raised against strange and subhuman agitators victorious in Europe and Asia. In the end the specific details of antitrust legislation, pure liberalism of course, reflect the devastating impact of the irrational terror inspired by Whiggery's "discovery of America."

3. The Theory of Success and Failure

Behind the politics of economic policy there lay of course the larger cosmos of Horatio Alger with all of its ethical problems, its psychic anxieties, and its driving energies. Toryism in Europe was not merely a strategic bogey or a technique for rationalizing property rights: it was an ethical scheme which opened the door, especially in England, for an escape from the driving impact of the competitive system on the part of the "successful" man. Nor was socialism a bogey merely or a technique for challenging property: it too was a theory of status, rescuing the working class from the liberal sense of "failure" and rationalizing its position in terms of a creed of cosmic optimism. But in the world of Horatio Alger, where the compulsive power of Locke made both of these schemes unthinkable, "success" and "failure" became the only valid ways of thought, which is what really lay behind William James's disgust with the "bitch-goddess," though his own pragmatism was by no means unrelated to it. This relentless running of the Lockian race liberated, as Georges Sorel saw, *une energie exceptionnelle* in the American people,[7] but it saddled them too with inward psychic dilemmas characteristically their own.

At the bottom of all this there lay a critical paradox. When American Whiggery democratized itself it at once destroyed the elitist principle and exaggerated it. It exaggerated it in the sense that while the chance to become successful was made equal, and was indeed extended to politics, so that Alger could write of Garfield as he did of a business titan the difference between success and failure was magnified beyond belief. "The crowd is credulous, it destroys, it consumes, it hates, and it dreams—but it never builds." [8] These were not the words of Hamilton but the words of Herbert Hoover, and who can deny, especially when one recalls their Darwinian base, that they were even more heartless than anything to be found in the early Whiggery? At the same time, while the material gap between the top and the bottom of American society was actually widened, the shattering even of the Hamiltonian distinctions of the earlier time meant that culturally it was more unified than ever, so that the heroes of the Hoover cosmos, instead of going beyond national good and evil personified it perfectly. They were victors in a race every good "American" was trying to run, which is why Mencken, a real disciple of Nietzsche, found little solace in their presence. One of them, Carnegie, once happily remarked: "Everybody in America reads the same news the same morning, and discusses the same questions." [9]

Now it is this rise of a race of giants in an intensified democratic setting which gives to the status issue a vividness greater than it had ever had in the American liberal world. Obviously a giant might arise who would not enjoy with Carnegie reading the same news as was read by the pygmies he had mastered. He might long for higher things, but lacking the Tory outlet, barred, as Ashley put it, from "securing a baronetcy, buying a country estate, founding a family, and ending his days with the rustics bobbing to him and a Debrett on the study table," [10] where was he to find such things? He might go to Europe outright and possibly end up in the House of Lords as William Waldorf Astor did, or he might marry off his daughter to purchasable European nobility as Collis P. Huntington did. He might even follow the path of Carnegie and buy an Old World castle, or the path of William Randolph Hearst and bring one all the way home. But within the American world itself there was no escape from the race even for those who won it, and any attempt to escape, to claim the feudal privilege in any way, as George Baer once did when he referred to the "infinite wisdom of God," was bound to be blasted by the Progressive with the very language the Whig habitually used against him: as being outside the American ethos. Thus the painful resort of the American "aristocracy" was an ever increasing display of material wealth itself, which indicated not removal from the race but merely victory. Veblen traced the "conspicuous consumption" of his era back to the feudal concept, but actually it was a frantic effort to compensate for the absence of the concept in the spirit of the national life. This is why "emulation," another Veblenian theme, could be so universally engaged in: the rustic could not emulate the baron but anyone could keep his bank account a secret until the sheriff arrived and pretend that he was a Lockian winner rather than a Lockian loser.

But now as always the problem of America's "frustrated aristocracy" did not lie merely in unsatisfied desire. It lay also in the conditions attendant upon maintaining one's position even as a bourgeois victor. For without some other status, there was always a danger that everything would be lost if financial position were gone, and so it was necessary to keep on running in the Lockian race lest someone else crowd you out from behind. When Elbert Hubbard said that "to stand still is to retreat" and that "superior men see no end to work," is not this what he really meant? [11] Ashley actually traced America's trust development to the psychic tensions implicit in success: "For the nerves of the American businessman have at last revolted and demanded some decently comfortable measure of stability." [12] The trust solution, needless to say, if it soothed nerves at the top, shattered them at the bottom, since the chance of rising in the American world was inhibited by it. But that is another story.

An elite suspended between aristocratic frustration and bourgeois anxiety is bound to have some limitations, and one of these was that it did not always display the highest degree of responsibility. If it was "un-American" to be feudal, why should one bother with feudal paternalism? Power, as once again Ashley saw, came to be an end in itself for the new American giant, "his essential reward," which gave him the feeling, as with Pullman, that a "principle was involved" when labor unions struck. [13] Even William Graham Sumner worried about this, though he had nothing to say in favor of unions, and after arguing at one point that the "mercantile" class ought to give up once and for all the idea of aping aristocrats, he finally conceded that some interpenetration of feudal with mercantile habits might do a lot for bourgeois leadership. [14] And yet if paternalism did appear, what would happen to the Darwinian struggle? Obviously Sumner was fighting with himself here, which shows how acute the issue really was. Brooks Adams, worrying always about the quality of capitalist leadership, betrayed the historic impulse of America's "frustrated aristocrat," but nonetheless he touched a relevant issue in the Horatio Alger world.

And yet the trials that Lockian "Americanism" imposed on the Whigs who originally discovered it were nothing as compared with those it imposed on the Progressives who fell victim to its charm and its terror. If the Whig was "un-American" when he tried to escape the tensions of the liberal race by translating "success" into aristocracy, the Progressive was doubly so when he tried to escape them by translating "failure" into anything that looked like proletarian solidarity. The irony of this, as always, is that the Progressive did not even use the class symbolism of Lloyd George, let alone the symbolism of Marx which rationalized the position of the working class in terms of an apocalyptic theory of misery and salvation. Far from inheriting the earth, all he wanted to do was to smash trusts and begin running the Lockian race all over again. But even the pathetic hope of Brandeis was blasted with an outpouring of liberal irrationalism. The very idea of organization, whether it be in labor unions or in the Progressive movement itself, was denounced as "un-American."

We must remember here that the whole new Whig strategy depended in a sense on the atomism of the democratic capitalist doctrine. The "discovery of America" did not dissipate Hamilton's motivational theory, that the "mob" was immensely self-interested. What it did was to smash the "mob" into a million bits, so that its fierce acquisitive passion, instead of being expended against property, would be expended against itself in the quest for property. Spencer, as it were, absorbed the passions of Plato, which is why, as soon as a few American atoms began to crystallize, the Platonic fear arose again. Life, said Elbert Hubbard, was "struggle," but class struggle was certainly not included in it. "All attempts," indeed, "to build up class hatred in this country must fail. We stand for cooperation, reciprocity, mutuality." Hence labor unions [15] drew a "line of demarcation between capital and labor" which straitjacketed the incipient millionaire; and the whole Progressive movement, to use the language of Harding, rather than that of Hubbard, was based on an idea of "grouped citizenship" alien to the American spirit.[16] At worst, of course, Gompers and Brandeis were "socialistic."

Thus there was no escape from "failure" save in the eternal effort to become a "success." Hubbard said: "Life without industry is guilt." [17] And guilt was indeed the consequence of running behind in the Lockian race, for the "failure" was damned not only because he was in the mass after the fashion of Carlyle but also because being an "American" he did not get out of it. There was only one saving concept here, the concept of luck or as ultimately translated into the American vernacular, the "breaks," upon which even Alger relied. Mr. Russel Crouse has noted how frequently Ragged Dick came to riches as a result of falling asleep in the snow and being found by a portly widower or rescuing a child from disaster and winning eternal gratitude.[18] But even this Machiavellian *fortuna* was earned by a prior energy, never being vouchsafed apparently to Luke the Loafer, so that it actually rationalized rather than mitigated the tensions of the liberal cosmos. How could it serve as a substitute for the cosmic solace that Marx and Engels gave to the "failures" of Europe?

4. The Issue of Conformity

And so it was not always easy to be an "American." Half-articulated, lurking just beneath the surface of Carnegie's joy, there was a vivid pattern of anxiety, frustration, guilt. And yet, for all of the structures that one might level against it, for all of the pure documentation it gives to the bourgeois image of Erich Fromm, can one doubt that it was an indispensable facet of the very virtues that "Americanism" had? Could one conceive of the religion of opportunity without it? Could one imagine those driving energies and mass ambitions that so impressed Sorel without the peculiar psychology it implied? The law of compensation works in every social personality: feudal, and indeed, as we are now beginning to discover, socialist as well. When we depict the tensions of bourgeois man, so superlatively illustrated in "Americanism," we have to realize that we are dealing with an eternally debatable proposition. If in America the negative side of the picture deserves stress because of underemphasis, that does not in the end alter the point.

But another question can be raised: not about the inner content of the creed but about its compulsive nationalism, not about Locke but about "Americanism." Once again we are back at the ancient American problem of liberal uniformity, far more striking now that even the frills of the earlier era have been stripped away and "success" and "failure" chain everyone alike to the single ethos. What Santayana called the historic American impulse to "follow the crowd" * took on even keener meaning in the

* One is reminded here, almost inevitably, of some of the recent brilliant work of David Riesman.

time in which he lived. And is not this the genuine pathos of the frustrated aristocrat and the frustrated proletarian that, quite apart from the validity of their cosmologies, they could not embrace them if they chose?

It is not accidental that Sumner should sense this problem, for not only was the crusty Yale professor given to clashing with the Alger creed he helped so much to build, as in the famous issues of plutocracy and the tariff, but he had, as we have seen, echoed the Tocquevillian lament in his own studies of the national past. "The trouble is," he wrote, "that a democratic government is in greater danger than any other of becoming paternal, for it is sure of itself, and ready to undertake anything, and its power is excessive and pitiless against dissentients." [19] This was the kind of statement which inspired John Chamberlain to dub Sumner one of the first of the Menckenites. And yet notice how closely it resembles the very creed of compulsive "Americanism" itself. This shows us something important, that the individualist premise itself was capable of yielding, Hegelianwise, a protest against its own tyranny in the nation. And here we have precisely the sentiment which flowered in Learned Hand and Zachariah Chafee during the redscare panic after the First World War. The logic of liberalism led to a perception of its own coercive dangers.

But in general this was not the case. We must remember that for the most part the tyranny of the "success-failure" ethos did not define itself in terms of jail sentences or even in terms of conscious frustration. It was a silent quality in the national atmosphere, not so much blocking alien decisions as preventing them from ever being made. It is a great advantage for a political movement to be able to exploit a power of this kind, and when Whiggery was able to do so, surely it was amply repaid for the miseries it had endured during the Hamiltonian time. America's law of Whig compensation was a kind one. It was a sort of Horatio Alger story in and of itself. And yet that story will not have been told in full until we examine more closely the American democrat who was enslaved to the Whig and the American socialist who was isolated by both. The fate of these figures rounds out the logic of Whig supremacy during the era after the Civil War when the Whigs "discovered America."

CHAPTER NINE

Progressives and Socialists

1. *Liberal Reform in America*

One can use the term "Liberal Reform" to describe the Western movement which emerged toward the end of the nineteenth century to adapt classical liberalism to the purposes of small propertied interests and the laboring class and at the same time which rejected socialism. Nor is this movement without its ties to the earlier era. If there is a link between Progressivism and the Jacksonian movement, there is a link also between the Jacobinism of 1848 and that of the French Radicals. The socially conscious English Liberals at the turn of the nineteenth century had their progenitors even during the age of the First Reform Act. But the American movement, now as during that age itself, was in a unique position. For swallowing up both peasantry and proletariat into the "petit-bourgeois" scheme, America created two unusual effects. It prevented socialism from challenging its Liberal Reform in any effective way, and at the same time it enslaved its Liberal Reform to the Alger dream of democratic capitalism.

The fate of America's socialism was thus deeply interconnected with the fate of its Liberal Reform, as both were involved in the triumph of its reconstructed Whiggery: we are dealing with an equation of interdependent terms. Because the Progressives confronted no serious challenge on the left, they were saved from a defensive appearance, were able to emerge as pure crusaders. And yet this very release from the tension of the European Liberal reformers was reflected in a peculiar weakness on the part of the Progressives themselves, which was their psychic susceptibility to the charm and terror of the new Whiggery. America's "petit-bourgeois" giant, in other words, if he would not flirt with Marx, was in constant danger of falling into the hands of Elbert Hubbard. And who can deny that the Progressive movement has a spottier history than anything to be found in the Liberal Reform of Europe? During the dizzy decade of the 'twenties, when Alger and the American Legion locked hands against the background of Bolshevism, Republican Presidents were not only elected but even the Democratic party reshaped itself in their image. If the Catholic Church was a refuge for Brownson after 1840, the left bank of Paris provided a refuge for many of his successors during the age of the stockmarket boom. Flight from the American liberal world itself, the technique of the "frustrated aristocrat," became the technique as well of the "frustrated radical."

But moments of utter collapse are not all that we have to consider. What sort of program did the American Progressive advance even during the vivid days of the New Freedom and the Bull Moose? The answer in general is obvious enough. He advanced a version of the national

Alger theme itself, based on trust-busting and boss-busting, which sounded as if he were smashing the national idols but which actually meant that he was bowing before them on a different plane. Wilson, crusading Wilson, reveals even more vividly than Al Smith the pathetic enslavement of the Progressive tradition to the "Americanism" that Whiggery had uncovered. To be sure, there is a quaint academic touch in Wilson's Algerism, which inspired him to depict "what it means to rise" by reference to Princeton freshmen and priests in the Catholic Church during the middle ages, but in essence he is as sound as a chamber of commerce orator. So is Teddy Roosevelt, although here we find, if not the atypical atmosphere of the classroom, the rather unusual bombast of a frustrated Nietzschean in the American setting. Certainly the contention of Croly that there was a great and "fundamental difference" between the New Freedom and the New Nationalism can hardly be defended, when we consider their common allegiance to democratic capitalism, and William Allen White had one of his keenest insights when he described the chasm between them as the chasm between Tweedledum and Tweedledee. One need not deny, of course, that both movements called for social measures such as hours legislation and workmen's compensation which were not entirely within the ambit of "Americanism" and which in their own small way offered a hint of the European Liberal reformers. But these were loose marginalia, lacking a definite rationalization other than that which the Alger scheme afforded, and certainly without the concept of a permanent "working class" or a permanent "social debt" such as the English Liberals and the French Radicals hurled against reactionary capitalism and Toryism.[*]

Which brings us again to the crucial significance of ideology: the Algerism of the Progressives was no more due in the last analysis to the boom of the time than was the Algerism of Whiggery. Boom sustained it, as it did the other, but after the crash of 1929 it would not disappear but would go underground to serve as the secret moral cosmos on the basis of which New Deal pragmatism moved. It was an expression of the dogmatic Lockianism of the nation, which is why it has a very peculiar pathos. Essentially, though of course in modified form, the American Progressive confronted the same realities as confronted the European Liberal reformers: the irreversible rise of a proletariat, the irreversible inequity of the capitalist race. But in the irrational grip of "Americanism," and not yet having learned through the agony of the crash the New Deal technique of burying ethics and "solving problems," he could not look these frightening facts in the face. He could not speak of "proletarians" or "capitalists" or even "classes." He could not see what every Western Liberal reformer saw with ease. Come what may,

* European Liberal Reform was not, of course, all of a doctrinal piece, and one can refer to it as a whole only in the sense that it sought generally to transcend the earlier individualism. There is a world of difference between Mazzini's nationalist idealism, influenced by the utopian socialists, and Bourgeois' theory of solidarity, influenced by French sociology. And there is a lot of difference between both and the collective idealism of T. H. Green and his liberal followers. What is involved in all cases of the "New Liberalism" is a frank recognition of the need for collective action to solve the class problem (though in fact this action was not always taken on a comprehensive scale). The image of Horatio Alger, for all of the effort of the movement to retain the core of individualism, was alien to it.

he had to insist that the Alger formula would work if only given a chance.

Here we have the clue to the whole trust obsession of the time. We think of the trust as an economic creation of American history, and we fail to see that it was just as much a psychological creation of the American Progressive mind. Granted that America now superseded England as the home of the "great industry," to use the words of Ashley,[1] it is still a fact that the relative concentration of economic power was greater in almost any part of Europe than it was in America. And yet the European Liberal reformers, though they blasted "monopoly"—the English in the case of the tariff and land, the French in the case of large business in general—did not make the same fetish of the symbol that the American Progressives did. They spoke of other things, the large alignment of classes. The truth is, the trust in America was in significant part an intellectual technique for defining economic problems in terms of a Locke no one dared to transcend. If the trust were at the heart of all evil, then Locke could be kept intact simply by smashing it. It was a technique by which a compulsive "Americanism" was projected upon the real economic world.

But this technique, simple as it seems, was not without its problems. As time went on more and more of economic fact had to be obscured in order to make it work. Representative minds like Lloyd and Brandeis were fairly good at this, which is why the surface of their thought does not show the problem clearly. It is in figures apparently more complicated, men like Croly and Ward, where the tension between reality and projection suddenly explodes to the surface, that we see the agony it involved. These were the courageous minds of the Progressive era, Comtians indeed, men who dared to think of "planning." But put their Comtism alongside Comte himself, and what do you find? A pathetic clinging to "Americanism" which in the case of Croly led to practically unintelligible rhetoric when the crucial questions were posed, and in the case of Ward led to a queer "sociocracy" half based on the very Lockian animism that Comte so vigorously assailed. Granted that the European Liberal reformers, even in France, did not advance the Comtian state, still they were a good deal closer to it than anything we find in these American iconoclasts. Is it any wonder then, if these intellectual heroes suffered so, that the common man should flee in his leisure hours to the fantasy Bellamy offered? It is only a superficial paradox that a utopia based on perfect planning should sell so widely in an age that struggled for perfect individualism. The dream is the subconscious wish: utopias are mechanisms of escape. Could there be any sweeter release for the tormented trustbuster then to dream of a perfect trust, a trust so big that it absorbed all other trusts, so big that the single act of its nationalization collectivized all America? Moreover notice this: there was nothing "un-American," "socialistic," or "alien" about this vision. "On the precise contrary," as the good Dr. Leete himself said, "it was an assertion and vindication of the right of property on a scale never before dreamed of." [2]

Surely it is not accidental in the light of this that American socialism was isolated. Actually, though the whole of the national liberal community sent the Marxists into the wilderness, the final step in the process which did so was the nature of American Liberal Reform. For what is the hidden meaning of all this compulsive "Americanism," with its rejection of the class and social language of the European Liberal reformers, if not precisely the burning of every conceivable bridge between Progressivism and the socialist movement? A man could move from Lloyd George's defense of the working class to socialism, as many Englishmen in fact did. A man could move from Bourgeois's theory of solidarity to socialism, as many Frenchmen did. But how could a man move to Marx from a Progressivism which even in its midnight dreams ruled out the concepts of socialism? Here we see why the American socialist movement could not cut into the Progressive vote appreciably, save in areas like the German-populated Wisconsin, for it was the drift of disenchanted Liberal reformers into the socialist camp which accomplished this process in Europe. It was the discovery by labor that Liberal Reform did not go far enough which produced the Labor party in England and the rise of Socialism in France. To be sure, there was in one sense less objective ground for such a drift in America, since it cannot be said that Progressivism permitted vestiges of the feudal order and feudal ethos to survive as European Liberal Reform did, since such vestiges were not here to begin with. Everywhere in Europe, in MacDonald's England hardly less than in Kautsky's Germany, socialism was inspired considerably by the class spirit that hung over not from capitalism but from the feudal system itself. On the other hand, since we are dealing with mythological assets and liabilities, we can also note that Progressivism paid for this advantage by an inability to dominate the socialists in a campaign against the old feudal institutions, a technique which European Liberal Reform took over from

European Whiggery. The real issue remains, however, that the vital point at which the American world isolated socialism was the point at which Progressivism compulsively embraced the Alger ethos.

And yet we must not dismiss this irrelevant European analysis too easily, since it was soberly reflected in the American socialist literature, which suggests that if the socialists were isolated by the mechanism of the national life they did little enough to sweeten their lot. Of course, their persistent use of the European concepts of Marxism when the nation was frantically ruling them out of its mind displays their behavior in the broadest way. But when we consider their own internal struggles, the battles over which they expended the colossal energies dammed up by political failure, we see how completely they were dominated by the European patterns of thought. For if the whole issue of collaboration with the "bourgeois reformers" took a unique shape in America, this did not prevent them from fighting, line by line and issue by issue, the European battle over the question. Even before the formation of the Socialist party in 1900 the struggle between Guesde and Jaurès arising out of a Dreyfus affair America never saw was dutifully fought out by the American Marxists, with De Leon, the eccentric half-genius of the movement, emerging as the leading "impossibiliste" of the New World. And, of course, when around 1910 the Socialist party split into two wings over the reform question, Victor Berger and the Milwaukee socialists, followers of Bernstein in a world Bernstein never knew, emerged as the leading "bourgeois collaborators." If the American socialists were determined not merely to advance the basic "un-Americanism" of the socialist scheme but also its secondary, interstitial, and post-Marxian "un-Americanism," is it surprising that their fate was even worse than that of the Southern "feudalists"?

One final point, a queer anticlimax to this whole age of rampant Lockian nationalism. The age produced in the ranks of American Progressivism and socialism a sparkling array of social science students of America: Beard, Smith, Parrington, Boudin, Myers. But did these men, who were to cast so long a shadow over our thinking, grasp the America in which they lived? The answer is predominantly negative in every case, but a curious distinction is involved. The Progressives failed because, being children of the American absolutism, they could not get outside of it, and so without fully seeing that Locke was involved everywhere, they built their analysis around a titanic struggle between "conservative" and "radical" which had little revelance to Western politics as a whole. They stood, as Bryan and Wilson themselves did, a unanimous age upside down and interpreted it in terms of cosmic conflict. But these men, as I say, were children of America: this was not true of the Marxists. The latter were children of Europe, "un-American" to begin with, outside of America, equipped with meaningful Western categories: feudalism, capitalism, liberalism. Why did they fail to comprehend the nature of the American liberal world, determined as it was by the absence of the primitive feudal factor in the Marxian scheme? Here lies the real intellectual tragedy of the time, but the reason for it is obvious enough. If an understanding of the American liberal world led to the grim conclusions for socialism we have uncovered here, why should hopeful activists look them squarely in the face? After all, Trotsky's law of combined development, which stressed the skipping of the liberal stage by Russia, was designed to rationalize that country's immediate plunge into the socialist revolution. Would he have developed the same law if it led to the opposite conclusion? What was needed if the Western historical orientation of Marx was to be effective was someone with that passion for gloom which characterized "frustrated aristocrats" like the Adamses all the way over at the other end of the political spectrum. But in the messianic world of Victor Berger, this was too much to ask. The age that "discovered America" in its social thought was doomed, as any other age in the national history, never to see itself.

2. *The Progressive Tension*

Once we grasp the conflict between a projected "Americanism" and a real social world that was beginning to deny it, we see that it is the pervasive agony of the whole Progressive mind. It is a symphonic theme which keeps coming out everywhere, in ideas apparently unrelated, in issues that seem as far apart as natural right and the question of bosses, the prelude always to Bellamy's mad utopian flight from the tension it involved. The Progressive mind is like the mind of a child in adolescence, torn between old taboos and new reality, forever on the verge of exploding into fantasy.

We see this in the very primitive question of community, the big issue in Western Europe as the collective ethos of the new liberalism supplanted the individualism of the old. Reacting against a harsh Darwinian world, many of the Progressives turned like T. H. Green to idealism or like Mazzini to spiritual nationalism. But having

237

turned in this direction, they could not follow through, for to arrive at the communitarian doctrines of the new European liberals, let alone of the socialists, would have spelled the end of the Alger taboo. And so they were like pitchers forever winding up but never throwing the ball. Lloyd and George, both heavily under Mazzini's influence, stressed the Duties of Man with a passion, but at the end we find them oddly enough with Jefferson. According to George, indeed, once the single tax were instituted and land monopoly abolished, we would approach not only the world of Jefferson but the "promised land of Herbert Spencer." [3] What was happening here, of course, was that Mazzini's nationalism, which sought to override Locke with a concept of community, was being canceled out, willy-nilly, by the compulsive power of another kind of nationalism based on Locke himself: "Americanism." George was a philosopher in psychic chains, and when he sadly rejected Bellamy's concept of community (interestingly enough, another kind of nationalism) as within the "domain of religious thought' rather than practical affairs, one feels that a spark of the original idealism in him must still have yearned to embrace it.

Consider the concept of natural right, another primitive starting point for political thought. We know what Sumner thought of this concept: it was inherently collectivist in nature, giving one man a claim upon another through the instrument of the state. And yet the paradox of Sumner's position is not that the Whiggery he defended joyously rediscovered the nature concept for use in a Lockian way, against the state, but rather that his very Progressive enemies used it in the same fashion.

Where is the subtle Rousseauan transformation in the natural rights idea which we find in English idealism, for example, to be found in American Progressive thought? Surely not in the Spencerian climax of George. Surely not in the Jeffersonianism of Wilson. Surely not in Teddy Roosevelt. Sumner, though his angry passion would not have been wasted in the world of Green and Hobhouse, was clearly wasting it here. When Veblen said that the American farmer identified nature with the "live and let live" principle of the eighteenth century, he could have said the same thing about the urban component of the Progressive psyche as well. Natural rights, in other words, were no more transformed in Progressive thought than the idea of community was fulfilled. Is it necessary to add that Marxism, which held that natural rights of any kind were a transient class projection, failed to fit into a picture of this kind?

The trust emerges as the specific institutional vehicle for this whole tension. Why, after all, reach community or transform natural right? If the trust is what is bad, you can stay at home with Locke simply by smashing it. But the formula is all too simple and all too neat. Like a hidden volcano, the original question explodes within the context of the trust issue itself, for what if some trusts are inevitable and others efficient? Then the impulse to leave home becomes so keen that only the most agonizing intellectual discipline can control it: you have to draw distinctions between good and bad trusts, and you have to do it even if you are Roosevelt, Herbert Croly to the contrary notwithstanding. It was brave of Croly to reject the Sherman Act completely, but his political hero from

Oyster Bay hardly dared to go so far.* And then, of course, we have Bellamy again, who with his big trust provided the great escape not only on this count but in a curious sense on the deeper philosophic count that lay behind it. Did not the trust itself in Bellamy provide the technique for reaching a kind of Rousseauan community? It is as if a mechanical gadget solved the puzzle of Plato.

It does not take a deep analyst to see that the whole issue of "direct government," that passionate symbol of the Progressive days, was involved root and branch in this problem. Why smash bosses and elect senators directly? Why get rid of Croker and Quay? The answer was: to give every last individual an equal chance to govern, and if you throw in the initiative, referendum, recall, and long ballot, to give him a chance to govern in practically every situation. Here was the equity of the Alger world flowering into politics, a program related to the log-cabin concept of the presidency which Alger himself embroidered in the case of Garfield, although there the hero started as a canal boy. Indeed the political energies premised by Progressivism were no less astounding than the economic energies it premised, so that the good American was not only a frantic economic dynamo rising to the top after trusts were shattered but a frantic political dynamo voting by referendum and recall after bosses were shattered. George, at least, had the sense to see that this was asking too much of any man, even an American, and he rejected direct democracy on the ground that it called for excessive interest on the part of the individual. And yet, with characteristic Progressive turmoil, he worried about

* In practice at any rate, Roosevelt instituted twenty-five indictments under the Act.

bosses, even suggesting that the day might come when a "Boss of America" appeared, a grand Caesaristic culmination of everything, which reminds one, although he never worked it out in the same way, of the big Bellamy Trust.

But this is only a surface correlation. Down deeper there was the specific connection between economic power and political corruption, which made the abolition of both simultaneous questions. Needless to say, the fact that the Progressives were dealing with perversions of the democratic process itself, rather than aristocratic and quasi-aristocratic institutions like the House of Lords and the French Senate such as confronted the European Liberal reformers, permitted them to move with unusual ease from economic to political questions. They were always, here as everywhere else, entirely within the bourgeois world. The point of connection, of course, was the charge that trusts and monopolies extracted special benefits from the state, a process Ward called "maternalism," so that a restoration of the true "American" world automatically called for elimination of the political corruption which its economic corruption inspired. Wilson especially was fond of making this point, together with his attack on "the trustee theory" of economic power advanced by Baer and Carnegie in their own different ways, and he even warned against too much state regulation on the ground that then "big businessmen" would "have to get closer to the government even than they are now." [4] But, of course, if regulation was the only way out in a world where wealth was inexorably being concentrated, you were back again in the realm of politics to the same dilemma you confronted in the realm of economics. "Americanism" produced its problems everywhere, blocking off, one hardly needs to say, the road into the Russian Revolution that the greatest muckraker of them all, Lincoln Steffens, dared alone to take.

But it might be argued, in the political arena did not Progressivism actually challenge "Americanism"? What about the attack on Constitution worship and the Courts? Do we not find here the very spirit of iconoclasm, the moving into forbidden areas, the shattering of what Croly called the "sacred character" of the fundamental law? One might reply that even the wildest Progressive revision of the Constitution would not have changed it much. But that is not the real point, which is this: the purpose of blasting legal "Americanism" was to attain Progressive "Americanism," so that the taboo involved was shattered on the surface only to reappear at the bottom. Brandeis, the Great Dissenter on the bench, was after all Brandeis, the great conformist in the realm of trustbusting Algerism. And if Holmes pursued a fine relativistic line, which might conceivably have sanctioned all sorts of things, including French solidarism and German socialism, at least in the states, the fact was that these philosophies did not come to the bench for his judgment. The apparent bravery in the realm of legal institution did not carry over into the large social outlook. It did not emancipate the Progressive from the central tension of his social thought.

To be sure, law embodied more than the rule of reason in the Sherman Act: it embodied barriers to a mass of regulation which went in fact beyond the Alger world. The Lochner case involved a law which premised the permanent existence of workers and employers. So did the Debs case, and many others. But did not these display, as with good and bad trusts, the struggle of the Progressive mind to retain John Locke and still to recognize developing social fact? Do we not find here, projected into the realm of state economic policy, the old, old problem? Surely, as George saw, the passionate affirmations in favor of direct democracy were not in any sense passionate affirmations in favor of extended state power: these two issues must never be confused. An agonized reluctance, enhanced by the sight of their own Jeffersonianism thrown against them in the service of laissez faire, characterized the outlook of Progressivism toward the positive legislation advanced everywhere by Western Liberal Reform. Bellamy, who sent the whole issue up in flames by regulating everything, came as a genuine relief.

The attitude toward socialism remains, however, the final test of Progressive "Americanism." Here we need not expect an inner tension, since it is the indomitable drive to stick to a nationalistic Locke which inspires the peculiar pathos of the Progressive mind. What we ought to expect, and what indeed we find, is a rejection of the Marxian creed no less fanatical than the one in Whiggery itself. When W. D. Howells said that socialism "smells to the average American of petroleum, suggests the red flag, and all manner of sexual novelties, and an abusive tone about God and religion," [5] he had in mind, with good reason as we have seen, even his fellow Bellamy enthusiasts. The issue, of course, is this matter of the "petroleum" odor, for the European Liberals opposed socialism as well, only with much the same concepts that socialism itself used, which meant that, instead of being horrified by the atmosphere of Marx, they could easily drift into it. We are brought directly to the isolation of socialism.

3. *Socialism in the Wilderness*

It is good for the analyst of the American liberal world, if not for the socialists themselves, that they were men of such fine European courage. Of course, they compromised a bit: they would be inhuman if this were not the case. When for a moment some of them dissolved and joined the "nationalist" movement of Bellamy, were they not compromising pathetically, as if the American fantasy, which as we know was American enough, could ever be the same as the European theory of Marx? Even within the context of socialism, moreover, and even in De Leon the revolutionary, we occasionally find a curious twisting of Marxian doctrine in order to satisfy the Alger ethos. But by and large the sins were remarkably few, and Spargo noticed the charge against even reform socialism that it sought "to apply to American life judgments based on European facts and conditions." [6] All in all the movement went doggedly ahead, even without feudal remnants, even without the power to make a serious impact on Liberal Reform. So that one might say it has the same relationship to the general pattern of Western Marxism that a postage stamp has to a life-size portrait: all the lines are there, all the features, but the size is very small.

It is not surprising that when the American socialists did begin to twist their Marxism a bit they did it with reference to the great American fetishes of the trust and direct democracy. Needless to say, Marxism, even of the Kautsky-Bernstein variety, which stressed the educational impact of the democratic process on the proletariat, did not yearn for anything like the long ballot, and yet the Socialist party again and again made it a crucial part of the Marxian scheme. One might call this, if he were in a satirical mood, "Jacksonian socialism," and ask how direct democracy would work under socialism when it could hardly work under capitalism where the business of government was comparatively small. But it was the trust issue which really played havoc with the American socialists, not because socialism did not blast monopoly but because its approach to it was radically different from anything the Progressives advanced. First of all, it did not blast monopoly in order to establish individualism, but rather to establish collectivism, so that when Atkinson spoke of creating "opportunities" by smashing trusts he was really being the worst thing in the socialist book: "petit-bourgeois." Even Jaurès, when he modified French socialism to satisfy the peasant, did not go as far as this. Ironically enough, moreover, it was the "impossibiliste" De Leon who integrated Atkinson's trustism into the Marxian historical theory. He said that he agreed with Bryan and Roosevelt that America had once been a land of freedom and that trusts had changed it when of course Marxism held that no capitalist society at any time, even in its early fluid stages, was ever really free.

But these sell-outs to "Americanism," considering its devastating impact upon the socialists, can easily be excused. Certainly they did not—by means of borrowing from Liberal Reform rather than challenging it, a kind of inversion of the European process—lead to any serious socialist inroad into the Progressive vote. To be sure, they helped the socialists in 1912, but this triumph could not last and even then it was minor compared to the Progressive enthusiasm on which it so obviously fed. The idea that Wilson could have been driven out of New

Jersey by Debs as Clemenceau was driven out of Paris by Guesde and Lafargue is of course fantastic. Even the pressure that the Independent Labor party in England put on the liberals before the World War was out of the question. Even after Bellamy wrote his American introduction to the *Fabian Essays*, the average American still, as he said there, "conceived of a socialist, when he considered him at all, as a mysterious type of desperado, reputed to infest the dark places of continental Europe and engaged with his fellows in a conspiracy as monstrous as it was futile, against civilization and all that it implied." [7] Nor was this the sort of hatred of "the continental agitators" that the English Marxist Hyndman used to entertain. That was a natural British distaste, as with Mill, for the Blanquist, putschist nature of radicalism across the channel, not a dislike of the socialist scheme itself. The American view involved the very foundations of socialist thought.

The fact that Progressivism could not be accused of compromising with an original feudal ethos, of failing to complete the original liberal campaign, was of course critical in the socialist fiasco. If Helen Lynd can list as one of the sources of the incipient English socialism of the eighties the "leaders and followers" pattern of British life, and if Adam Ulam can list it as one of the sources of the rise of the Labor Party itself, pointing out that labor could have bargained with the Liberals for specific policy measures,[8] is not the lesson for America clear? Could Debs argue that socialism was essential to abolish the class spirit emanating from Henry Adams? If the socialists were not lured in the direction of Progressivism by the desire for a united front against Adams, and thus avoided one of the significant European sources of internal factionalism, this was small consolation. In the long run Jaurès and Briand, as well as Guesde and Sembat, gained more than they lost from the Millerand question at the time of the Dreyfus affair. Without the *ancien régime,* the issue of collaborating with the Radicals against it would not to be sure have split French Marxism, but French Marxism would not have existed either.

In any case, the question of collaborating with the Radicals, so to speak, was fought out by the American socialists as well, thus sending them even farther into the wilderness they occupied in a liberal society. Of course the matter of "bourgeois collaboration" extended much beyond the issue of a united front against reaction. There were aspects of it, indeed, which were given a peculiar vividness by the nature of American liberal society. In a land where labor was truly bourgeois, the issue of what Lenin called "trade union consciousness" was indeed interesting: witness De Leon's battle against Gompers. In a land where democracy had been established early, the issue of what Bernstein called the "partnership" of liberalism was also vivid: witness Berger's plea for peaceful change. But these interesting intellectual twists were purchased at the price of isolation, so that if "parliamentary idiocy" was fascinating in a very parliamentary country, the term was also meaningless there.

There is this parallel between the problem of Progressivism and the problem of socialism: both were in the grip of fetishes, "Americanism" on the one hand, Marxism, or "Europeanism" if such a term exists, on the other. But if these are in some sense similar psychological experiences, "word-worship," to use a term of Henry Carey's, they were antagonistic in a profound way. The word of Alger excluded the word of Marx, so that in a community of the blind and half-blind a significant logic was in play. Word-worship is peculiarly bad for scholarship, which is why the social science both of Progressivism and American socialism failed in its analysis of America. And that is our next problem.

4. *The Problem of Historical Analysis*

The European word of Marxism need not, of course, have been applied as the American Marxists applied it: instead of using it to impose a European pattern on America they could have used it to discover the irrelevance of the European pattern here. But since they failed to do so, for good reasons of struggle and activism, their analysis boiled down to something that, in flavor at least, had a curious resemblance to the starkly nativistic orientation of Beard and the Progressives. After all, is not a struggle between "conservative" and "radical," or "aristocrat" and "democrat," whatever these terms may really mean, much like a "class struggle"? Ironically, on the social science plane "Americanist" Progressivism and the Marxian socialism it so passionately excluded blended into a kind of common iconoclasm, with men moving interchangeably between the two. Beard had to repudiate the charge that he was influenced by Marx.

There is, to be sure, little talk of "Americanism" in the work of the Progressives. But also there is little talk of "liberalism," save in the vague sense that anyone who wants to go forward is a "liberal," which means that the blind subjectivism inherent in the former concept was at work in the usual way. The European Liberal reformers, fighting Tory reaction and socialism as well as the tradition of Whiggery, could easily see the historic milieu in which they moved, even though they missed the origin of socialism, attributing it to the objective conditions of the "social question" alone. But fighting only Whiggery in a world where everything else was blacked out, why should the Progressive intellectuals understand their milieu of agreement at all? And so, as we know, at the very moment when everyone in the nation was worshiping at the Alger shrine, a situation of moral unity without parallel in the West, they came forth with a cosmic social struggle.

There is more than a touch of comedy in this, for the Progressive scholars were not content with working with the "conservatism" and "radicalism" of their own era. In the mood of unconquerable "realists," they plowed back to the ideological phantoms of the Hamiltonian era, documenting them out of the lurid speeches of the Fathers themselves, so that even the progress their contemporaries had made in the "discovery of America" was buried from sight. There was, to be sure, a peculiar strategic value in this enterprise. In an age when Hamilton had flowered into McKinley it did the latter little good to expose the fact that he had once been Hamilton. This not only made him an absolute "conservative" but an absolute villain as well. Needless to say, Hobhouse, even if he had wanted to, could not have used the same technique to discredit the modern disciples of Brougham, since to the right of Brougham there had always been Wellington, which changed the iconoclastic picture entirely. Had he pointed out that the men who pushed through the First Reform Act were men of property who feared the populace, as Beard did in connection with the framers of the Consti-

tution, he would have shocked no one. Had he uttered
J. Allen Smith's dictum, "Constitutional government is not
necessarily democratic," [9] he would have been accused of
being platitudinous. But the larger point, of course, is that
the Progressive historians, working with the concept of
social revolt, fortified with a mass of erudition all the
misunderstandings the average American in the midst of
"Americanism" had about himself. They discovered a genuine American "revolution," they unearthed a "class conflict" between "agrarian and capitalist," they forgot the
Southern reaction, and they made the rise of American
democracy practically impossible to understand.

In one sense it is strange that the group analysis of
Arthur Bentley should have been included in the "realism"
of the Progressive movement, for it contradicted the
theory of Beard and Gustavus Myers. A multiplicity of
interests is a different affair from the contest between
"conservative" and "radical," and if the battle between
Hamilton and Jefferson is the image of American politics,
how can the Smoot-Hawley tariff be the image of it also?
The truth is, Bentley went deeper than Beard, for the free
and easy play of pressure groups was a real characteristic
of the American liberal world, inspired by the moral settlement which underlay it and hence obscured class lines.
And yet there is a reason, not usually noticed, for lumping
Bentley with Beard, since the "group" was used by the
former in the same absolute way that "conservative" was
used by the latter. The followers of Bentley rarely observed that their analysis was a reflection of the relative
conditions of America's liberal life, although the evidence
they used was almost always American, and they therefore
assumed that they were talking mainly about "politics,"

or as the term now goes, "political behavior," rather than about America. Had they tried the group approach in connection with the English Labor party or the French Radicals, they would have found themselves defining the "group" in all sorts of odd ways, being forced to avoid the obvious overwhelming fact that class and ideological forces were at the heart of European politics, feudal as it was in origin. In other words, the Progressive might have gotten a hint of his absolute "Americanism" out of the Bentley theorists, but not much more.

But the truly Progressive scholarship was the scholarship of Beard and Smith and, it might be asked, what was lost in their enslavement to a liberalism so absolute that it could not see its relative self? The answer lies in the simple fact that provincial horizons are never intellectually justifiable. But it lies also in the fact that Beard and his disciples thus betrayed Progressivism, for they did not explain that movement to itself, which is surely the first task of any fighting social scholarship. Ironically, Marx and Engels, with their theory of "superstructure," told the European proletariat more about its psychic solidarity with the European bourgeoisie than the Progressive critics told America's "petit-bourgeois" giant about his solidarity with the Whigs. In the long run did it help the American democrat to be notified that America's political checks and "judicial oligarchy" were the product of "conservative" action when, despite his periodic outbursts against them, he had out of his own individualist fear collaborated in their support? Did it help him to know that he had forever been at war with "big business" when, out of his own capitalist lust, he had worshiped it, and was doing so more now than ever? What this simplistic analysis did, as the lurid theory of Taylor had done in the earlier era, was to fashion a conscience for the American democrat that impulse could not meet and thus to saddle him in the end and with confusion and a secret sense of shame. It was to make the shock and agony of Brownson a permanent and periodic phase of Progressive experience.

The socialists might have corrected all this for the Progressives, but since they were bent on establishing the presence or potential presence of their own peculiar "radicalism," proletarianism, they failed significantly to do so. There can be no doubt that there were other reasons, apart from activism, which prevented American Marxists from exploring the implications for America of the absence of the feudal factor in the Marxian scheme. Concentrating on labor and capital within the bourgeois order, for one thing, meant that the Marxist necessarily viewed feudalism as an antique phenomenon. This orientation was even true of Marx and Engels themselves who predicted socialism in America and yet explicitly noted the fact that America had skipped the feudal stage of Western development. Moreover the instinctive tendency of all Marxists to discredit ideological factors as such blinded them to many of the consequences, purely psychological in nature, flowing from the nonfeudal issue. Was not the whole complex of "Americanism" an ideological question? But after all of this has been said, the simple refusal to face unpleasant facts stands out as crucial. Let us recall again that a law of combined development did appear in Russia when the facts it seemed to produce were pleasant.

To be sure, however blind he was about history, it was not always easy for the American socialist to whistle in the American dark. Usually he conceded that he was in the poorest position of any Western socialist, holding that this was due to transient material prosperity, in line with the Marxian materialist emphasis. Noting that "until quite recently" it was easy for the worker to become a capitalist in America, and that land had been abundant, Spargo traced the whole of the socialist isolation to passing economic circumstances. The fact that a thousand strikes a year were taking place showed that the circumstances were passing.[10] De Leon, possibly because being more revolutionary he was more impatient, could not always tolerate even this analysis. Pointing out that capitalism was "full-orbed" in America, he argued that the revolution would come most quickly here, avoiding the unpleasant fact that where capitalism is "full-orbed" even the people who are supposed to make the revolution are inveterate capitalists. "Plutocracy," another point made by practically all socialists, did not prove anything. So long as the American millionaire stood at the apex of the Alger scheme he did not symbolize the fulfillment of the Marxian hope.

The historical insight lost by this frenzied optimism is clearly revealed in the familiar socialist effort to root socialism in the American past. When De Leon cites Jefferson as the "great confiscator," [11] how can he grasp the nonrevolutionary nature of American life? Even Veblen, outside the strategic compulsion of Marxism, was forever making the same mistake. Though an acute observer of the capitalist spirit in America, he lumped the "American Declaration of Independence, the French Declaration of the Rights of Man, and the American Constitution" in the same liberal category.[12] But the eighteenth century was of course not the only thing at stake. Given this orientation, which obscured the relevance of the nonfeudal issue, how could American socialism understand anything about its fate? How could it understand the crucial importance of the absence of surviving feudal elements? How could it understand the nature of its failure to make an impact on Progressivism? How could it understand its odd link with the fate of the Southern "feudalists"? In the end Marxist theory paved the way for socialist disappointments as Progressive theory paved the way for Progressive disappointments, which is another way that the two "radicalisms," one nativistic and the other alien, seemed to blend together. A valuable historical analysis, which might have laid bare much concerning the American liberal world, went unused.*

And so one is bound to say again that this age which "discovered America," which made a conscious fetish out of the national liberalism, did not actually see itself. But in the last analysis, is this so paradoxical? Was there anything in the period, either on the side of Whiggery or the

---

* The question is bound to be raised: In terms of the whole concept of a liberal society, what is the general estimate of Marxism? On the one hand there is a negative view of Marxism stemming from the fact that socialism is traced ultimately to the *ancien régime* as well as to capitalist growth. On the other there is an affirmative view of Marxism stemming from the breadth of its categories as compared with those of the Progressives. These two view are not incompatible, even if the first has implications for economics and ideology which, when carried to their logical conclusion, are damaging to the basic metaphysics of the Marxian scheme. Categories can still be useful even if they are misapplied. However one may legitimately ask, after all of this watering down has taken place, whether there is much more of Marx left than the Western concepts of class which one can find practically everywhere in the Western literature. I would not deny this. The only reason for insisting on the peculiar utility of Marxism here is that it happened to be the one manifestation of the European viewpoint which had followers in America. For additional material on the problem of Marxism, see pp. 277-83.

side of Progressivism, which made this larger national perception a strategic necessity? Social thought, even scholarship, has a lazy way of rising only to the level required of it and, the truth is, America could get along with its old subjectivism. You did not need an objective comparative analysis of the nation to make Whiggery triumph, to enforce the categories of Algerism, to produce the quality of Progressivism, or to send the socialists into the wilderness. All of this could be done without it, better of course without it, and above all the nation could live in comparative ease and prosperity. We say of the Progressive era that it was a time of tumult, but in our own age we know what tumult is, and few of us would be willing to date Armageddon at 1912. Above all we know the meaning of world involvement, as the age of Alger did not know it, and this is the real force driving toward objective national analysis. But before we come to this, we have to consider the Great Depression, which brought the American democrat to power again, finally reversing the law of Whig compensation that governed the era of Carnegie and Harding.

PART SIX

Depression and World Involvement

CHAPTER TEN

The New Deal

---

1. *The Triumph and Transformation of Liberal Reform*

If the Great Depression of the 'thirties suggested anything, it was that the failure of socialism in America stemmed from the ideologic power of the national irrational liberalism rather than from economic circumstance. For however "objective" the conditions for the Marxian apocalypse now became, what emerged to deal with the economic problem was a movement within the framework of the liberal faith, or in other words, a movement which belonged to the genre of Western Liberal Reform. What emerged was a movement, familiar now for fifty years in Western politics, which sought to extend the sphere of the state and at the same time retain the basic principles of Locke and Bentham. We find again the European correlations we found during the Progressive period.

And yet, despite the wealth of social legislation going beyond the Alger premise apparent in the New Deal, which identifies it even more closely than Progressivism with the doctrine of the English Liberals and the French Radicals, its connection with European Liberal Reform is hidden by a whole series of false fronts. For one thing, it is "radical," while the European movement, now on the defensive before socialism and communism, is not: the blackout of Harold Laski makes Sir Herbert Samuel a first-rate iconoclast. For another, it is pragmatic while the European movement is philosophic, since even the normal Liberal Reform departures from Locke cannot be tolerated consciously by the absolute mind of the nation. Of course the deflated Whiggery of the Republicans tries to expose the non-Lockian nature of much of the New Deal, tries to precipitate the moral crisis that would inevitably come if Americans thought they were "un-American," but it fails. The experimental mood of Roosevelt, in which Locke goes underground while "problems" are solved often in a non-Lockian way, wins out persistently. And who will deny that this, even more than the isolation of socialism, is a tribute to the irrational liberal faith of America? Eating your cake and having it too is very rare in politics.

Few contrasts are more striking, and indeed more misleading, than the contrast between the "radical," aggressive mood of Liberal Reform in the American New Deal and the "conservative," defensive mood of Liberal Reform in Western Europe during the 'thirties. The English Liberal party is now a fragment of its former self as a result of the combined assaults of Toryism and the Labor party. The French Radicals, though stronger than the English Liberals, are also caught between the fires of right and left during the age of the United Front. Everywhere in the Radical camp there is a heightening of the old philosophic turmoil and indecision, as the need for even more collective action becomes patent. The term "Radical" becomes in many quarters a term of contempt, a symbol of shilly-shallying and the building of impossible halfway houses. How different is the tone of the American New Deal! Here there is a feeling of high adventure, a sense of iconoclasm, genuine "radicalism." The young men who in Europe become socialists and communists in America for the most part become New Dealers. Liberal Reform here has all of the youth and energy that Marxism has across the Atlantic.

And yet, as we are sometimes told, youth and energy are matters of perspective. Of course there is a substantive issue here which cannot be blinked. America came late to positive social legislation, so that the New Deal might reasonably be said to reflect some of the radical excitement of Europe at the turn of the century. There is a good deal of truth in Helen Lynd's remark that the American experience is usually the English experience delayed by fifty years. Moreover in the context of a prior devotion to Horatio Alger, which Europe never had, any amount of Liberal Reform was bound to seem iconoclastic. But compared to the larger mechanics of the American world, these are actually minor points. What makes the New Deal "radical" is the smothering by the American Lockian faith of the socialist challenge to it. Nor does the meaning of this lie merely in the fact that Roosevelt was not seriously compared by many Americans with Norman Thomas and Earl Browder who of course were more radical than he was. It lies mainly in the fact that he did not need to *reply* to them, as English Liberals and French Radicals had to reply to socialists and communists. This meant that he did not, as the Europeans did, have to spell out his liberal premises and hence create the atmosphere of indecision which this necessarily involved. Compelled to reply only to the dispossessed Whiggery of Hoover on the right, which of course was glad to call him "radical," he could look like the man the Hearst papers, after Hearst's change of heart, made him out to be. Poor Norman Thomas, instead of being able to deride the New Deal as indecisive, was forced to complain that many Americans accepted it as socialism itself.

Hence there is an unwritten history of New Deal social thought which, if we are speaking in Western terms, it is only fair to write. What would Roosevelt have said had he indeed been compelled to take Thomas and Browder seriously? What would he have said had the American Socialist party been the English Labor party or the American Communist party been the party of the United Front in France? Obviously under such circumstances Roosevelt would be speaking very strange language indeed. He would be defending private property, he would be assailing too much "bureaucracy," he would be criticizing the utopian mood in politics. After pleading for the TVA and the SEC and the HOLC, he would proceed to qualify his faith in the state by an attack on the larger radicalism which faced him to the left. In other words, instead of being "radical," he would be half radical and half conservative, which is precisely the unfortunate position that the Liberal reformers of Europe were compelled to occupy. Instead of enlisting the vigorous passions of youth, he might easily be described as a tired man who could not make up his mind: a liberal who tried to break with Adam Smith but could not really do so.

But fully as significant as this "radical" result of not having to reply to socialism is the pragmatic result. Had Roosevelt said, "we have to go beyond Locke but not as far as Marx," and had he translated Locke into "Americanism," which was of course its meaning here, he would have alienated many of his followers from him, and not because of his indecision. "Americanism" was gospel, the very thing which made socialism alien, and any conscious transgression of it, even the transgression of Europe's "New Liberalism," of Ramsay Muir and Sir William Beveridge, was highly unpalatable. So from the standpoint of his survival the fact that he did not need to leave Locke openly was far more important than the fact that he did not need to stop short of Marx openly. In other words, the crucial thing was that, lacking the socialist challenge and of course the old corporate challenge on the right such as the European conservatisms still embodied, he did not need to spell out any real philosophy at all. His "radicalism" could consist of what he called "bold and persistent experimentation," [1] which of course meant nothing in terms of large social faiths and was indeed perfectly compatible with "Americanism." Good Americans like Edison and Alexander Graham Bell were experimenters. So were the pioneers. When asked concerning his social philosophy, Roosevelt once said that he was a Democrat and a Christian, which meant, needless to say, that he was as good an irrational Lockian as Grover Cleveland.

Of course, as we know, many of the bold and persistent experiments of Roosevelt involved substantive departures from the liberal faith of a considerable kind. There is no need to overwork the point. The New Deal left a lot of free enterprise standing, and much of its state action, from spending to trustbusting, was designed to fortify rather than to weaken free enterprise. But a problem still remains of liberal convictions held in the face of nonliberal innovations, best illustrated by the rugged individualism of the American farmer who is supported on all sides by the state, which must surely fascinate any social psychologist. It is what lies at the bottom of the belief many Americans even now have that America is a "free enterprise" country, an idea the rest of the world seems glad to share with them. But whatever might be said psychologically about the collectivism that pragmatism could build on Locke in America, politically it has had crucial uses, some of them quite apart from the major one of permitting the New Deal to survive in the land of "Americanism." It permitted the Democrats, when war prosperity came, to lapse back into some of the language of Harding. And it permitted the Republicans, when the New Deal "solutions" became irrevocable, to accept them. After all, neither the party of reform nor the party of conservatism need be seriously affected by mere technical gadgetry. One of the hidden uses of political pragmatism in a liberal society is thus its effectiveness as an instrument of party accommodation.

And yet, for the most part the Republican view of the New Deal during the 'thirties was not based on this happy acceptance of it. It was based on an attempt to expose the very mechanism by which pragmatism hid the departure from Locke. It was based on an attempt to set off exactly that explosion which would have taken place had America philosophically confronted its deviations from the liberal ethic. This was the whole meaning of Hoover's cry of "American Individualism," carried forward by Hearst and Dies. But we must not assume that that cry was really philosophic, even though it meant a measuring of New Deal action by abstract standards. For save in the case of a few men like Lippmann, it was almost entirely nationalistic, Locke as usual having been transformed into Biblical fetish. Actually what we find during the New Deal era are two irrationalisms fighting with each other: the explicit "Americanism" of Hoover on the one hand, the sublimated "Americanism" of Roosevelt on the other.

Under such circumstances the failure of Marxism was as inevitable as it ever was during the Progressive era. We need not deny that a number of "intellectuals" (the very term sounds alien of course in a liberal society) turned to socialism and communism. We need not deny that in certain cases they exercised influence, even in the Roosevelt administration. But the drift of the New Deal was to frustrate them even more than the earlier Marxists, for surely it was harder to take isolation in a time of crash than in a time of boom. Norman Thomas complained bitterly of "a kind of American progressivism which calls itself practical because it has no general principles." [2] Max Lerner assailed the New Deal as "temporizing and blundering" and called for "a concerted effort at economic planning." [3] Actually there is an odd sense here in which the Marxists were close to the Hooverians, for both were trying to impose on the experimentalism of the New Deal a sense of theoretical direction. But if the Marxists recognized the pragmatic character of the Roosevelt program, this did not mean that they understood its meaning. Not even the light that the Marxist analysis minus the feudal factor might have shed on the situation was ever vouchsafed to them. For now, no more than in the age of De Leon and Spargo, were they willing to give up the dream of ultimate victory, so they were driven willy-nilly to force America into the European pattern rather than to see the way in which it differed from it. The result was that not even those doctrinally outside the world of "Americanism" were able to appreciate the mechanism of its viability during the depression era: its remarkable transformation of Liberal Reform, its resistance to the terror tactic of Whiggery, indeed its exclusion of socialism. Like so many of their predecessors, Roosevelt, Hoover, and Thomas were actors in the drama of a liberal society none of them understood.

2. *Roosevelt in Europe*

Of all the twists and distortions that America has imposed on Western political movements, it is doubtful whether any have surpassed in subtlety those experienced by American reformist liberalism when, freed of a serious socialist challenge on the left and inspired to assail Social Darwinism,* it came in power in 1932. One is reminded, in a kind of inverted way, of the elitist Whigs during the early years of American history who, lacking feudal enemies to fight, appeared on the American scene much like the feudal reactionaries themselves: lacking Marxists to fight, the New Dealers looked much like the Marxists themselves. But in this case as in the other we cannot be

---

* There is no need to deny, despite the experimental mood of the New Deal, that this attack produced a certain amount of ideological ebullience. Roosevelt repudiated the "man of ruthless force." Wallace spoke of a "cooperative" way. However, we must guard against interpreting these slogans in such a way as to obscure the centrally pragmatic character of the New Deal experience and the deep national need stemming from liberal convictions for it. Nor is this merely because modifying Spencer is a good deal different from giving up Locke. Mainly it is because the scattered polemical outcries of the American political battle, now as during the Jacksonian era, are in themselves deceptive. When set in the context of Western intellectual history, the most important things in American thought turn out, again as during the Jacksonian period, to be taking place beneath the surface.

266

satisfied with what the lights and shadows of American politics permit us to see. We have to put Roosevelt, as earlier we put Alexander Hamilton, in the Western context of which he was a part. If in the course of the process he seems less "radical," while Hamilton seems more so, this can hardly be helped.

Take the question of property rights. Private property was sharply defended by the English Liberals who, even more than the French Radicals because England was not historically a land of small holdings, dreamed of popularizing property, as Ramsay Muir put it,[4] as an alternative to nationalizing it: spreading it out so that all could have the Lockian experience of fulfillment that it brought to the individual. Surely Roosevelt, had he ever needed to attack the plea of Norman Thomas or Earl Browder for nationalization, would have gone at least as far as Muir. Probably farther. For there was, of course, little in the New Deal program which did not, in some way, rely on the liberal theme. The TVA, as Norman Thomas lamented, was the only full instance of public ownership, and the rationalization of this, as everyone knows, was in terms of the inspiration it gave to private initiative. But why, when Hoover and Landon are the only men you are really worried about, embark upon a Lockian defense of the property right? In America, instead of being a champion of property, Roosevelt became the big antagonist of it: his liberalism was blocked by his "radicalism."

The issue of "class conflict" presents us with much the same story. Who would think of Roosevelt as a philosopher of class solidarity? And yet, had the American Socialist party been anything like the French or the English, that is what Roosevelt, at least a large part of the time, would surely have been. It was of the very essence of the reformist Liberal position in Europe that it should stress the solidarity of the nation as against the class theories both of the right and the left. In English thought this idea had a long and honorable history, going back to Green and Hobhouse, who replaced Benthamism with an idealist theory of community consciousness—a theory which was bound to be nourished more than ever by the Liberals as the Labor party emerged. Had the New Deal been seriously challenged by such a theory, Roosevelt too, instead of being a "traitor to his class," might easily have become an arch-opponent of class war. Imagine Roosevelt debating with Thomas: can anyone doubt that this would have been one of his themes? And yet, of course, the actual picture, since such a debate never took place, was a wholly different one. It was Roosevelt himself, especially after 1936, who was blasted as the fomenter of class antagonism. One could have seen that something was curious here on the basis of the very terminology he used, not terms like "capitalist" and "working class" but terms like "economic royalist" and the "forgotten man" which were obviously the peculiar categories of a peculiar community. But that made little difference: they sounded "radical" enough, as Thomas lamented, to take the thunder away from socialism.

If it is hard to conceive of Roosevelt as an apostle of class unity, it is even harder to conceive of him as a sharp critic of bureaucracy, red tape, and incipient planning dictatorships. And yet what of Sir Archibald Sinclair whose collective aims were even wider than those of the New Deal but who blasted the "officialdom and Government" [5] implicit in the Labor philosophy. The issue of bureaucracy, like many other things, is quite a matter of degree. And for all of the talk of "planning" generated by Tugwell and others at the outset of the New Deal, there was clearly a degree of it which even these New Dealers would have repudiated with a liberal passion. But alas, as always, there was nothing to bring to the surface this last-ditch Lockian spirit because the leftist challenge was inconsequential. Norman Thomas wanted the railroads nationalized instead of regulated under the ERA, but Roosevelt did not deliver a fireside chat pointing out how much red tape and how much deadening of initiative nationalization would bring. Thomas wanted the dairy corporations seized by the state, but Roosevelt did not plead against bureaucratizing the American farmer. The face of the New Deal was always turned rightward, where the only real American enemy lay, and from that quarter there came at it a blast on the score of bureaucracy and dictatorship which defined the categories of its polemical life.

There is no need to carry this analysis on indefinitely, but a final issue ought to be discussed: the issue of "utopianism," of doctrinaire thinking. One can hardly pass this up because of the "Brain Trust" quality of the New Deal and because, too, it touches America's twist of perspective at perhaps its most vital point. European reformist liberalism, of course, assailed the Marxian movement for its apocalyptic dream, and declaring for limited reform, it actually began to acquire a Burkian touch alien to its historic origins. Such, surely, was the real ethos of the American New Deal. But given again the fecklessness of Marxism on the national scene, and given also a nonphilosophic, nonintellectualistic tradition, which also played its part here, the New Deal emerged as a daring effort in the doctrinal field. In Europe college professors had always contributed something to politics, but when in America Roosevelt relied on them heavily for the first time, and when it was only the grass roots speechmaking of Hoover and Landon they had to assail, the result was striking enough. Who can forget the cap and gown and the mad professorial eyes that were the delight of the Republican cartoonist during the New Deal days? Marx in the British Museum could scarcely have been depicted in a wilder light.

What emerges then in the case of the New Deal is a liberal self that is lost from sight: a faith in property, a belief in class unity, a suspicion of too much state power, a hostility to the utopian mood, all of which were blacked out by the weakness of the socialist challenge in the American liberal community. And yet this radicalization of the New Deal, though it provided ammunition for the Hooverite attack, in the end was tied up with Roosevelt's very success. For when the moral cosmology of New Dealism sank beneath the surface, what appeared, of course, was that happy pragmatism which usually refused to concern itself with moral issues at all. And this, in turn, permitted, the American democrat to go about solving his problems without the serious twinges of conscience which would surely have appeared had he felt that his Lockian "Americanism" was at stake. In one sense this put him, from the angle of experimental freedom, far ahead of the European Liberal reformers or even the European socialists. During the 'thirties it used to be the fashion to lament with Thurman Arnold the way in which folklore and fixed ideas stood in the way of social change.[6] But the truth is, the age was much freer of fetish in America than it was in Europe where ideological categories reigned. Where in England or France or Germany could you find the free-wheeling inventiveness typified by the NRA, the TVA, the ERA, the WPA, the SEC, and all the other New Deal alphabetical combinations and recombinations? What Thurman Arnold failed to see was that the technical pragmatism he wanted was nourished by the very "folklore" he blasted. An irreversible ethics made all problems technical.

Now we must not assume that we are dealing here with a devious propaganda strategy on the part of New Deal propagandists, a scheme they deliberately cooked up for selling European Liberalism or European socialism to Americans without assaulting their nationalist conscience: no doubt among a few "intellectuals" this consideration was present. But for the most part (and this superlatively includes Roosevelt himself) the New Dealers were themselves taken in by the process involved, being proud of their pragmatism and seeing no more clearly than the great Dewey himself the absolute moral base on which it rested. Henry Wallace, the most articulate and reflective of the New Dealers, spoke of an "American Way" distinct from that of Europe in which "plain men" would deal with problems as they came up.[7] Stuart Chase, the author of A New Deal before the New Deal appeared, spoke of the "third road," untouched by the doctrinaire mentality, which was peculiarly open to Americans.[8] But why this luxurious peculiarity? Why this fine freedom from Europe's moral turmoil? When the question was answered, which was rarely enough, a hackneyed issue like America's abundant resources was usually wheeled out. The truth is, it would have shocked the New Deal "radicals" themselves to learn that their American technical freedom stemmed from something very old: the American liberal faith.

In the end, when war came and the Truman prosperity appeared, it did the New Dealers no harm to have been swallowed up in this mechanism. For then, having been responsible merely for the solving of "problems," they could themselves happily adopt a modified version of the Alger ethos, attributing its strength indeed to the very problems they had solved. Were not Truman's speeches during his second administration an odd blend of the fighting Roosevelt and the complacent capitalist oratory of Herbert Hoover? Surely such a synthesis would have been impossible if the New Deal had been defined in anticapitalist ideological terms.

3. *The Strategy of a Deflated Whiggery*

But needless to say, even though the Dewey and Eisenhower Republicans themselves were to profit from the same technique, their Hooverian predecessors during the New Deal blasted it, trying to create precisely that ideological upheaval which it served to avoid. Robbed now of the golden charm of the Alger dream, left only with its "Americanist" thunder, Whiggery became more querulous, more scriptural, more nationalist than ever. Of course, there is a line of progression here. At one extreme you have a liberal philosopher like Walter Lippmann, using little nationalist thunder and concentrating, almost as if he moved amid the abstractions of Europe, on the liberal argument itself. Then comes Hoover, a bit of a theorist but mainly an "Americanist" thunderer. And finally, of course, there are Hearst and Dies, in whom thought is gone and thunder is about all that remains. Given the money and power behind this patchwork of disintegrated Whig thinking, it is a tribute indeed to the American pragmatic mechanism that it managed to withstand the turmoil in the national conscience it tried to stir up.

I have said that Lippmann (in the *Good Society* era of course) smacked of the European spirit, but this ought not to be misinterpreted. He was not European in the sense that Baldwin and the French conservatives were European, any more than Hoover and Dies were. Nor was he wholly outside the "Americanist" identification of the New Deal with "alien" departures from the Lockian creed, since he contended that any planning leads in the direction of total planning, i.e. the totalitarian states of Russia, Italy, and Germany.[9] But Lippmann's defense of liberalism, if it utilized the bogey of foreign totalitarianism, was for the most part devoid of American nationalism. It was theoretical, philosophic, relying, as we know, on the Austrian school of Von Mises and Hayek. And here is a most interesting set of relationships. The class-conscious Toryism of Europe could absorb only a bit, and even that incongruously, of the diehard John Brightism preached by the Austrians. Austria itself with its statist tradition found it for the most part irrelevant. But America, a liberal community, found it usable, so that Hayek after the Second World War scored himself a more vivid literary success here than Lippmann had during the New Deal. What they used to say about England, that it was the home of dead German philosophies, would have to be altered in this case to apply to America: it is the home of dead English philosophies retained by Austrian professors.

Though Lippmann was a philosopher rather than a polemical thunderer like Hoover or Hearst, he was not for this reason an especially acute critic of the American scene. Necessarily, given his approach, he spoke of liberalism in universalistic terms: as the wisdom of the ages. He based his defense of laissez faire on the rule of law, an excellent thing to do when Alger's pot of gold was rather dim, but he did not tie this in with the American tradition of legalism. Above all he did not tie in liberalism itself with the peculiar American situation, which meant that he praised the classical liberals for destroying the economic restrictions of the *ancien régime* when the peculiar species of New Deal collectivism he was assailing came of course from the fact that this had not happened here. What we are reminded of by Lippmann is that "discovery of America" which the Whiggery of Carnegie, in the midst of its nationalism managed to accomplish: "Americanism" was a terror tactic but this was because it actually came from a valid historical insight.

Hence Hoover has, in a sense, to be accounted a better historian than Lippmann. He spoke not of individualism but of "American Individualism," which was a good deal more to the point. At the same time this insight went up so quickly in nationalist smoke that little came of it. What could Hoover do? Could he embroider the historic individualism of American life at the moment of its starkest collapse? Habit, to be sure, inspired some wild incongruities. In 1932, in a speech only a few miles from the great strike at Gastonia, he said that America trains "the runners" and that the winner is always the man of "the greatest ability, the strongest character." But these versions of the Alger race were quickly, embarrassedly, superseded by modifications of it. After all, Algerism had never meant "greed in economic agencies," "business exploitation," or even "laissez faire." It must have been a great relief to shift to the purely negative assault on the New Deal: the "American Way." Here happily, moreover, the issue was not alone that Roosevelt was introducing alien concepts of collectivism. The depression itself was somehow alien, for referring to the collapse of trade in 1931, he said that had it not been for "events in other lands we would have recovered months ago." [10] What could be neater than to be able to label not only the New Deal that dispossessed you but the Depression which began under your own regime as a foreign conspiracy? This covered everything: your sins as well as the sins of others.

Hearst and Dies come with a kind of Greek inevitability, the final sloughing off of speculation and the emergence of pure "Americanism." In our own time even a New Dealer would have to concede that the "Trojan Horse" concept had more to it than one thought during the New Deal days. And yet the original progressive response was valid enough in substance: here was a wild tactic of terror, satirizing itself in the pursuit of the Shirley Temples of Hollywood. Of course fascism was a bogey here as well as communism, but the former never served the purpose of the latter, even in an age like the 'thirties when the first responses of the nation to the Russian Revolution had worn off. There were a number of Americans who with Ambassador Childs liked the fact that the trains ran on time under the fascists, which may itself not be out of line with the efficiency side of the liberal ethos. It is interesting that the term "fascist" was itself often applied to Dies, Hearst, Huey Long, Father Coughlin, and Gerald

L. K. Smith. Here was indeed a rich and intricate lunatic fringe, but without going into the infinite possibilities for analysis it offers, one thing stands out. This was not the "fascism" of Germany or Italy nor the fascisms of Mosley or the Action Française. What all of these European movements had in common was a general faith in hierarchy and authoritarianism, and if they were anticommunist, it was in that spirit. The American "fascists" were all "Americanists" to the hilt, i.e. "democrats," however much they differed among themselves as to "sharing the wealth" or Protestantism or Catholicism. When Long said that fascism would come to America denying that it was fascism, he had, needless to say, a valid insight into the American ethos. But more of the fascist question in a moment.

It is surely a tribute to the pragmatic mechanism on which the New Deal turned that it was able to withstand the turmoil in the national Lockian conscience that this whole trend of "Americanism" tried to stir up. It did not, of course, withstand it entirely. There were many in the nation who were influenced by it: we must not forget the millions who voted for the Republican candidates who fell at each New Deal election. But by and large the Rooseveltian technique of sublimating "Americanism" and "solving problems" worked. Put another way, the non-philosophic approach of the nation worked. They said of Hoover that he was an engineer, bred in the practical life, but the truth is, as Tugwell shrewdly saw, he was a moralist, hurling liberal abstractions against the real engineers of the time: the New Dealers.[11] His frustration was well described by Albert Jay Nock who described his own. Noting that Americans did not see that the New Deal was dangerously converting social power into political power, an adaptation of Spencer peculiar to Nock, he said sadly: "The point is that in respect of the relation between theory and the actual practice of public affairs, the American is the most unphilosophic of beings . . . so long as he can listen to the pattern of litanies, no practical inconsistency disturbs him—indeed, he gives no evidence of even recognizing it as an inconsistency." [12]

But for the Republican party, what in the end would have been the advantage of the American democrat recognizing "inconsistencies" ? Theoretically, of course, it would have made the New Deal impossible, for America would have recoiled against being "un-American." But something had to be done: capitalism itself was at stake, as many of the New Dealers said. Would the Republicans have gained if the nation had clearly delineated its departures from the national liberal scheme? After all, they had little philosophic viability in their approach. They could not, as English Tories like MacMillan and even Baldwin did, accept social reform in the honorable name of paternalism. Whiggery, as we know by now, was far away from that, with Hoover explicitly denouncing the "feudal type of mind." [13] The fact is, by defining New Deal policies in amoral terms and hence making it easy for the Republicans ultimately to accept them, Roosevelt helped to save the Republican party. In this sense he was a better friend of Dewey and Eisenhower than Hoover himself.

4. *The Failure of Marxism*

The American Marxist learns nothing and forgets nothing, and if evidence of this were ever needed, the New Deal era provides it aplenty. Despite the peculiar mechanism of their isolation, the Marxists fought out with a fine in-

tegrity every one of the battles which split apart their
brethren abroad. Trotskyites blasted Stalinists, cherishing
an American branch of the Fourth International and insisting on a puristic version of ancient texts. Stalinists offered the friendly hand of the United Front to the Socialists, and being rejected they assailed the party of Thomas
with a venom no less than that which they expended on
the party of Cannon and Schachtman. And while all these
European tempests were taking place, not a single socialist analyst appeared ready to apply the Marxian analysis
minus the feudal force to America.* Indeed Max Lerner,
one of the milder of the Marxists, heavily under the influence also of Beard and Veblen, assailed "exceptionalism," here no less than in Spain or China, because it might
deny "to Marxism the main area of radical experience." [14]
As in the Progressive time, activism vitiated understanding, even Marxian understanding.

The scattered insights of a Thomas ought not to be
taken too seriously. If he perceived accurately the pragmatic nature of the New Deal, if on one occasion he
could even lament that Marxist terms were not "self-ex-
planatory" in America,[15] all this does not mean that he
had given up hope for the socialist prophecy in the New
World. Neither did the remarkable Granville Hicks who
was so anxious to ground Marx in the American experience that he almost sold out to Martin Dies: "My thesis
is not that I am as good an American as you; that is
too modest a claim; I maintain that I am a better American." [16] Hicks indeed, though often brilliant as a literary
critic, had a genius for evading the constructive uses to

* For a critical evaluation of the uses of Marxism on this count see
p. 254n.

which Marxian analysis might be put in the American scene. He defined the "middle class," in Western terms, rather than in terms of the general Aristotelianism which Lippmann at one stage used, which was sound enough, but he missed completely the historic implications of a middle class America because of his concern with the decline of individual property holdings and the rise of an "objective" proletariat. He was much taken with Lewis Corey's proof on this count, which in more than a single socialist heart kept the flame of hope alive.

What was lost here of course was the whole meaning of a nationalistic bourgeois dogma, but this is even better revealed in the issue of fascism which inspired the United Front tactic on the part of the Communist party. According to the socialist analysis, all the way from Max Lerner to William Foster, fascism would rear its head in America mainly when the proletarian thrust would come. It would be the response of capital to socialism. But as a matter of fact whatever might be termed "native fascism" had its main strength in the "Americanist" ethos which excluded the possibility of a socialist victory. This was the ethos behind much of the antilabor vigilantism historically in the nation. It was capitalized upon by men like Coughlin and Gerald L. K. Smith, mongrel as were the social strains they represented. An outright fascist like Lawrence Dennis came close to seeing this point. And surely after the Second World War eclipsed the depression and brought Russia into the picture, the Marxists themselves were bound to see it. The pressure of conformity is strong in America now, the Marxists have fallen upon evil times, but not because of their victory: because of a national liberal faith which prevented their victory from ever coming.

Given these optimistic assumptions, and a hatred of the "exceptionalism" which would exclude America from the Marxian apocalypse, it is not surprising that American history and politics were turned upside down for the purpose of dramatizing conflict. Here the most brilliant figure is Lerner. At an earlier point I showed how Progressivism and Marxism arrived at similar theories of American internal struggle, even though the one was nativistic in its orientation and the other Western. Lerner exploits this similarity very well indeed. As a Marxist bent on seeing the socialist victory, he assails "secessionists from world history," lumping American liberalism with European liberalism.[17] As a Progressive uninterested in any categories but those which come out of America itself, certainly a form of "secessionism," he fortifies this very prejudice with the Beardian struggle between "radical" and "conservative." Of course there are ticklish problems here. The latter struggle has little to do with the struggle between aristocracy and bourgeoise, or bourgeoisie and proletariat, presumably the great issues of "world history" as Marx defined them, and its actual characteristic of course is that it is projected entirely within the bourgeois cosmos. But at any rate it is a struggle, and if one is tired of the "radical-conservative" dualism one can use instead "majority" and "minority." Although the latter is just as irrelevant to Marxian categories of conflict as the former, just as "exceptionalist," to use the hated word, it still can be dramatized fairly well. Along with Edwin Mims, who developed this line of analysis in extreme fashion,

Lerner described the battle it involved as one of "life and "death." [18]

Now had Lerner actually applied Marxian categories to a nonfeudal society, he would have discovered of course that the distinctive thing about the battle between majority and minority within the liberal system was precisely the fact that it was not a matter of life and death: that it was forever dissolving into common agreements. But if one wanted emotionally to identify that battle with the battle between the liberal system and other systems, so that Marxism might still be in possession of the "main area of radical experience" in America, this obvious lesson of Marxism itself had to go overboard. Lerner's Supreme Court analysis, which was the prototype of much of the leftist legal criticism, illustrates the result. Here was an institution which, from the day that Hamilton foreshadowed Marshall, was nourished by the liberal unanimity of the nation. Its very capacity to restrain the majority lay in the liberal fear the majority had. The horror of the nation in the face of Roosevelt's effort to pack the Court showed the force of that fear even during the tempestuous New Deal days. And yet, in order to establish an American pattern of conflict, the Court was interpreted as an instrument of the minority in the historic struggle to the death. Like Corwin and others Lerner spoke of the American "symbolism" of Court and Constitution, the religious worship of both, but the moral solidarity which obviously nourished this was never related to the pattern of conflict he mainly stressed.* A Beardian Marxism, if one

---

* In discussing the New Deal Court struggle the late Mr. Justice Jackson, then Solicitor General, skirted the truth without knowing it. At one point he said: "Struggles over power that in Europe call out regiments

can use the term, rescued historical analysis for the coming socialist apocalypse.

Under such circumstances the persistence of the socialist passion, despite the flanking movement of the New Deal, and even the persistence of the internecine socialist battles, had definite meaning. If the Marxian railroad train is bound to arrive in America as in Europe, the immediate number of passengers is not important, and everything depends on whether you are connected with the right branch of the road or not. Hence the hope even of the Trotskyites in the Socialist Workers Party, even of the Lovestonites and all the rest of the splinter groups which mushroomed on the American scene. Hence, too, the passion, quite apart from European influence, with which Stalinists and Socialists responded to these deviations, for when the conviction of inevitable success is more significant than the number of followers even the smallest item of doctrine becomes a crucial matter. Remarkably enough, the inevitability orientation of Marxism served peculiar psychic purposes in a land where Marxism had little chance of serious victory.

But in the end of course the isolation of the Marxists gains its significance from the way in which it illustrates

of troops, in America call out battalions of lawyers." At another: "It is surprising that it [the Court] should not only survive but, with no might except the moral force of its judgments, should attain actual supremacy as a source of constitutional dogma." *The Struggle for Judicial Supremacy* (New York, 1949), pp. x, xi. What Jackson did not see was that lawyers instead of troops appeared in America because its struggles were not quite the same as those of Europe. And this was due to the fact that the "moral force" of the Court did not stem from the Court itself but from an ethical settlement which its adjudicative function symbolized. It would indeed be mysterious if the supremacy of the Court came simply from the fact that it was a court.

the persistence of the American liberal habit in the face of the most serious economic difficulties. When one contemplates the pragmatization and radicalization of Liberal Reform in America during the New Deal era, shutting out the doctrinaire pleas both of Whiggery and the socialists, one sees the desperate ingenuity which a liberal community will use to maintain its link with the past. In light of this one can easily wonder whether any purely domestic crisis could shake the national faith, whether innovations even larger than those the New Deal dreamed of could not be made on the basis of the mechanism it used. But for better or for worse, that is not the issue we face, since the age of purely domestic crisis apparently is over. America's new world involvement explodes at once the handy pragmatism and the submerged Lockianism which governed the New Deal era.

CHAPTER ELEVEN

America and the World

1. *Foreign Policy and Domestic Freedom*

It is in the deepest sense the payoff of the American experience that during the twentieth century America should
suddenly be catapulted to the heart of world politics and
should emerge as the leading national power in the struggle against the Communist revolution. No insularity in the
West, not even the English, has been so acute as the
American: no international involvement, again not even
the English, has been so deep. But there is a danger that
the simple contrast between isolation and intervention,
striking as it is, will hide the most serious issues. Fully
as significant as the fact that modern America finds itself in the big wide world while the Founding Fathers
managed to escape from it is the tradition that modern
America brings to its new role—the tradition of escape
itself, of a nonrevolutionary nation as compared with a
Europe that has emerged out of revolution and an Asia
that is now undergoing it. The problem that America now
faces emerges out of the first issue, but whether it will
solve it or not, and how successfully, may well depend
on the second.

Now this is a matter both of the success of American

policy abroad and the fate of American freedom at home: the two are tied up in an intricate knot. It is a principle applicable to all countries, of course, that the struggle for national survival leads to the constriction of internal freedoms. But the American problem is more subtle than this, for the psychic heritage of a nation "born equal" is, as we have abundantly seen, a colossal liberal absolutism, the death by atrophy of the philosophic impulse. And in a war of ideas this frame of mind has two automatic effects: it hampers creative action abroad by identifying the alien with the unintelligible, and it inspires hysteria at home by generating the anxiety that unintelligible things produce. The redscare, in other words, is not only our domestic problem: it is our international problem as well. When the nation rises to an irrational anticommunist frenzy, it replies to the same instinct which tends to alienate it from Western democratic governments that are "socialist." When it closes down on dissent, it answers the same impulse which inspires it to define dubious regimes elsewhere as "democratic." This is the peculiar link that a liberal community forges between the world and domestic pictures: its absolute perspective, its "Americanism."

On the world plane itself, however, "Americanism" has had a dual life, which has confused many observers. First of all, from the time of Jefferson onward, even before its articulation by the triumphant Whiggery of Horatio Alger, it has been characterized by a strong isolationist impulse: the sense that America's very liberal joy lay in the escape from a decadent Old World that could only infect it with its own diseases. This was the spirit that pervaded most men even during the revolutionary age of American history.* And yet, in the twentieth century, "Americanism" has also crusaded abroad in a Wilsonian way, projecting itself headlong over the strange and ancient societies of Europe and Asia. The explanation is actually not hard to find. Embodying an absolute moral ethos, "Americanism," once it is driven on to the world stage by events, is inspired willy-nilly to reconstruct the very alien things it tries to avoid. Its messianism is the polar counterpart of its isolationism, which is why Harding and Wilson are both "Americanist" thinkers, and why, as Mr. George Kennan has recently noted, Americans seem to oscillate between fleeing from the rest of the world and embracing it with too ardent a passion. An absolute national morality is inspired either to withdraw from "alien" things or to transform them: it cannot live in comfort constantly by their side.

Viewed in these terms, it is ironic that America should emerge on the world scene when wars have become revolutions and are fought with the weapons of ideology. A keg of moral dynamite to begin with, the American liberal faith has gradually exploded under the impact of this situation. It has traveled abroad with "Americanist" democracy, and it has purified itself at home with the same doctrine. Actually, to be sure, we have not seen the full effect of this until now: the imperial episodes at the turn of the century and the First World War did not bring it completely to view. But even there the mechanism of the American liberal absolutism can clearly be watched at work, preparing for the responses that the current expansion of the Russian Revolution have evoked. And it is,

* See pp. 35-6.

of course, that Revolution which has fixed the categories of modern ideological war.

But what is the escape from this? Must a liberal community, in addition to all of the massive problems of diplomacy and freedom any great nation faces in the modern world, be saddled forever with the peculiar limitations of its own perspective? No one now can fully answer these questions, but if the answer is to be a favorable one, it can come from only one source: the world involvement itself. For if that involvement intensifies nationalist blindness in some, it serves to educate others, and it is one of the thankful aspects of the situation that is fated to produce an A. Mitchell Palmer and a Senator McCarthy that it is fated also to produce a Woodrow Wilson and a Wendell Willkie. There has been, in other words, throughout the twentieth century an impulse to transcend the American perspective evoked by the very clash of cultures which has closed it down, and as the case of Wilson shows, the two tendencies have usually fought it out within the single American mind. "Americanism" is at once heightened and shattered by the crashing impact of the rest of the world upon it. And so, curiously enough, the answer to the national blindness that the new time produces is the national enlightenment that it also produces: the race between the two is a fateful one indeed. Which is to say that America must look to its contact with other nations to provide that spark of philosophy, that grain of relative insight that its own history has denied it. This is the real meaning of that "coming of age" of America that Van Wyck Brooks and his friends used to talk about in the 'twenties. It could not happen then, but if it is going to happen at all, I believe that it will begin happening now.

2. *Imperialism: Bryan and the Expansionists*

The two-edged effect of the American liberal absolutism—hampered insight abroad and heightened anxiety at home—scarcely reveals itself during the imperial episodes which ushered America onto the world stage at the turn of the century. For one thing imperialism, despite the high knowledge of subject peoples which it requires for its success, is at bottom a fairly simple international venture: domination by force eliminates a lot of ticklish problems of cultural understanding. McKinley had his spiritual turmoils but who will argue that he faced, even on a smaller scale, the substantive issues that later confronted Wilson and Truman? The very pleasant simplicity of the imperial formula is, of course, one of the sad heritages that Western diplomacy now confronts in the East. Moreover, McKinley was involved in no ideological war unless it was a war within the United States over the imperial enterprise itself. The Filipinos posed no threat to the American way of life, Aguinaldo had no agents in Washington or San Francisco, and the current of moral passion, such as it was, came entirely from the American side. This, together with the absence of any real sense of national danger even during the Spanish-American War, let alone the imperial engagements which followed it, precluded the flowering of the witch-hunt tactic on any serious scale. Bryan and the Anti-Imperialist League had a freedom to shout, complain, and organize that the opponents of American military action have never had since.

As a matter of fact, the ethos of the American liberal absolutism was heavily weighted against imperialism, which actually gave to Bryan and his followers a stronger grip on "Americanism" than it gave to militant spirits like Mahan and Teddy Roosevelt. Since the days of Adam Smith the liberal creed had assailed colonial expansion, and while Liberals like Jules Ferry and Sir Edward Grey ultimately embraced imperialism, the passion of a Gladstone even during the later era vividly revealed the logical hostility of the liberal and imperial concepts. But if Gladstone and the Little Englanders were speaking for a single ideology, Bryan was speaking for a national faith, and this, as always, was a much more powerful business. Moreover it so happened that the only revolution the American liberal community had experienced was a revolution against imperial domination, which had produced a Declaration of Independence of great symbolic value. Thus Bryan was able to embark on a peculiar "Americanist" witch hunt of his own. Touring the country in 1900 he said that the Republican party was trying to "imitate European empires," that it had accepted the "European idea," that like the Englishmen fighting the Boers it really believed in the "monarchical" principle.[1] The imperialists were not only non-Jeffersonian, but being so, they were something even worse: alien.

This ironic "Americanist" outburst against imperialism, a nationalism consuming nationalism which could only occur in America, led the partisans of the new imperialism to stress other concepts of American destiny toward which, in any case, they had a certain bent. Of course they could always say in response to Bryan, as Beveridge did, that America's domination of the Philippines or its Dollar Diplomacy in Latin America was sharply to be distinguished from foreign "autocratic" movements since its mission was really to extend Lockian liberty. But exactly how this mission was to be accomplished even Woodrow Wilson, who before the World War cherished it most, never really said. As soon as we begin to explore America's imperialist messianism we see that the heavy drift of it lies in other directions: Anglo-Saxon superiority, as with Josiah Strong, organic national interest, as with Mahan and Roosevelt and Croly. Roosevelt warned against basing American policy "not on the firm ground of national interest but on the treacherous sands of international democratic propagandism"—a direct repudiation of the Wilsonian idea.[2] In other words, cold hard power considerations, the considerations that in England a Tory like Disraeli could accept but a liberal like Gladstone could not, ought to be supreme. Disraeli and Teddy Roosevelt: here is an interesting pair. Can it be that the large number of "frustrated aristocrats" among the imperialist thinkers, Brooks Adams and Beveridge and Roosevelt himself, is to be explained in terms of a longing for the iron spiritual ethos that a liberal world denied them? If this were true, it would, of course, be the best proof, by inversion, that Bryan had gotten hold of the real spirit of bourgeois America as regards imperialism.

There is no denying, of course, that we are dealing here with a tangled ideological situation. The Rooseveltian strenuous life, if it had a Tory touch in one way, was tied in with American thought in several others. The Darwinian framework of the nationalist, economic, and racist theories of imperialism was not without its receptive base in a land whose development had led it to embrace Herbert Spencer on an unprecedented scale. Mahan, when he spoke of national rivalries, had behind him at least the good Horatio Alger principle of competition. And when the issue boiled down to the quest for markets, as at one point or another it almost invariably did, the spirit of Alger flourished more easily than ever. Even the theory of racial supremacy, and this quite apart from any Darwinism, found a twisted root in American life. An ethnic mélange, a submerged class of Negroes: here was fodder for a thousand corner drugstore Gobineaus, and one has to admit that it seemed to serve its purpose better than the lower classes of France on which Gobineau was forced to rely. The blood and thunder imperialists could ground themselves on a fair amount of oblique American analogy and submerged American prejudice.

But the fact remains that all this was basically alien to the national liberal spirit: it had to work within and around it. Mahan believed in competition, but the competition of sublime organic national entities was unfamiliar to the American mind, and moreover it swallowed up the atoms of Horatio Alger's world and jelled them into a solidary whole that they did not like at all. It had been one of Sumner's central passions to assail the Germanic idea of state and nation, to blow up into individualistic bits what Mahan wanted to create. True, Mahan had a certain amount of support among academic thinkers like Burgess and Woolsey, men steeped in European scholarship, but of what national influence were they? Who read them outside the classroom? Moreover, it was no minor sin to obscure the uniqueness of America by listing it as a "nation" or even as part of the Anglo-Saxon or Germanic "race." Wasn't the whole meaning of "Americanism" that America was a peculiar land of freedom, equality, and opportunity? Wasn't this the supreme message of Andrew Carnegie, however much he himself may have believed in Anglo-Saxonism? And insofar as American racial prejudice went, let us not forget the fate of ante-bellum Southerners like Fitzhugh and Josiah Nott: the prejudice of loose elements in a liberal community is a lot different from the massive and uniform democratic faith by which it lives. It is revealing that the Republicans who joined the anti-imperialist movement, men like George S. Boutwell and Senator Hoar, were almost invariably Republicans of the older generation who could not forget the work of Lincoln and the Civil War.

Thus in a liberal community the imperialist drive at the turn of the century was hamstrung by a unique nationalism: national liberalism. Arming themselves with "Americanism," and untroubled by a military or ideological menace from without, the followers of Bryan lived a comparatively free and easy life. The Anti-Imperialist League, far from going underground, had branches openly in all parts of the country, enlisting the allegiance of many of the most prominent men in the country. If the press was predominantly imperialist, Bryan could run on the ticket of a national party in opposition to military ventures abroad. And when the Secretary of War tried to stop Edward Atkinson from sending anti-imperialist propaganda to the soldiers who were actually fighting in the Philippines, a howl of protest went up which forced a withdrawal of the action and discredited the McKinley Administration. Atkinson, one outraged editorial writer said, was being victimized by a "rule of blood and iron." [3] A strange contrast indeed with later days.

And so the imperialist time was an oddly deceptive in-

troduction to the problem of America's liberal absolutism
as it was going to shape up in the field of foreign affairs
in the twentieth century: it elicited no "Americanist" scare
at home and it did not contribute to a peculiar blindness
abroad. Indeed on the latter count, if anything it helped
a bit: the qualms of conscience that Bryan had, despite
the brutality of the suppression of Aguinaldo and despite
the record of Dollar Diplomacy, cushioned the impact of
American imperialism. The American record, comparatively, is not a bad one, and if this is traceable to many
factors, not the least of which is the massive set of resources America still had at home, it is traceable in part
as well to the fact that national domination is peculiarly
distasteful to the dogmatic liberal mind. But this was introduction only: a different pattern would begin to unfold
once the structure of Europe collapsed in 1914.

3. *The First World War and the First Redscare*

What the World War and its Russian Revolution after-
math did was to color American policy with the conscious
ethos of the American liberal faith and thus to take away
from its opponents any real polemical grip on "Americanism." Of course, this made America's intentions finer: a
later Woodrow Wilson, by our own norms at least, is to
be preferred to an earlier one and certainly at any time
to a Josiah Strong. But this very shift had the effect of
projecting the limitations of the American liberal perspective onto the world scene and at the same time, by generating the national moral passion, striking hard at the
lone dissenting spirit. We must not, of course, attribute
all problems to "Americanism": Lloyd George and Clemenceau made their own mistakes in foreign policy and

neither of them, despite their lesser attachment to "Making the World Safe for Democracy," presided over societies unridden by war hysteria. But after this has been said, the peculiar American blindspots of Wilson are evident, and the peculiar quality of America's liberal hysteria, especially as the Bolshevik Revolution succeeded the war itself, cannot be denied.

The shift from the imperial pattern to the pattern of world war could hardly be more dramatic. The obvious fact is, of course, that the ideas of national self-determination and democracy superseded those of imperialist control. But as if to make the contrast more perfect and thoroughgoing, the whole Teutonic bent of much of the earlier imperial racist doctrine was suddenly smashed to bits: Beveridge had spoken of the civilizing mission of the "English Speaking and Teutonic Peoples" and Burgess had absorbed the one into the other. But now, of course, the Teuton became the "Hun," and if George Creel blasted him with the subtle arts of journalism, John Dewey and Ralph Barton Perry blasted him with the even subtler arts of philosophic discourse. The "backward peoples" of the East and elsewhere, had they been concerned with this issue, might have derived a fine ironic joy from seeing half of the people who were supposed to civilize them suddenly denounce the other half as barbarians since their origin. Where, indeed, after 1914 was a "backward person" to turn with any real assurance of being civilized? But the main point, of course, is the new definition of American policy in terms of the Lockian faith which was not only facilitated by making the war a crusade for "democracy" but also by blasting Germany as a breaker of treaties and hence violating the fundamental principle of contract. The nation rose in a single chorus, apart from the few non-Lockians like Randolph Bourne, as American boys shipped abroad to fight for the American faith.

The policy of Wilson in peace, so striking a contrast to the realpolitik of the Old World and ultimately so abject a victim before it, was shot through and through with the absolute "Americanism" on the basis of which the war was fought. His central dilemma, what Walter Lippmann called the "inner contradiction" of his thought, is by now a commonplace: the attempt to apply to a world in crying need of integration and on the brink of capitalist decline the political formulas of nationalism and free trade that the nineteenth century evolved.[4] But to say merely this, to classify Wilson as a decadent disciple of Gladstone, is not only to miss the American contribution to his perspectives but actually to obscure it. Wilson's blindness was not only philosophic, it was empirical as well, the product of a peculiar historic experience. If he missed the enormous social upheavals that were impending in Europe, as his friend George Record told him, this was half due to the fact that the concept of social upheaval was alien to the American mind. If he exalted national self-determination, he did so not only because he worshiped Bright and Mill but because for a nation "born equal" the Declaration of Independence symbolized the essence of liberation. Wilson said that he had a sample American heart, which was true, and that America was the sample democracy of the world, which was not. These convictions, fully as much as abstract liberalism, shaped the "inner contradiction" of his thought.

It is interesting how Wilson's world policy reflected his domestic Progressivism. One can, to be sure, make out a case in realpolitik for that policy: its stress on free trade and equal opportunity for nations was remarkably well suited to America's new economic supremacy enhanced now by a merchant marine and a strong position in foreign markets. But the common reliance on a free play of interests in the domestic and the international spheres is too obvious to go ignored. Wasn't Wilson smashing the Austro-Hungarian Empire into bits much as he would smash an American trust? Wasn't he depending on an automatic harmony as clearly in the one case as he was in the other? Actually Wilson's enslavement to the American experience reflected not only its original nature but the very stage of its internal development. We have already seen that American Progressivism, of all the liberal reform movements of the West, was alone preoccupied with attaining a Horatio Alger world. The two other reformist liberals who sat down with Wilson at Versailles, Lloyd George and Clemenceau, were not bent on that objective at home: they had accepted, theoretically at least, the principle of social control.

But if Wilson was "American," he was only, as it were, half so, and this has a lot to do with the final crushing defeat he experienced. I do not mean this merely in the sense of his uncompromising utopianism with respect to the League of Nations and its consideration by the American Senate. That is an interesting story even within the confines of his own social thought. For if the League was for him a kind of Robespierrian flight—"If it won't work it must be made to work"—and if his treatment of the Senate was as unbending as anything to be found in the Republic of Virtue, he himself was a lover of Burke in his social thought and usually took the errors of the French

Revolution as a starting point for his analysis of modern history. For a man who defined even his Darwinism in Burkian terms, there was surely something odd, explicable perhaps in terms of an opposing Presbyterian conscience or a sense of the need to compensate for concessions at Versailles, about the fact that Colonel House was forced to remind him that "Anglo-Saxon civilization was built upon compromises." [5] His hard doctrinaire mind, taken as a whole, was not of the American type.

And yet to the extent that it sought to define and reconstruct alien things in terms of an American image it was fully in the national tradition, which is the real point that ought to be stressed in connection with his half-way Americanism: the other half was a withdrawal from alien things, the spirit of Bryan and now of Harding, the polar counterpart of the crusading impulse. It was the insurgence of this isolationist "Americanism" which in the end shattered Wilsonian "Americanism." When Harding said in 1920 that he did not want to "menace the health of the republic in Old World contagion," and that "One cannot be half American and half European or half something else," [6] he expressed in his own characteristic prose the old Jeffersonian drive, which Wilson before 1914 had himself shared, of the American liberal community: Hebraism, separateness. And this, of course, coincided with the death of the Progressive movement and the rise to power for its dizzy decade before collapse of the democratic Whiggery of the post-Civil War era. So Harding's "Americanism" is at once the "Americanism" of isolation and the "Americanism" of Whiggery. This point is crucial, for both were the peculiar instruments of imposing the redscare mentality on the nation after the outbreak of the Russian

Revolution. Which means that Harding's nationalism is actually three faceted: isolationism, Whiggery, and liberal hysteria. In the internally intricate history of the American liberal absolutism the Senator from Ohio will always occupy a fine symbolic place.

This brings us to the heart of the domestic situation: the impact of the American faith at home. Needless to say, with "Americanism" as the country's banner in a vast national war, Randolph Bourne did not enjoy the freedom of Edward Atkinson during the Philippine conquest. The rule of "blood and iron" that was decried when Atkinson was hindered for a brief moment from disaffecting our fighting troops fell on Bourne and the Socialists with a terrific actuality, and there was no Anti-War League led by outstanding national figures, comparable to the Anti-Imperialist League, to protest their fate. The Sedition Act, as it was interpreted by the courts, would have put Atkinson in jail within twenty-four hours. And yet, for all of the absolute liberalism of the war against Germany, the faith of the nation does not show itself so starkly in connection with it as it does in connection with the redscare which followed it. This is not merely because the Kaiser's agents were "spies" rather than revolutionaries and the German enemy, for all that could be said about its "autocratic" ideas, did not represent the same ideological threat to the liberal faith that Communism did. It is also because on the plane of war alone it is hard to disentangle the peculiar force of the American liberal dogmatism from the domestic tyranny that war involved everywhere. Bertrand Russell is, after all, some sort of English counterpart to Randolph Bourne.

This is why Bourne himself, with his eyes on the concept of the State, missed a lot in the very atmosphere that struck him down. What he said was true enough: war was in some sense the "health of the state," it intensified the "herd current" in society, it struck at deviations that in peace were tolerable. But to reduce the issue to "romantic patriotic militarism" was to obscure its ideological component, which in a liberal society was crucial.[7] The redscare ultimately brought this out. Of course, for a moment the Kaiser and Lenin were intermingled in the American demonology, as Zachariah Chafee has brilliantly shown in his study of the collapse of free speech at the time. Judge Van Valkenburgh, addressing the jury which convicted Rose Paster Stokes, a Bolshevik sympathizer who opposed the war, denounced the Russian Revolution as "the greatest betrayal of the cause of democracy the world has ever seen," [8] although the Espionage Act had nothing to do with it. He was one of many American judges of the time, responding to the "vague fear" that Mr. Justice Holmes perceived and above all to the American general will upon which their peculiar power depended.

But it is as the redscare pulls away from the war situation and begins to blossom on its own—as what Louis Post called the "Deportations Delirium of 1920" begins to develop—that the distinctive force of the American liberal absolutism begins to stand out. This is not to say that in other Western countries the Bolshevik Revolution was greeted with none of the panic that the war itself inspired: in England the great coercive powers of the wartime Coalition were hurled against strikers burning with the Bolshevik inspiration and even Ramsay MacDonald's government tried to hinder Communist journalism. But who will compare this situation with the one over which Attorney General Palmer presided? The MacDonald government was a socialist government after all, it was forced to recognize the Soviet Union, and it retreated ignominiously from its order against the radical writings of J. R. Campbell. And in France simultaneously, for all of the fear of Bolshevism there, a Radical government was returned based in part on Socialist support. This is a far cry from the New York situation of late 1919 when five pathetic Socialist members of the New York Legislature were thrown out of that body. A far cry, too, from the happy raiding of Palmer, the exclusion of socialist literature from the mails, the deportations delirium, and the wave of Hardingesque "Americanism" which followed it. As always, logically enough, the situation boiled down to this: the American liberal community contained far fewer radicals than any other Western society but the hysteria against them was much vaster than anywhere else.

We must not assume that the substitution of Republican "Americanism" for Democratic "Americanism" wholly explains this movement: it is what they had in common that really produced it. True, the embroidering of the Bolshevik menace was a natural technique for a Whiggery which had since the Civil War tried to discredit its opponents by labeling them as "socialist" and "un-American." But this technique was possible only because the nation as a whole was inherently sensitive to the symbol of socialism, and Wilson was as much a party to this sensitivity as Harding was. He denounced Bolshevism as "poison." [9] It was under his aegis that American interventionism in Russia took place,* and indeed it was the isolationism of Harding which did much to end that intervention. The heart of the matter lay in the American general will, which is what produced the distinction between America and Europe and what, in an odd sense, made the deportation approach to Communism quite instinctive. After all in a land where Communism is truly "alien," what is more sensible than to get rid of it simply by throwing out the men who brought it over? Western Europe could not adopt this approach, needless to say, because it had originally produced Marxism, if not in England in the seventeenth century then surely on the continent in the eighteenth or the nineteenth. The fate of Emma Goldman was peculiarly symbolic of the whole situation.

The redscare mentality displays the American absolutism in its purest form. When in 1921 Secretary of State Hughes rejected a Soviet overture for the opening up of trade with America he said that trade rested on production and that production would be impossible in Russia since it depended on "firm guarantees of private property, the sanctity of contracts and the rights of free labor." [10] Herbert Hoover, as Secretary of Commerce, had used much the same language a few months before. Both men of course were identifying the process of production itself with the procedures of American capitalism, and it would be hard to find in Wilson's blindspots abroad anything to transcend such an identification. But this was sober technical analysis: the fury appeared when one moved to the realm of morals. And here, in addition to what the Bolsheviks actually professed in their antagonism to the liberal

---

* Reluctantly to be sure.

system, the imagination of the nation conjured up such principles as the nationalization of women (the "Decree of the Saratov Soviet") in order to intensify its response. Under such circumstances it was just as easy to remove the Bolsheviks from the human race as it was to remove their economic organization from the realm of productive mechanisms. Figuratively Senator McCumber was right when he called the Bolsheviks "beasts," [11] but one has the uneasy feeling that he was also speaking literally, as Aristotle might when describing a being outside the state.

This then was the domestic culmination of the "Americanism" in terms of which the war had been defined and the peace had been negotiated. It was the reflection in fear at home, despite the triumph of the isolationism which accompanied it, of the hope we had projected abroad. George Kennan has spoken of "our inveterate tendency to judge others by the extent to which they contrive to be like ourselves." [12] There is a lot more to this principle. It is peculiarly easy for us to judge others by ourselves because, especially since the Jacksonian upheaval, we have been so much alike. And in a time of ideological war the judgment of others by our norms brings, by automatic reflex, the passionate and fearful intensification of those norms as they apply to ourselves as well. In other words the American liberal absolutism lies at the heart of the problem, linking as always the issue of world insight with the issue of domestic freedom.

4. America and Russia

Even now, when it is apparent that the Bolshevik Revolution represents the most serious threat in modern history to the future of free institutions, it is no mistake to assail the redscare of the A. Mitchell Palmer age. In Progressive circles there has been some doubt about this, as if now it might be necessary to rethink or to undo the reaction against the Bolshevik hysteria which set in with the late 'twenties and the 'thirties. But the truth is, as Communism has swallowed up large portions of the globe and its threatening character has been made plain, the anti-Palmer spirit is more important than ever, not merely to distinguish between authentic fear and liberal hysteria at home but in order to meet the revolutionary challenge abroad. In an age when not only Europe but Asia is involved in American diplomacy the blindspots of "Americanism" pose a peculiarly complicated problem, and in an age when the Communist threat is of a long-range type the irrational inward passion of "Americanism" is as grave a threat to domestic freedom as any we have ever faced. This is the ironic end product of a Second World War originally fought against fascism, of a historic phase which began in the late 'thirties simply with an argument over isolationism.

Isolationist "Americanism" went through certain agonies before it was smothered by the Second World War. If the memory of Jefferson and Bryan were not available to remind us that this peculiar form of American absolutism was not the property of Whiggery alone, the New Dealers would have provided evidence enough of this fact. During the 'thirties many progressives embraced the idea passionately, sometimes in terms of an Oxford Oath pacifism common to the West, sometimes in terms of the profit theory of war that the Nye Committee advanced, and often in terms of a peculiar nationalism associated with the concept of planning. The "New Isolationism," as

Raymond Buell called it, was excellently reflected in the neutrality legislation of the 'thirties. Actually, whatever might be the world outlook of Roosevelt or Hull, the implicit devotion of the New Deal to a dogmatic liberal mentality rejecting "alien" things fits in here. It was not accidental that some of the New Dealers, men like Stuart Chase, Jerome Frank, and Charles Beard, blossomed forth with an America First philosophy in the end. Chase, perhaps thinking of that "third road" which he defined as America's peculiar prerogative in 1931, simply said that this country had a pattern for social survival while Europe, Asia, and Africa did not.[18]

But the impact of fascism, especially during the Spanish War, began to corrode progressive isolationism and to supplant it slowly with an international feeling. Willy-nilly this took on the Wilsonian logic by which "Americanism," when it does not retreat, goes abroad. "What the United States is today," Lewis Mumford wrote, "the world itself might become tomorrow if the menace of fascism and imperialism and class exploitation were lifted. . . ." [14] Even Wilson did not go as far as this. But on the whole it was chastened "Americanism" that was projected onto Europe with America's entry into the war, defined largely in negative terms of beating the Axis and there was actually criticism to the effect that American aims in fighting had not been clearly enough defined. And yet if anyone thought that the American liberal perspective had died, that the propensity of the nation to define world issues in terms of its own experience had disappeared, the postwar era was enough to disenchant them. Many of the problems raised by "Americanism" in the occupation of Germany and Japan are well known, but it is the battle against the Communist revolution in its current phase which has brought to the fore the peculiar orientations of a nation "born equal."

It is the absence of outright war, or the presence of what we call the "cold war," which makes these orientations plain; for military struggle, as Waldo Frank has somewhere written, is the great simplifier, reducing complicated social issues to the simple lines of the battle chart. Because the current struggle against Communism is in significant part an ideological competition for human loyalties, it has brought into the plainest view America's psychological pattern. One of the issues it involves is the issue of a social "message" to compete with the appeal of Communism in various parts of the world. Since the American liberal creed is a submerged faith, even in its Alger form, it is obviously not a theory which other peoples can easily appropriate or understand. Its very absolutism depends of course on this aspect of its character. At the same time this is not antithetical, as we have seen, to a crusading "Americanism" based on the absolute mood which this very character of American thought inspires. Hence the question is not whether our history has given us something to "export" but whether it has given us the right thing. And this question has to be answered in the negative. If we want to meet the action of Communism on this score, our job, in addition to repeating the Declaration of Independence, the "American Proposition," as the *Fortune* editors put it, is to transcend the perspective it contains.[15]

There has been a lot of whistling in the dark on this whole question. Not only have we been told that our history provides us with an "American Proposition" applicable to all countries East and West, but we have also been told that it is we, not the Russians, who are the most "revolutionary" nation on earth. Nothing is farther from the truth and we may as well face the fact. It is the absence of the experience of social revolution which is at the heart of the whole American dilemma. Not only does this produce the quality of our absolute thinking, Locke never having been contrasted with Filmer and hence never with Marx, but in a whole series of specific ways it enters into our difficulty of communication with the rest of the world. We find it hard to understand Europe's "social question" and hence tend to interpret even the democratic socialisms of Europe in terms of our own antiradical fetishism. We are not familiar with the deeper social struggles of Asia and hence tend to interpret even reactionary regimes as "democratic." We fail to appreciate nonpolitical definitions of "freedom" and hence are baffled by their use. Needless to say, all this plays into the hands of Russian Communism which, grave as is the threat it poses, is nonetheless a genuine ideology of social revolution.

The domestic phase of this national subjectivism follows by the usual logic, and it is familiar to all of us: the redscare. Exaggerated as this phenomenon may be abroad, there can be no doubt that it represents the most frightening closing down of "Americanism" at home that we have yet experienced. It is keener than the Palmer drive precisely in proportion as the Communist threat which elicits it is keener. It is wider than the Dies hysteria just as the element of reality it involves is wider. It has charged the atmosphere of the national life with a fear that has become familiar. We cannot interpret it in terms of a single politician, whether he be McCarthy or someone who might succeed him. The hope has always been raised that by discrediting the personal villain in the redscare drama

the drama itself would end. This is as delusive as the belief on the international plane that "we are the most revolutionary nation on earth." For it is of the very essence
of our unusual response to Communism, whatever its
immediate sources may be in national groups or political
alignments, that it reflects an absolute "Americanism" as
old as the country itself. Some of its apostles may indeed
fade from the political scene, but so long as the historic
forces which call it into being continue to exist, they will
be replaced by others hardly less energetic.

Nor ought we to be misled by the peculiar position of
the New Deal in the redscare pattern. If the mission
of the anti-Communist hysteria is in significant part to
discredit the American Progressive movement, still that
movement has always contributed heavily to its ultimate
strength. I have mentioned the isolationist "Americanism"
which characterized much of New Deal thinking on the
international plane in the early years. But more significant is the deeper irrational liberalism of the New Deal
movement which was responsible for its whole pragmatic
orientation, for its whole aversion to systematic social
thought. Whatever one might say about the socialist and
communist intellectuals who entangled themselves with
the New Deal, these were the dominant moods of its
life and, as we know, they infuriated the leftist intellectuals themselves. It is ironic that the Progressive tradition
should be discredited by an "Americanist" tide of which
it was itself a part, but the same thing happened to Wil-
sonism after the First World War. If the Progressive tradition is to become a fighting weapon against the redscare hysteria, against American conformism in its current
frightening phase, the soul-searching that leads to an un-

derstanding of this fact is an experience it has got to go through.

But the larger forces working toward a shattering of American provincialism abroad as well as at home lie of course in the world scene itself. Will these affect the counterpressures stemming from the same source? Will the insight of a Willkie or a Stevenson offset the end of insight a McCarthy inspires? There is nothing in an analysis of American history which gives us a final answer to this question; we are left hanging in the air concerning it. But surely, whatever the outcome, this is the largest challenge the American liberal world has faced, and the payment for meeting it effectively is more than mere survival in an age of world turmoil. It holds out the hope of an inward enrichment of culture and perspective, a "coming of age," to use the term of the 'twenties again, which in its own right is well worth fighting for. What is at stake is nothing less than a new level of consciousness, a transcending of irrational Lockianism, in which an understanding of self and an understanding of others go hand in hand. Nor can one omit the large consequence for the whole free world which this would involve. For if America is the bizarre fulfillment of liberalism, do not people everywhere rely upon it for the retention of what is best in that tradition? It would be an all too easy defense of "neutralism" to say that Western Europe, having originated both liberalism and socialism, confronts them twisted alike in America and Russia by laws of "combined development." The fact is, Russian development has turned its back on the Western concept of personality while American development, what ever its provincialism, rests still on that concept. Perhaps this has something to do with the distinction between "overleaping" a historical stage and fleeing it. In any case, given the totalitarian nature of Russian socialism, the hope for a free world surely lies in the power for transcending itself inherent in American liberalism.

Can a people "born equal" ever understand peoples elsewhere that have to become so? Can it ever understand itself? These were the questions which appeared at the beginning of this book: inevitably also they are the questions which appear at the end.

Notes and Index

Notes

CHAPTER ONE

1. L. Hacker, *The Triumph of American Capitalism* (New York, 1940), p. 279.
2. See the brilliant comments of B. F. Wright in "Political Institutions and the Frontier," *Sources of American Culture*, ed. D. R. Fox (New York, 1934), pp. 15-39.
3. J. Jameson, *The History of Historical Writing in America* (Boston, 1891), p. 138.

CHAPTER TWO

1. Alexis de Tocqueville, *Democracy in America*, ed. F. Bowen (Boston, 1873), vol. ii, p. 123.
2. *Rededicating America* (Indianapolis, 1920), p. 137.
3. In J. L. Blau (ed.), *Social Theories of Jacksonian Democracy* (New York, 1947), p. 58.
4. "Dissertation on the Canon and Feudal Law," in John Adams, *Works*, ed. C. F. Adams (Boston, 1856), vol. iii, pp. 447-465.
5. Quoted in D. Walther, *Gouverneur Morris* (New York and London, 1934), p. 76.
6. Samuel Adams, *Writings*, ed. F. H. Cushing (New York, 1904-1908), vol. ii, p. 164.
7. John Adams, *Works*, vol. iv, p. 55.
8. Quoted in H. Niles (ed.), *Principles and Acts of the Revolution in America* (New York, 1876), p. 56.
9. *Surveys Historic and Economic* (London and New York, 1900), p. 406.
10. Cf. M. Einaudi, *The Physiocratic Doctrine of Judicial Control* (Cambridge, Mass., 1938).

313

11. Quoted in John Adams, *Works,* vol. ii, p. 522.
12. Thomas Jefferson, *Writings,* ed. P. L. Ford (New York, 1892-1899), vol. iii, p. 231.
13. *The Pulpit of the American Revolution,* p. 311.
14. John Dickinson, *Writings,* ed. P. L. Ford (Philadelphia, 1895), p. 316.
15. Cf. B. F. Wright, Jr., "The Early History of Written Constitutions in America," in *Essays in History and Political Theory in Honor of Charles Howard McIllwain* (Cambridge, Mass., 1936), pp. 344 ff.
16. Quoted in J. Shapiro, *Condorcet and the Rise of Liberalism* (New York, 1934), p. 223.
17. *An American Dilemma* (New York, 1944), p. 7.
18. *Observations on the Importance of the American Revolution* (London, 1785), p. 69.
19. *Encyclopedia of Social Sciences* (New York, 1937), vol. ii, 645. By the same logic, we have never had a "Liberal Party" in the United States.
20. *Democracy in America,* vol. i, p. 58.
21. W. Sombart, *Quintessence of Capitalism* (London, 1915), p. 306.
22. Quoted in V. Parrington, *Main Currents in American Thought* (New York, 1927-1930), vol. i, p. 200
23. The letter, dated 1778, is printed in Price's *Observations,* p. 95. For a general discussion of the problem, see O. and M. Handlin, *Commonwealth: Massachusetts* (New York, 1947), and L. Hartz, *Economic Policy and Democratic Thought* (Cambridge, Mass., 1948).
24. Some of the finest work on this subject is being done by Professor Carter Goodrich of Columbia. See his recent articles in the *Political Science Quarterly.*
25. *Encyclopedia of Social Sciences,* vol. xv, p. 199.
26. M. G. Jean de Crèvecoeur, *Letters from an American Farmer* (London, 1926), p. 40.
27. Quoted in *Principles and Acts of the Revolution in America,* cited above (n. 8), p. 46.
28. *Theory of Politics* (New York, 1854), p. 262.
29. C. Nettels, *Roots of American Civilization* (New York, 1938), p. 315.
30. Quoted in A. G. Keller (ed.), *The Challenge of Facts and Other Essays* (New Haven, 1914), p. 318.
31. G. Santayana, *Character and Opinion in the United States* (New York, 1924), p. 210.
32. *Second Treatise on Civil Government* (Oxford, 1947), p. 29.
33. C. L. Becker, *Freedom and Responsibility in the American Way of Life* (New York, 1945), p. 16.
34. *The Challenge of Facts and Other Essays,* p. 304.

CHAPTER THREE

1. C. Beard, *The Rise of American Civilization* (New York, 1930), p. 294.
2. C. Becker, *Freedom and Responsibility in the American Way of Life* (New York, 1945), p. 10.
3. M. Farrand, *Records of the Federal Convention* (New Haven, 1911-1937), vol. i, p. 215.
4. *The Life and Works of Thomas Paine*, ed. W. M. Van der Weyde (New Rochelle, N. Y., 1925) vol. ii, p. 121.
5. G. R. Minot, *The History of the Insurrections in Massachusetts* (Boston, 1810), p. 33.
6. J. Morley, *Burke* (New York, 1894), p. 130.
7. E. Bax, *The Last Episode of the French Revolution* (London, 1911) pp. 107, 109.
8. M. Farrand, *Records*, vol. i, p. 82, *The Discovery of Europe*, ed. P. Rahv (Boston, 1947), p. 3.
9. J. Adams, *A Defence of the Constitutions of Government of the United States of America*, London, 1787, p. viii.
10. M. Farrand, *Records*, vol. i, p. 448.
11. *Ibid.*, p. 400.
12. *Ibid.*, p. 402.
13. The *Federalists*, ed. M. Beloff (Oxford, 1948), pp. 41-48.

CHAPTER FOUR

1. *Education of Henry Adams*, Mod. Lib. ed. (New York, 1931), p. 33.
2. *Works of Rufus Choate*, ed. S. G. Brown (Boston, 1862), p. 419.
3. *Speeches on Questions of Public Policy*, ed. J. E. T. Rogers (London, 1869), vol. i, p. 227.
4. Max Farrand, *Records of the Federal Convention* (New Haven, 1911-1937), vol. i, p. 87.
5. *A Letter to the Hon. Daniel Webster* (Philadelphia, 1837).
6. J. Story, *Miscellaneous Writings* (Boston, 1946), p. 327.
7. *Works of Rufus Choate*, p. 422.
8. Quoted in A. M. Schlesinger, Jr., *Age of Jackson* (Boston, 1946), p. 327.
9. *Social Theories of Jacksonian Democracy*, ed. J. L. Blau (New York, 1947), p. 302.
10. Quoted in Th. Rothstein, *From Chartism to Laborism* (London, 1929), p. 96.
11 J. T. Horton, *James Kent, A Study in Conservatism* (New York-London, 1939), p. 255.

12. B. F. Wright, *Source Book of American Political Theory* (New York, 1929), pp. 369, 373, 382.
13. See L. Hartz, *Economic Policy and Democratic Thought* (Cambridge, Mass., 1948), pp. 56 ff., 292-293.
14. Quoted in Schlesinger, *Age of Jackson*, p. 270.
15. Edward Everett, *Orations and Speeches* (Boston, 1836), p. 297.

CHAPTER FIVE

1. *Democracy in America*, ed. F. Bowen (Boston, 1873), vol. ii, p. 191.
2. *Ibid.*, pp. 191-192.
3. *Farming and Democracy* (New York, 1948).
4. Quoted, M. J. Dauer and H. Hammond, "John Taylor: Democrat or Aristocrat," *Journal of Politics*, vol. vi., 1944, pp. 381, 390.
5. Quoted, J. Dorfman, *The Economic Mind in American Civilization* (New York, 1946), vol. ii, p. 663.
6. J. Taylor, *An Inquiry into the Principles and Policy of the Government of the United States* (Fredericksburg, Va., 1814), pp. 50 ff.
7. J. Taylor, *Arator* (Petersburg, Va., 1818), p. 33.
8. Quoted, H. Schneider, *A History of American Philosophy* (New York, 1946), p. 121.
9. Quoted, L. Hartz, "'Seth Luther: Working Class Rebel," *New England Quarterly*, vol. xiii, 1940, p. 412.
10. G. Santayana, *Character and Opinion in the United States* (New York, 1924).
11. Quoted, C. Merriam, *A History of American Political Theories* (New York, 1920), p. 164.
12. J. Taylor, *Construction Construed and Constitutions Vindicated* (Richmond, Va., 1820), p. 34.
13. G. Camp, *Democracy* (New York, 1859), p. 14; R. Hildreth, *Theory of Politics* (New York, 1854), p. 255.
14. *United States Magazine and Democratic Review*, 1837-1838, vol. i, p. 3.
15. C. Beard, *Economic Origins of Jeffersonian Democracy* (New York, 1915), p. 418.
16. Quoted, *Social Theories of Jacksonian Democracy*, ed. J. S. Blau (New York, 1947), p. 74; J. Taylor, *An Inquiry into the Principles and Policy of the Government of the United States*, p. 70; quoted, B. Hammond, "Jackson, Biddle, and the Bank of the United States," *Journal of Economic History*, vol. vii, 1947, p. 6; quoted L. Hartz, *Economic Policy and Democratic Thought* (Cambridge, Mass.), p 77.
17. New York *Tribune*, April 12, 1848.

18. B. Hammond, "Jackson, Biddle, and the Bank of the United States," *Journal of Economic History*, vol. vii, 1947, pp. 2, 9 ff.
19. *Democratic Review*, vol. xii, 1843, p. 377; quoted, J. Dorfman, *Economic Mind in American Civilization*, vol. ii, p. 66.
20. *Social Theories of Jacksonian Democracy*, ed. J. Blau, p. 57.
21. *Democratic Review*, vol. xiii, 1843, p. 129; G. Camp, *Democracy*, p. 14.

CHAPTER SIX

1. *Southern Literary Messenger*, vol. xxxvii (1863), p. 723; *Sociology for the South* (Richmond, 1854), p. 209.
2. J. Calhoun, *A Disquisition on Government*, ed. Cralle (New York, 1943), p. 4; *Sociology for the South*, p. 119; *Harper on Slavery*, p. 6.
3. *De Bow's Review* (New Orleans, 1857), vol. xxii, p. 137-138.
4. *Selections from the Writings and Speeches of William L. Garrison* (Boston: 1852), p. 259.
5. *Speeches* (Boston and New York, 1905), p. 127.
6. *Harper on Slavery*, in *The Pro-Slavery Argument* (Charleston, 1852), p. 4; George Fitzhugh, *Cannibals All!* (Richmond, 1857), p. xv.
7. *Disquisition*, p. 62. Calhoun refers neither to slavery nor the sectional struggle explicitly in *Disquisition*, but the import of his remarks is obvious.
8. Quoted, *De Bow's Review*, vol. xxiii, 1857, p. 349.
9. *Ibid.*, 347.
10. *Cotton Is King*, ed. E. N. Elliott (Augusta, 1860), p. 318.
11. *De Bow's Review*, vol. xxiii, 1857, p. 348.

CHAPTER SEVEN

1. K. Marx and F. Engels, *Communist Manifesto*, in *A Handbook of Marxism*, ed. E. Burns (New York, 1935), p. 47.
2. See Wilfred Carsel, "The Slaveholders' Indictment of Northern Wage Slavery," *Journal of Southern History*, vol. vi, 1940, pp. 505 ff.
3. *De Bow's Review*, vol. xxiii, 1857, p. 345.
4. W. Harper, *Harper on Slavery*, in *The Pro-Slavery Argument* (Charleston, 1852), p. 6.
5. Henry Hughes, *Treatise on Sociology* (Philadelphia, 1854), *passim*.
6. W. Channing, *Slavery* (Boston, 1835), p. 26.
7. *De Bow's Review*, vol. xxii, 1857, p. 136.
8. *Cannibals All! or, Slaves Without Masters* (Richmond, 1857), p. 127.

9. G. F. Holmes, "'Theory of Political Individualism," *De Bow's Review,* vol. xxii, 1857, p. 138.

10. *Cannibals All! or, Slaves Without Masters,* p. xv.

11. See *ibid.,* p. 359.

12. J. Dorfman, *The Economic Mind in American Civilization* (New York, 1946), vol. ii, pp. 809-825.

13. Quoted, J. S. Bach, Jr., "The Social Thought of the Old South," *American Journal of Sociology,* vol. xlvi, 1940, p. 187.

14. See E. Ruffin, *The Political Economy of Slavery* (n.p., 1953), pp. 6-8.

15. *Ibid.,* p. ix.

16. Quoted, J. Dorfman, *The Economic Mind in American Civilization,* vol. ii, p. 906.

17. *Cannibals All!,* p. 60.

18. *Ibid.,* p. 61.

CHAPTER EIGHT

1. S. Chase, *A New Deal* (New York, 1931), p. 62.

2. Quoted, B. Twiss, *Lawyers and the Constitution* (Princeton, 1942), p. 53.

3. W. Harding, *Rededicating America,* ed. Frederick E. Schortmeier (Indianapolis, 1920), p. 109.

4. E. Hubbard, *Little Journeys to the Homes of Great Business Men,* George Peabody (East Aurora, N. Y., 1909), p. 72.

5. Quoted, B. Twiss, *Lawyers and the Constitution,* p. 149.

6. A. Carnegie, *Triumphant Democracy* (New York, 1893), p. 32.

7. Introduction to G. Gatti, *Le Socialisme et l'Agriculture,* p. 20.

8. H. Hoover, *American Individualism* (New York, 1934), p. 24.

9. A. Carnegie, *Triumphant Democracy,* p. 22.

10. W. Ashley, *Surveys Historic and Economic* (New York, 1900), p. 409.

11. E. Hubbard, *The Motto Book* (East Aurora, New York, 1920), p. 24.

12. W. Ashley, *Surveys Historic and Economic* (New York, 1900), p. 385.

13. *Ibid.,* p. 409.

14. W. Sumner, *What Social Classes Owe to Each Other* (New York, 1883), pp. 103-105.

15. E. Hubbard, *The Closed Shop or Open Shop* (East Aurora, N. Y., 1910), p. 24.

16. W. Harding, *Rededicating America,* p. 45.

17. E. Hubbard, *The Motto Book,* p. 9.

18. H. Alger, *Struggling Upward and Other Works,* ed. R. Crouse (New York, 1945), introduction, pp. viii-ix.

19. W. Sumner, *What Social Classes Owe to Each Other,* p. 32.

CHAPTER NINE

1. W. Ashley, *Surveys Historic and Economic* (New York, 1900), p. 385.
2. E. Bellamy, *Equality* (New York, 1913), p. 12.
3. Quoted, J. Dorfman, *The Economic Mind in American Civilization* (New York, 1949), vol. iii, p. 146.
4. W. Wilson, *The New Freedom* (New York and Garden City, 1913), p. 201.
5. Quoted, J. Dorfman, *The Economic Mind in American Civilization*, vol. iii, p. 152.
6. J. Spargo, *Socialism* (New York, 1906), p. 139.
7. G. Shaw, *et al, Socialism; the Fabian Essays,* with introduction by E. Bellamy (Boston, *c.* 1894), p. ix.
8. H. Lynd, *England in the Eighteen Eighties* (New York, 1945), p. 110; A. Ulam, *Philosophical Foundations of British Socialism* (Cambridge, Mass., 1951).
9. Quoted, J. Chamberlain, *Farewell to Reform* (New York, 1932), p. 208.
10. J. Spargo, *Socialism* (New York, 1906), pp. 143, 144.
11. Quoted, Olive M. Johnson, *Daniel De Leon* (New York, 1935), p. 24.
12. T. Veblen, *The Vested Interests* (New York, 1920), p. 20.

CHAPTER TEN

1. Quoted, R. Hofstadter, *The American Political Tradition* (New York, 1951), p. 310.
2. N. Thomas, *America's Way Out* (New York, 1937), p. 131.
3. M. Lerner, *It Is Later Than You Think* (New York, 1939), p. 19.
4. *Liberal Magazine,* vol. xliv, London, 1936, p. 526.
5. *Ibid.,* p. 315.
6. T. Arnold, *The Folklore of Capitalism* (New Haven, 1937).
7. H. Wallace, *Whose Constitution?* (New York, 1936), p. 295; *New Frontiers* (New York, 1934), p. 276.
8. S. Chase, *A New Deal* (New York, 1932), pp. 242-252.
9. W. Lippmann, *Inquiry into the Principles of the Good Society* (Boston, 1937).
10. Quoted, R. Tugwell, "Mr. Hoover's Economic Policy," *John Day Pamphlets,* No. 7 (New York, 1932), pp. 7, 14; H. Hoover, *The Challenge to Liberty* (New York, 1935), p. 6.
11. R. Tugwell, "Mr. Hoover's Economic Policy," p. 5.

12. A. Nock, *Our Enemy, the State* (New York, 1935), p. 26.
13. H. Hoover, *The Challenge to Liberty*, p. 156.
14. M. Lerner, *It Is Later Than You Think*, pp. 62, 82.
15. N. Thomas, *As I See It* (New York, 1932), p. 20.
16. G. Hicks, *I Like America* (New York, 1938), p. 4.
17. M. Lerner, *It Is Later Than You Think*, p. 82.
18. *Ibid.*, p. 91.

CHAPTER ELEVEN

1. W. Bryan, *Speeches of William Jennings Bryan* (New York and London, 1909), vol. ii, pp. 23-30.
2. Quoted, W. Leuchtenberg, "Progressivism and Imperialism: The Progressive Movement and American Foreign Policy, 1898-1916," *Mississippi Valley Historical Review*, vol. xxxix, No. 3, December, 1952, pp. 483, 501.
3. Quoted, F. Harrington, "The Anti-Imperialist Movement in the United States," *Mississippi Valley Historical Review*, vol. xxii, No. 2, September, 1935, pp. 211, 225.
4. See W. Diamond, *The Economic Thought of Woodrow Wilson* (Baltimore, 1943).
5. T. Bailey, *Woodrow Wilson and the Lost Peace* (New York, 1944), pp. 307, 324.
6. W. Harding, *Rededicating America* (Indianapolis, 1920), pp. 106, 188.
7. Quoted, L. Filler, *Randolph Bourne* (Washington, 1943), pp. 123-125.
8. Z. Chafee, Jr., *Freedom of Speech* (New York, 1920), p. 58.
9. Quoted, W. Diamond, *The Economic Thought of Woodrow Wilson*, p. 177.
10. F. Schuman, *American Policy toward Russia since 1917* (New York, 1928), p. 202.
11. *Ibid.*, p. 123.
12. G. Kennan, *American Diplomacy, 1900-1950* (Chicago, 1951), p. 135.
13. S. Chase, *The New Western Front* (New York, 1939).
14. L. Mumford, *Men Must Act* (New York, 1939), p. 149.
15. *U.S.A., The Permanent Revolution*, by the editors of *Fortune* with the collaboration of Russell Davenport (New York, 1951).

Index